Organizational Diagnosis

ORGANIZATIONAL DIAGNOSIS

A Practical Approach to Company Problem Solving and Growth

Andrew O. Manzini

amacom
American Management Association

*This book is available at a special
discount when ordered in bulk quantities.
For information, contact Special Sales Department,
AMACOM, a division of American Management Association,
135 West 50th Street, New York, NY 10020.*

HD
58.8
.M29

Library of Congress Cataloging-in-Publication Data

*Manzini, Andrew O.
 Organizational diagnosis.*

  *Bibliography: p.
  Includes index.
  1. Organizational change. 2. Problem solving.
I. Title.
HD58.8.M2633   1988   658.4   88-47709
ISBN 0-8144-5778-9*

*© 1988 AMACOM, a division of
American Management Association, New York.
All rights reserved.
Printed in the United States of America.*

*This publication may not be reproduced,
stored in a retrieval system,
or transmitted in whole or in part,
in any form or by any means, electronic,
mechanical, photocopying, recording, or otherwise,
without the prior written permission of AMACOM,
a division of American Management Association,
135 West 50th Street, New York, NY 10020.*

Printing number

  10   9   8   7   6   5   4   3   2   1

To
Serena,
. . . just for being there

Acknowledgments

This book builds on the work of many outstanding practitioners who have pioneered the concept of organizational diagnosis and championed its utility over the years. I have been most influenced by a towering figure in the field: Harry Levinson of the Levinson Institute. I owe him a debt of gratitude for the inspiration and encouragement he provided me in the early years of my practice in this area, and for helping me to recognize that I should not seek simplistic solutions to complex business problems.

I am also indebted to my friends and colleagues who, over the years, worked (and suffered) with me on dozens of diagnostic projects in many organizations. Robert F. Walton, Thornton Jenness, and David C. Silver participated with me in conducting one of the most comprehensive diagnoses ever attempted. Their support and confidence were instrumental in making that happen. Of particular importance was the contribution of the late José Sánchez, whose boundless enthusiasm and exceptional personal efforts encouraged us to navigate in uncharted waters and made us believe that a comprehensive diagnosis could indeed be done. Little of the original diagnostic work that we were able to accomplish would have been possible without the efforts and support of many co-workers, among whom were Timothy J. Ryan, George Keller, Barbara Bauer, Al Bazemore, and three distinguished academicians—Drs. Noel Tichy, Ian Macmillan, and Michael Tushman. A particular debt is owed to the hundreds of managers in many organizations who gave generously of their time to share with us their experiences and their perceptions about their environment, and who gave us the benefit of the doubt that was so crucial to establishing the diagnostic technique in the repertoire of management tools of these organizations.

Finally, I thank Adrienne Hickey, senior acquisitions and planning editor at AMACOM, who would not take no for an answer, persuaded me to write this book, provided merciless and justified criticism, and worked with me during the publishing process.

Introduction

This book is the result of many years of work in business organizations—companies with a heritage, a predictable mode of behavior, and a concern for ensuring their own survival—and studying these organizations as living systems. It is also a record of the real experiences of real people in real organizations—people who have engaged in a powerful process of introspection over a prolonged period, sharing their feelings about their efforts to cope with an increasingly complex environment. My extensive exposure to a multitude of difficult business issues and problems, coupled with systematic observation of managers in action, enabled me to formulate a practical approach to organizational diagnosis. It can be used by all managers interested in improving the effectiveness of their organization, without reliance on specially trained consultants.

An organizational diagnosis is a systematic process of gathering data about a business organization—its problems, challenges, strengths, and limitations—and analyzing how such factors influence its ability to interact effectively, and profitably, with its business environment. A properly conducted organizational diagnosis can not only help you deal with a multitude of mundane problems, such as low productivity, poor morale, and interdepartmental conflict, but can also help you get a grasp on strategic issues such as mission, goals, market positioning, and dealing with competition.

In many ways, however, the strongest and most positive effects of such a diagnosis do not concern the findings, but the process. People gain significant insight into the organization and themselves as they research, interview, and organize their data. Such a project can be a cathartic experience; many who participate come to believe that the process would have been personally significant and satisfying even if it had not generated change. And a study like this can be an energizer. People gain new pride in the organization, new confidence in themselves, and new zest for their work.

Today's manager, and the human resources professional in an advisory and support role, is overwhelmed by a mass of literature that attempts to provide guidance for and "new" insights aimed at organizational improvement. The predominant thrust of such material is to improve the repertory of a manager's technical skills, ranging from strategic planning to human resources management, and it usually seems to imply that learning a fairly complex canon of theories will lead to salvation. This is not the case with this book. In promoting organizational diagnosis, I submit that a harried manager can temporarily take respite from such education, since he or she is in the same situation as the old farmer who refuses to buy more books on farming, because his real problem is that he doesn't farm as well as he knows how to.

The central thesis of this book is that the solution to many organizational problems lies within the company itself—with its own people. If you create an environment that encourages people to communicate their perceptions about problems and issues that prevent the company from being as effective as it can possibly be, and that solicits their input about what could be done, you tap a reservoir of talent that is more than adequate in most circumstances. People working in an organization *know what's wrong,* and in most cases, they *know how the problem can be fixed.* Likewise, people are very much aware of the fact that the world is changing and that something needs to be done in order for them and their organizations to cope effectively with such change. Yet top managers insist on taking upon themselves the burden of steering the organizational ship without the benefit of feedback about which way the wind blows that can be readily obtained from the people who work the sails. Organizational diagnosis is a vehicle for obtaining valid and useful data not only about a company's problems but also about potential solutions. Such a methodology is both usable and cost effective.

This book is intended for use in the real world by managers and human resources professionals who are not necessarily schooled in scientific methods; the suggested methodology is therefore based on the meaningful use of data gathered by employees from employees—since employees are the people who are most affected by the issues and problems being scrutinized. A diagnosis conducted by members of an organization, rather than by outside consultants, has a better chance of generating data valid to the participants, which in turn generates commitment to change. Certainly, valid data can be generated by consultants. The only problem is whether the data will also be considered valid by the people in the organization. And that's what really counts.

In order to illustrate how people respond during a diagnosis, I have drawn material and quotes from an extensive number of past projects that I have directed. This use of real-world settings will lend immediacy to the examples and will expose (in a positive context, I hope) the challenges, the ill-founded assumptions, the mistakes, the pain, and the occasional triumphs of people charged with managing organizations in a complex environment. You will note that quoted commentary and remarks by actual people involved in projects (or comments typical of such people) are scattered throughout the book and appear slightly darker than the rest of the text.

The questions that this book poses are weighty: How serious are you about your job as a manager or an adviser to managers? How deeply do you understand the organization before you intervene? How willing are you to invest in yourself, sustain ambiguity and inadequacy, and embark on an extended learning experience, not through theory, but through the practice of your profession as a manager?

The purpose of this book is to explain a relatively new technique, and to encourage you, as a manager or a person in a support role, to work with greater sophistication, tempered by how things really *are* in organizations and not by some unrealizable ideal of what they should be. You are asked to increase the significance of what you do and to develop your understanding of what's involved in large-scale organizational improvement and change. In the process, perhaps you will be able to gain some insight into the kind of feelings and experiences that are likely to accompany an organizational diagnosis. This book may serve as a guide, and also as a means of coping with some of the inevitable pain-inducing issues, helping you to accept them as a natural part of the process and thus contributing to a renewal of your own self-confidence and development.

Contents

List of Figures   *xix*

Part I*   *Organizational Diagnosis: Origins and Concepts   **1**

  1 Organizational Diagnosis: A Valuable Management Tool   **3**

      The Need for New Approaches   3
      Classic Developmental Processes   5
          Strategic Planning   5
          Organizational Design   6
          Management Development   6
          Organizational Development   6
      Organizational Diagnosis: A Powerful New Tool for Improvement and Development   8
          The Value of Diagnostic Techniques in Today's Business Environment   8
          What a Diagnosis Is Not: The Distinction Between "Process" and "Content"   10
          The Diagnostic Cycle   11
          Diagnostic Models and Approaches   12
      The Organic Approach to Organizational Diagnosis   13
          The Focus of Organizational Diagnosis   15
          The Scope of Organizational Diagnosis   16
          The Phases of a Comprehensive Diagnosis   16

Part II*   *Plan and Organize the Diagnostic Project   **21**

  2 Preliminary Assessment and Startup   **23**

      Define Your Role as a Diagnostician   23
          Analyst   24
          Expert or Problem Solver   24
          Behavioral Scientist or Technologist   24
          Facilitator   25
      Understand the Reasons for the Diagnostic Project   25
          Diagnosis for Remedial Purposes   25
          Diagnosis for Developmental Purposes   29

Analyze the Political Environment   30
- To What Extent Is the Sponsor or Company Management Invested in, or Responsible for, the Way Things Are?   30
- Is the Sponsor in a Position of Sufficient Authority to Legitimize the Project With Other Key Managers?   30
- Who Are the Significant Players Making Up the Critical Mass? Is It Necessary to Get Them Involved as Part of the Diagnostic Team?   31
- Does the Situation Require the Establishment of an Organizational Development Council?   32

Present a Detailed Proposal   33
Obtain Final Approval to Proceed   34
Organize the Project   35
- Establish a Political Support System   35
- Establish an Administrative System   38
- Assemble the Diagnostic Team   43
- Train the Diagnostic Team   45

Part III   Collect and Process Diagnostic Data   49

3 Data Gathering   51

Organize the Logistics of Interviewing   51
- Confirm the Availability of Interviewers   51
- Notify the Respondents   52
- Match Interviewer with Respondent   52
- Schedule the Interviews   54

Develop a Reference Data Base   58
- Perform Background Research   58
- Interview Key Management Personnel   59

Develop the Main Data Base   61
- The Process of Diagnostic Interviewing   61
- The Interview Procedure   63
- Important Considerations   64
- Open the Interview   64
- Work on Data Generation   65
- Possible Problems During the Interview   67
- Close the Interview   68

Review the Interview Process   68

4 Process Collected Data   70

Establish Administrative Tools   70
Transcribe Notes   71
Control Paper Flow   71
Review Volume and Progress   72

Contents   xv

        Organize Collected Data   72
            Review the Transcripts   72
            Code the Data Cards   74
        Select the Team for the Balance of the Project   76
        Prepare for the Analysis and Interpretation   77
            Develop Issue Categories   78

Part IV Analysis and Interpretation   81

5 Corporate History and Culture   83

        Corporate Culture as a Reality   83
        Historical Development and the Shaping of a Corporate Culture   84
        Corporate Indoctrination: Passing on Culture, Values, Assets, and Liabilities   85
        A Framework for Analyzing Corporate History and Culture   87

6 Planning, Strategy, and Structure   90

        General Planning Practices in the Organization   90
        Strategic Planning   91
            Core Mission   91
            Environmental Scanning   93
            Scenarios and Strategies   95
            Strategy Implementation   99
            The Prospects of Strategic Planning   101
        Operational Planning   102
        Organizational Structure   103
            Extent to Which "Form Follows Function"   103
        Evaluation of Strategic Advantage   105
            Environmental Threat and Opportunities Analysis   106
            Strategic Advantage Profile   107

7 Organizational Resources   111

        Financial Resources   112
            Goals of Financial Management   113
            Financial-Statement Analysis   114
            Analysis of Financial Goals   115
        Technological Resources   118
        Physical Resources   120
        Human Resources   121
            Employee-Turnover Patterns   122
            Turnover Trend Analysis   123
            Performance Appraisal   125
            Management Development   128

8 Organizational Processes — 130

Leadership and Power Characteristics   130
   Types of Leaders   131
   Authority and Power   132
      Bases of Power   133
      Power, Influence, and Politics   134
Problem-Solving Practices   136
Decision-Making Practices   137
Reward Systems   138
Work and Productivity   138
   Assess Levels of Performance Deficiency   139

Part V Feedback, Action Planning, and Evaluation — 141

9 Complete and Deliver the Diagnosis — 143

Diagnostic Conclusions   143
   Summary of Significant Issues and Problems   143
   Indicators of Unresolved Issues and Problems   143
Present Phase of Organizational Crisis   144
Significant Organizational Strengths and Assets   147
   Aspects of the Organization That Should Not Be Changed   147
Diagnostic Recommendations   148
Presenting the Diagnosis to Management   148
   The Structure of the Diagnosis   148
   Prepare for the Presentation   152
   Deliver the Presentation   152

10 Action Planning and Evaluation — 155

Review the Diagnosis With Management   155
   Handle the Questions   155
   Reach Consensus on Major Issues or Problem Areas   157
Action Planning   157
Planning the Organizational Change and Development   158
   Reach Agreement on the Company's Core Mission   158
   Determine an Appropriate Response to the Identified Environmental Demands   159
   Project Into the Future   159
   Define the Desired Future State   159
Organizational Interventions   160
   Evaluate the Effectiveness of the Diagnosis   160
   Conduct an Evaluation Study   161

Part VI Diagnosis as a Management Tool — 163

11 Special Applications of Diagnostic Techniques — 165
    Diagnosis in Mergers and Acquisitions   165
    Diagnosis to Analyze Problems in Diversification Strategy   175
    Diagnosis in Team Building   180
        Family-Group Team Building   181
        Project Team Building   185

12 Conclusion: Issues and Problems of Organizational Diagnosis — 191
    Predictable Problems in Diagnostic Projects   191
        Management Resistance   191
        System Resistance   192
    Conditions for Success   192
    Conclusion   193

Part VII Appendixes — 195

1 Examples, Forms, and Checklists — 197
    1.1 Sample Proposal Structure   198
    1.2 Master Project Checklist   202
    1.3 Master Interviewing Schedule   209
    1.4 Interview Data-Recording Guide   210
    1.5 Core Mission and Strategic Planning Issues Analysis   211
    1.6 Equipment Control Log   217
    1.7 Transcription Control Log   218
    1.8 Document-Review Control Cover   219
    1.9 Sample Diagnostic Report   220
    1.10 Sample Topical Analysis Summary   228
    1.11 Diagnostic Recommendations   230

2 Diagnostic Models and Intervention Methods — 234
    Behavioral-Science Models   235
    Special-Purpose Models   249
    Comprehensive Models   251

3 Organizational Diagnosis: An Experience — 258
    Background of the Organization   258
    The Diagnosis Is Commissioned   259
    An Organizational Development Council Is Established   259
    The Power Diagnosis   260
    The Study   260

Historical Methodology Applied to Organizational
  Diagnosis   261
Recommendations to Management   266
Review, Action Planning, and Implementation   267
Strategic Human Resources Forecasting, Planning, and
  Development Systems   268
Integration of Human Resources Development With Corporate
  Strategy   270
Conclusions   277

Notes   279
Bibliography   283
Index   287

Figures

2-1.	Invitation to the council.	33
2-2.	Memorandum to participant's manager.	36
2-3.	Memorandum to potential team members.	37
3-1.	Interview scheduling letter.	52
3-2.	Interviewer availability chart.	53
3-3.	Notification to respondents.	53
3-4.	Executive interview selection.	55
3-5.	Partial version of a filled-in master interviewer availability schedule.	56
3-6.	Sample opening statement.	57
4-1.	Sample "thank you" memo.	77
6-1.	SBU strategy selection.	98
7-1.	Six-year turnover analysis.	124
7-2.	Hires for growth and turnover.	126
7-3.	Cost of employee replacement (8 percent annual inflation).	127
9-1.	Phases of organizational crises.	145
A-1.	The organizational iceberg.	236
A-2.	An action-research model for organizational development.	241
A-3.	The six-box model for organizational diagnosis.	252

PART I
Organizational Diagnosis: Origins and Concepts

This introductory part places organizational diagnosis in perspective with other organizational change processes. In particular, it reviews how diagnosis has evolved from a technique utilized as part of the organizational development process to a major management technique in its own right. It also discusses why diagnosis has become such a valuable tool for managers interested in significant organizational improvement. Finally, this part introduces the method that is the principal focus of this book—the organic diagnosis—and outlines its planning and implementation phases. These phases are discussed in detail in the remaining parts of the book.

CHAPTER 1

Organizational Diagnosis: A Valuable Management Tool

A business organization is essentially a vehicle for producing profits for its owners. To secure the best possible return on their investment, the stockholders of a company, directly or indirectly, employ managers who are responsible for setting profit objectives and reaching them through the use of resources such as plants, equipment, and people.

The Need for New Approaches

In pursuing its goals, an organization interacts with its environment, an amorphous combination of shareholders, customers, competitors, financial institutions, markets, and the government—each of which represents a threat or an opportunity that needs to be dealt with in order for the organization to survive.

Theoretically, a company adapts to its environment as a result of systematic and explicit strategies formulated by its management. However, the dynamic nature of contemporary business also requires that a company's management try to *influence* its environment. This in turn demands built-in flexibility in the system, which can be achieved by having managers who discover opportunities, make rapid changes in a firm's strategy, and initiate the corresponding internal actions that are necessary to implement such changes.

Simple in concept, but difficult in execution, the process of managing a company is subject to endless scrutiny, second-guessing, postmortems, and evaluations by various concerned groups, which include academics, shareholders, the general public, and Wall Street. The gap between organizational theory and what really happens is sometimes significant, because the managerial response to business problems or environmental challenges is not always timely, appropriate, or effective. Certainly, many factors affect a company's ability to interact with its environment, among them the quality of its leadership, its effectiveness in perceiving reality, its resources, and its image in the marketplace.

Like people, organizations can suffer illnesses and manifest a variety of symptoms. Generally, such illnesses are transmitted by "carriers"—key figures who make major decisions but who are temporarily or permanently unable to cope with the demands of their roles. Being products of the system themselves, they affect and are affected in turn by the milieu in which they work, and can spread the infection to such an extent that unless it is checked and cured, the organization itself will be in jeopardy. The cure can be found only if the illness is acknowledged in the first place.

A company with a culture that makes it taboo to discuss certain facts that are not palatable to its leadership, or which sets boundaries on the extent to which people will be allowed to look at environmental realities, may restrict consideration of the very alternatives the organization must employ in order to deal with issues critical to its long-term survival. This type of situation is evident when an organization's managers are unable to resolve severe business problems, such as loss of market share, unsalable products, foreign inroads, decreasing productivity, and lower earnings. The managers seem to have run out of solutions, and they start blaming the fickle customer, the competition, the government, corporate raiders, or tough times.

If left unchecked, such conditions leave an organization susceptible to induced drastic changes, ranging from replacement of the leadership to mergers with or takeovers by stronger organizations. The net result is a postmortem reexamination of past practices, a predictable realignment of people and capital resources, and, it is hoped, a new strategic direction.

The story of the Chrysler Corporation under Lee Iacocca is an illustration of how new leadership and strategy can revitalize a company that most people had dismissed as moribund. This example of the successful use of radical surgery suggests to some corporate boards, the press, and occasionally the helpless stockholders that when something is no longer working in an organization, the existing leadership is somehow at fault and the solution is to replace them with people who may be more capable or who are endowed with fresh ideas.

To some extent, this Draconian approach is supported by the research of Elliott Jaques.[1] His conclusions are that people (i.e., managers) are endowed with certain innate capabilities that are predictable. He calls these "levels of abstraction," of which there are at least seven, each higher level progressively endowing the individual with significant additional work capacity, insight, and perspective. In essence, Jaques's work suggests that what really matters is having a chief executive with the requisite level of abstraction and work capacity to successfully lead the organization around whatever obstacles it may have to face in the environment. This hierarchy removes any excuses by implying that a manager properly matched to the requirements of the job should be able to anticipate problems, trends, and opportunities, and to act accordingly.

In practice, wholesale replacement of a management team is neither desirable nor realistic. It is a fallacy to assume (1) that successful management makes no serious mistakes and (2) that unsuccessful management is incapable of learning. The reality is that often the existing leadership is facing circumstances that prevent vital facts from emerging or from being considered as germane to the issues at hand, thus short-circuiting a problem-solving process that may have been successful in the past. Something—the organization's culture, the nature of the problem, new environmental factors, the people involved, or the filtering of information through the fabled twelve inches of lead surrounding the executive suite—induces in the organization's management a case of temporary blindness.

This affliction can be cured, provided the barriers that prevent a clearheaded and dispassionate examination of a problem and its causes are identified and removed. Techniques for identifying and removing such barriers do exist; in most situations, they help clarify the nature of the problems and provide the necessary additional insight that can enable a management team to redirect its organization toward renewed effectiveness, with relatively little trauma to the people in the system.

Classic Developmental Processes

It is possible to improve the effectiveness of an organization gradually and systematically, without restricting its freedom of action, provided its leadership is willing to allow certain interventions that are different—in nature and focus—from commonly accepted, orthodox management practices such as planning, directing, staffing, and controlling. The management literature is full of techniques that are purportedly designed to help managers scan the environment for relevant facts; these facts are subsequently "processed" so management will have a data base that will help in decision making and problem resolution. The most common of these developmental, future-oriented processes include:

- Strategic planning, also referred to as organizational planning, corporate planning, and business planning
- Organizational design
- Management development
- Organizational development

These differ in focus and emphasis, although they overlap considerably, and they eventually link with and impact on each other as they are used in organizations. These techniques are all essential elements of proper management of an organization, and we briefly discuss how and where they can have the most impact.

Strategic Planning

Also referred to as organizational planning, corporate planning, and business planning, "strategic planning" means creating a blueprint for change, development, resource allocation, and implementation of strategic plans. Such an activity focuses on:

- Examining internal organizational processes and related resources
- Clarifying the organization's main mission
- Examining the business environment and selecting relevant factors
- Integrating internal and external data
- Developing economic and environmental scenarios
- Developing strategies appropriate for dealing with the planned environment
- Developing, funding, and communicating the strategic plan

Organizational Design

This process is an effort to match structure with strategy, involving:

- Matching objectives, processes, and reward systems in a functional framework
- Looking at organizational stratification as an important element of design

Management Development

Sometimes confused with the generic term "training and development," management-development programs are designed to help prepare employees with management potential to meet their responsibilities in a highly competent and proactive way. Methods commonly used in management development include:

- *Performance appraisal*—assessing employees' past accomplishments
- *Evaluation of potential*—assessing future capabilities of candidates for management
- *Career management*—designing career paths and development plans for promising employees
- *Management succession*—planning to have the right people available at the right time and place, at the right price

Organizational Development

A somewhat controversial and sometimes unfocused body of knowledge originally based on the application of behavioral-science methodology, organizational development (OD) utilizes a repertory of techniques claiming to facilitate the development and implementation of programs that enhance the capability of an organization to meet its challenges.

Richard Beckhard, the noted consultant and author in the field of organizational development, provided the best-known definition:

> Organization Development is an effort (1) *planned*, (2) *organization-wide*, and (3) managed from the top, to (4) increase organization effectiveness and health through (5) planned interventions in the organization's "processes," using behavioral-science knowledge.[2]

Most organizational development work is accomplished through "interventions"—activities that involve the collaboration of a trained facilitator and the affected members of the organization. Early on, such interventions took the form of sensitivity training, team-building meetings, and heavy reliance on data provided by the people in the system itself.

Most OD interventions involve a series of steps, which include:

1. Data gathering
2. Diagnosis
3. Feedback to the organization
4. Action planning
5. Implementation
6. Evaluation
7. Reiteration, if necessary

Typical OD Interventions

Team building. Team building is one of the more often used interventions. It generally focuses on identifying and solving the work group's problems and on facilitating group interaction. The objectives of team building are (1) to develop sound processes for goal setting, performance planning, and problem solving so that appropriate action can be taken as necessary and (2) to maximize use of existing resources by encouraging participative management.

This is not to suggest that formal lines of authority are discounted. Far from it. Hierarchies exist, and they serve highly useful purposes. However, sometimes they are inefficient. Participative management is particularly effective when problems are ill defined and a solution requires various integrated outputs. Participative management is possible even when people are not equal in terms of knowledge or position in the hierarchy. People interacting in any given situation are just not equal. On this point, Frederick Hertzberg once pointed out that the only time we are equal is when we find ourselves in a situation in which we are equally ignorant.

To get things done in an organization, the involvement of people is critical. One of the value concepts underlying this assumption is that we should not make decisions that affect people without involving them in those decisions. In OD, participative decision making is encouraged, but with the proviso that everyone has a different position in the hierarchy.

Intergroup development. Another class of OD intervention brings groups of people together to reduce conflicts so that their efforts can be focused on a common goal or problem that affects all of them. This generally involves a front-end diagnosis conducted by the group members themselves, under the guidance of impartial facilitators; jointly setting priorities; working through the problems and issues, both as separate groups and as an overall team; and developing a plan that commits the groups to common action and problem resolution.

Process consultation. This type of intervention involves the use of a facilitator to help in the diagnosis, understanding, and resolution of "process" problems—that is, how the group members work together. Occasionally, the facilitator may get involved in resolving difficult one-on-one relationships. In this kind of activity, the participants usually deal in the here and now, with real, "live" problems.

Diagnosis. Diagnosing the problems is one of the first activities associated with OD. In fact, organizational development can be credited with institutionalizing the diagnosis as a regular and essential part of its methodology. Diagnostic studies can be remedial (concerned with finding problems and their solution) or developmental (concerned more with what needs to be done to help the organization become stronger and more successful). The scope of a diagnosis ranges from a scrutiny of whole systems to an examination of individual problems. In a diagnosis, an organization generally examines itself in terms of issue and problem identification: What is getting the job accomplished? What are the barriers to reaching the goals? What can be done?

Organizational Diagnosis: A Powerful New Tool for Improvement and Development

The Value of Diagnostic Techniques in Today's Business Environment

Organizational diagnosis is an extended form of the basic front-end, fact-finding activity that is a prerequisite for most OD efforts. Since the organizational diagnosis is intended to deal with large and complete systems such as a company, its scope is of necessity larger than that of OD, and for this reason, it can legitimately be treated as an intervention in its own right.

This method is designed to help eliminate managerial blind spots and, when accompanied by appropriate actions, can be an important factor in organizational recovery or development. Often, the organization's culture is at least partially responsible for the blind spot, although very rarely is it the only variable in a major organizational dysfunction. A properly conducted, comprehensive diagnosis, under the right conditions, can provide managers with valuable insights that may not have been obvious to them previously and that may lead to finding solutions well within the capabilities and resources of the existing leadership. Moreover, an organizational diagnosis can be used effectively for developmental purposes beyond problem solving: It can help prepare an organization to deal with significant planned change, such as diversification, acquisition, or change in market direction.

A comprehensive diagnosis can help an organization identify where it is today and why, where it wants to go, and how it will know when it gets there; moreover, it can help the organization find the means to reach its goal. This involves a fundamental reexamination of the organization—where it came from, how it got to be the way it is, and why its present manner of dealing with the business environment no longer works. Conversely, it can help clarify why an organization is particularly effective, in order, with planned deliberation, to continue the successful pattern of operation. Diagnosis can also help an organization assess what it needs to do to compete effectively in a new environment.

Traditionally, skilled internal or external consultants with a background in organizational development, finance, and strategic planning, often supplemented by selected line managers, have examined the cause of a particular dysfunction systematically and identified solutions that have been provided by the respondents; in most cases, these solutions were then implemented by the line managers themselves. In the following chapters we see how a meaningful diagnosis can be performed by an organization's own managers.

When organizational problems are examined by people who are not involved in their genesis, or who have no vested interest in the outcome, these problems can usually be traced back to a number of factors unique to the organization itself—its background, development, growth, values, culture, behavior, systems, and people. The diagnostic process starts by identifying the location of the "pain," what it is like, how long it has been going on, and what has been done about it.

Since much of diagnosis traditionally deals with problem solving, Harry Levinson, a noted pioneer in this field, insists that it is crucial at the beginning to ascertain whether pain really exists. Successful and prosperous organizations may wish to further improve teamwork, find breathing room to "think" about where they are going, or stem the loss of top performers who are being lured away by the competition. Often, however, this stated discomfort is indicative more of obstacles whose removal would be desirable, rather than the pain necessary to induce a meaningful change effort. If there is not sufficient pain, Levinson insists, there is no motivation to change, and he suggests that, in such cases, the wise consultant does not intervene.

Certainly, there is much truth to this assertion, but nevertheless we explore how a set of conditions can be created that will enable the planning of change in a developmental mode without the prerequisite pain as a motivator. Admittedly, it is more difficult to get managers to see the need for an intervention if pain is not there, but it can be done.

In a pure sense, it can be argued that any activity that includes data gathering as a prerequisite for action involves diagnosis. Indeed, diagnosis is a separate and at the same time inextricable element of the various activities and techniques used during the process of organizational improvement and change, and this relationship remains very much in evidence throughout this book.

Since this book focuses primarily on organizational diagnosis, it does not take issue with the fine points of whether organizational diagnosis is merely a subordinate technique or a significant tool in its own right. Moreover, diagnosis is treated in a broader context, in an attempt to integrate traditional, "soft" organizational development methodology with a more objective, data-based approach that examines issues and problems not always related to the behavioral realm.

What a Diagnosis Is Not: The Distinction Between "Process" and "Content"

It is important to understand that organizational diagnosis, by itself, is irrelevant unless specific outcomes are observed. The critical element is the attainment of organizational objectives. Perhaps the premise of diagnosis can be made clearer by discussing what such a process is not:

- *It is not putting out fires.* If fire breaks out, crisis intervention is a perfectly legitimate approach. In such a case, managers simply do not have the time to study the matter, deliberate, and reach group consensus.
- *It is not strictly remedial.* Organizational diagnosis is useful but somewhat limited in its ability to help in remedial situations. Rather, diagnosis is developmental in nature.
  - Diagnosis usually requires time.
  - Diagnosis requires commitment from all people in the system, not just a few. A diagnosis and subsequent OD effort in one department can be effective to the point at which they require interface with other departments. At such a stage, the process can be stymied by lack of understanding of and exposure to the relevant issues raised by other groups in the system. A common hypothesis suggests that change generates protective cohesion by work groups and that such behavior is attributable to fear and consequent resistance to change by the groups' members. In fact, resistance to change is a myth. Certainly, change is difficult to implement, and people do resist change if they don't understand it or haven't been involved in initiating it. Diagnosis can help in promoting such understanding.
  - Diagnosis is designed to deal not with individuals but with the organization as a whole. The intent is to help the company look at itself as a set of interdependent subsystems that together make up the whole.
- *It is not management consulting.* Management consulting is primarily "expert" consulting. It involves focusing on the content of the matter going into a system; working on a specific problem, often of a technical nature; and making specific, prescriptive recommendations. Diagnosis is mainly process oriented. It assumes that people within a system are already technically competent. A diagnostic intervention heightens the awareness of the organization's people as to what's going on so that they can make choices about the problems, issues, or challenges and find

their own alternative solutions. Those who engage in diagnosis don't tell people what to do; rather, they tend to observe and provide feedback on how things get done. If asked to, they may suggest alternative models of suitable processes.

The Diagnostic Cycle

The purpose of a diagnosis is not only to find the real problems facing the organization, but also to determine their causes so that management can plan solutions. Even though a diagnosis is a powerful consciousness-raising activity in its own right, its usefulness lies more in the action that it induces. Therefore, a list of the major elements of the diagnostic cycle must include the steps that naturally follow the diagnosis itself. The entire cycle consists of:

1. *Data gathering.* Collecting information through formal channels such as documents and reports, and from interviews with selected executives, managers, and employees. In some cases, interviews are extended to people outside the company, such as ex-employees, academicians, and researchers.
2. *Analysis.* Reviewing, categorizing, and analyzing the collected data in terms of their relevance to organizational problems and issues; this process can lead to conclusions about the organization's strengths and weaknesses.
3. *Feedback.* No matter which method is employed to conduct diagnosis, feeding back the results in all cases to management and the respondents. The feedback should not consist of raw data, but rather data organized within a conceptual framework. The objective of the feedback is to obtain a reasonable consensus on the facts and a shared way of thinking and talking about these facts.
4. *Action planning.* Exploring ways of closing the gap between "what is" according to the diagnosis and a desirable state that must be defined. During this stage, management uses the diagnostic data to formulate goals and objectives, as well as action plans designed to activate organizational resources in the desired direction.
5. *Implementation.* Carrying out the plans. The key to effective implementation is the degree of commitment to the change felt by the people who must carry out the plans. This stage sees the actual execution of action plans by the appropriate organizational units, working with designated resources.
6. *Evaluation.* Reexamining the data. This essentially returns the organization to the diagnostic phase. After the various interventions have taken place, has there been any change?

As we progress through a detailed explanation of the method, we will see how each major stage is an essential element for organizational improvement.

Diagnostic Models and Approaches

There are many established methods of conducting organizational diagnoses, all of which have their relative merits (see Appendix 2). Such models range from very simple interviews and surveys to major, complex, and time-consuming large-systems diagnoses. The people who engage in these techniques call themselves organizational development (OD) practitioners, diagnosticians, or analysts and may be consultants, specialists, academicians, internal staff personnel, or an organization's own line managers. In all cases, however, these people collect data, mostly from an organization's own members, in an effort to identify issues, better define problems, and seek appropriate solutions. The diagnosticians almost always recommend solutions, but it is up to management to implement them. In organizational development work, the consultant generally takes the role of data gatherer rather than problem solver. The OD consultant collects relevant data; arranges them in a meaningful pattern; feeds the data back to the client system, which may be management but more often is the respondents themselves; and helps it reach conclusions. The OD consultant may then act as a facilitator, assisting the client system to set priorities and implement its own solutions.

Consultants and analysts engaged in performing diagnostic studies seek to examine characteristic patterns and features of organizations. In practice, conducting an organizational diagnosis is not as simple as collecting facts and categorizing them in a meaningful pattern. As a general rule, diagnosticians find it necessary to adopt a model or structure that provides general guidance for conducting such an effort. This need for specific models is reinforced by certain realities about the data-gathering process in complex organizations.

First, more data are available than can possibly be collected and interpreted. Second, there are now more options regarding the kinds of data that can be collected. Depending on the scope of the diagnosis and the consultant's theoretical orientation, chances are he or she will focus on certain areas such as communications, interpersonal relations, or structural issues. In most cases, the consultant's choices about data collection follow a consistent pattern precisely because he or she favors a certain framework or model. Models affect the behavior of diagnosticians and the kinds of interventions they use, primarily because the model they select dictates the kinds of data they will seek and the type of action they are likely to recommend. Thus, a diagnosis could focus on identifying concrete business problems (for instance, we can't meet the schedule) or on resolving interpersonal issues (for instance, the reason we can't meet the schedule is we can't work together as a team).

Given the same symptoms, different models mean approaching the problem differently; this is the reason why, to many practitioners, the choice of model is so important, especially if the situation is complicated.

The main disadvantage of diagnostic models that are narrowly based is the possibility that the diagnostician may only detect problems and suggest solutions that best fit his or her own past experience, education, capabilities, and frame of reference.

Even though the results of such a diagnosis may be helpful, there is no guarantee that all the important issues and problems which should be examined and dealt with have in fact been addressed. For this reason, comprehensive models, which attempt to collect data from all sides, without built-in restrictions on the kinds of data that will be accepted, are generally better suited for general, organization-wide analyses.

This is not to say that focused diagnostic methods are less effective than comprehensive approaches. Far from it. Focused approaches are cost effective and elegant, particularly if the problem is relatively confined, such as a team that is having leadership problems. Moreover, experienced diagnosticians point out that the down side of comprehensive diagnostic methods is that they are expensive and time consuming. They should therefore be used only when the nature of the issues or problems is systemic, affecting most of the organization's units, particularly with respect to its interaction with a changing business environment.

The Organic Approach to Organizational Diagnosis

This section introduces the organic diagnosis, an approach that in many instances may be more cost effective and timely than established models. Organic diagnosis does not subscribe to any one theory; rather, it uses aspects of established diagnostic techniques that, in my experience, are particularly well suited for analyses both of large organizations and of discrete units within them.

Essentially, the organic diagnosis requires (1) limited background research and (2) relatively unstructured diagnostic interviewing of an appropriate number of subjects. The collected data are then arranged in related clusters dictated by the issues and problem categories relevant to the project or situation as they surface, resulting in an "organic" arrangement of data in a natural pattern. The mentioned frequency of given situations suggests that if enough people point out a problem or an issue, in all probability the problem or issue is important and should be dealt with.

The main advantage of such an approach is its relative simplicity, speed, and timeliness. Since this approach is not dependent on a particular model, it can be performed by most managers of all disciplines, and it minimizes the possibility of favoring particular solutions to a problem just because they happen to fit a consultant's theoretical orientation.

Being relatively simple to conduct, the organic diagnosis does not require highly trained consultants and can, in most cases, be performed by an organization's own managers. Moreover, this approach does not preclude the supplemental use of other data-collection methods, particularly research and paper-and-pencil surveys. Formal research to obtain background information from publications and documents can also be done, but as a complementary task that helps confirm the respondents' perceptions. The majority of this book deals with the details of how such a diagnosis can be successfully executed.

The organic diagnosis has parallels in other lines of work. Whenever a solution or a methodology for reaching a solution is dictated by the realities of the situation at hand, rather than by preconceived notions about what *should* be going on, the procedure is comparable to organic diagnosis. The difference in approach and results can best be explained through an illustration.

For example, two newspaper reporters from competing papers are assigned to cover a brawl that injured several students after a school basketball game in a northeastern city. One reporter, Jones, comes with his own and his paper's predisposition to find racial overtones to the disturbance, which was essentially a parking-lot fight between students from a predominantly black inner-city school and students from the host school, in a largely white suburb. This "fact"—the ethnic contrast between the two schools—and his newspaper's predisposed editorial policy are all Jones needs to write a story carrying the headline "Race Riot Erupts After Local Basketball Game."

The other reporter, Smith, arrives at the scene without preconceived notions of what happened or why, intent only on finding out the truth about the situation by examining the facts. Through interviews with participants and witnesses, Smith learns that the fracas was set off by an unsuccessful mugging attempt: Several local hoods attempted to rob a couple on their way to their car and were prevented from doing so by a dozen black youths leaving the game. Some local kids, misinterpreting the reason why some of "their own" were scuffling with outsiders, immediately jumped in and became involved in the altercation. In the confusion, others from both schools joined the fray, and the thieves escaped. Smith's headline: "Several Injured as Teens Foil Muggers."

Obviously, Jones's and Smith's stories carried entirely different evaluations of what occurred and why. A reader of the papers in which the two articles appeared would be justified in thinking that two different events were being described, one a sad commentary on our troubled times and the other a hopeful report of Samaritan behavior by young people.

To draw a parallel in another field of endeavor, there is an axiomatic prescription among successful trial lawyers for deciding how to present a case: "If the facts favor our side, present the facts; if the facts favor the other side, present the law; and if both the facts and the law are against you, appeal to the jury's emotions." Although the adage is somewhat tongue-in-cheek, it does suggest that simple facts can be corrupted quite easily by someone willing to do so. They can also be inadvertently misinterpreted if they are approached with prejudice or preconceived notions.

The openness and lack of hidden agendas prescribed by the organic diagnosis approach, while admittedly difficult to attain in practice, are worth trying, even if the reality inevitably falls somewhat short of the ideal. The philosophy encourages you to allow the process, methodology, or techniques of the solution to emerge from the realities at hand, not from set notions about a "best" way to achieve a reasonable approximation of the relevant facts.

Central to the organic approach is the idea that people's perceptions affect their behavior. Perceptions, of course, do not always correspond to facts. However, perceptions are reality to the perceivers and do play a significant role in determining their actions. Moreover, it can be safely assumed that if enough people perceive certain issues, problems, and circumstances in a similar way, those perceptions, even allowing a certain margin for error, are generally indicative of what is really happening.

As a manager interested in practicing organizational diagnosis on a regular basis, initially you might want to follow the suggested techniques. As you complete several projects and gain confidence, you are likely to formulate your own ideas about what works and what doesn't, and you will probably develop your own techniques. The organic diagnosis, by definition, allows you to do this, because it is an extremely flexible method; it acknowledges the practical reality that most people will organize the same data in different yet still valid ways. However, if you try to maintain an open mind, there will be a consistency of results even if the format changes. The important thing is that the collection and interpretation of the data reflect a sincere effort to be impartial and factual.

The Focus of Organizational Diagnosis

We have already mentioned that organizational diagnosis is an examination of what's going on and why, and that its focus is twofold: remedial and developmental. The distinction is important enough to merit further discussion.

Diagnosis for Remedial Purposes

Just as a medical diagnosis is an attempt to find the cause of a physical ailment so that appropriate treatment can be applied, an organizational diagnosis focuses on essentially the same result: to find out what has gone wrong in an organization to cause a problem, and to identify possible solutions that may have escaped the attention of management. Throughout this book we examine in depth how, when, and where organizational diagnosis can help a system deal with a variety of problems. This diagnostic focus is common in industry today, primarily because of a tendency to wait until something has gone wrong before dealing with it. However, we must not forget that diagnosis can be more useful if its focus is preventive and developmental.

Diagnosis for Developmental Purposes

An organizational diagnosis is most useful when its aim is to help management assess what needs to be done to improve the organization so that it stands a better chance of achieving ambitious objectives. In this context, the focus of the diagnosis is not so much on finding the cause of problems and solving them, but on assessing the organization in its present circumstances and on developing a forward-looking, proactive approach that changes what is no longer effective while preserving and enhancing the company's unique assets and strengths. This enables the company to examine relevant major issues as a means of preparing itself to deal effectively with the future. Thus, it must constantly be kept in mind that even though many examples in this book deal with problems, such an examination should lead to improvement rather than criticism. The specific problems, in most cases, will be ancient history, and evaluations will be of little value unless they result in lessons on how to avoid such problems in the future. The focus should be on how weaknesses can be overcome or minimized, and on how strengths and assets can be further developed and used to good advantage.

The Scope of Organizational Diagnosis

Whether its purpose is remedial or developmental, the scope of a diagnosis can range from a full-blown process that involves a close examination of an organization since its founding through the present to a here-and-now approach that concerns itself only with today and what needs to be done to strengthen the organization to meet challenges ahead.

In such endeavors, the truism "You get what you pay for" is indeed applicable. Even though the emphasis of this book is on practical, economical diagnostic applications, it must be recognized that the usefulness of a diagnosis depends on the quality and thoroughness of the data collected and the extent to which those data enable the unambiguous articulation of relevant organizational issues. For this reason, it can safely be said that, if at all possible, a comprehensive rather than an issue-specific diagnosis is most effective, particularly since its larger scope enables the organization to approach issues in a developmental rather than a remedial perspective. This book describes both comprehensive and issue-specific approaches to diagnosis. Given this information, you will then have to determine the scope that would be most effective for your particular diagnostic needs.

The Phases of a Comprehensive Diagnosis

The organic diagnosis, for all its flexibility, still requires a disciplined sequence of activities. The outline below shows each step of the process and the appropriate decision points. As previously noted, organic diagnosis is a practical, comprehensive, and powerful technique, primarily because it does not require exotic credentials and expertise. Any competent manager can deal with the methodology, provided the procedures are adhered to. The following overview of the process reflects the structure of the material in the rest of the book:

    I. Plan and organize the diagnostic project
        A. Preliminary assessment and start-up (1 to 3 months)
            1. Define your role as a diagnostician
                a. Analyst
                b. Expert or problem solver

        c. Behavioral scientist or technologist
        d. Facilitator
    2. Understand the reasons for the diagnostic project
        a. Diagnosis for remedial purposes
        b. Diagnosis for developmental purposes
    3. Analyze the political environment
        a. To what extent is the sponsor or company management invested in, or responsible for, the way things are?
        b. Is the sponsor in a position of sufficient authority to legitimize the project with other key managers?
        c. Who are the significant players making up the critical mass? Is it necessary to get them involved as part of the diagnostic team?
        d. Does the situation require the establishment of an organizational development council?
    4. Present a detailed proposal
    5. Obtain final approval to proceed
    6. Organize the project
        a. Establish a political support system
            (1) If possible, establish a council
            (2) Enlist the critical mass
        b. Establish an administrative system
            (1) Define the final scope of the project
            (2) Define major task areas
            (3) Finalize the list of respondents
            (4) Finalize resource requirements
            (5) Draw up interview or data-collection schedule
        c. Assemble the diagnostic team
            (1) Select the team members
            (2) Assign responsibilities
        d. Train the diagnostic team
            (1) Interview the critical mass
            (2) Conduct a workshop
II. Collect and process diagnostic data
    A. Data gathering (1 to 3 months)
        1. Organize the logistics of interviewing
            a. Confirm the availability of interviewers
            b. Notify the respondents
            c. Match interviewer with respondent
                (1) Considerations for matching interviewers and executives
            d. Schedule the interviews
        2. Develop a reference data base
            a. Perform background research
            b. Interview key management personnel
                (1) Part 1: The strategic issues interview
                (2) Part 2: The regular interview

3. Develop the main data base
    a. The process of diagnostic interviewing
        (1) Advantages of the interview method
        (2) Disadvantages of the interview method
    b. The interview procedure
        (1) Prepare the interviewer
        (2) Prepare the respondent
    c. Important considerations
    d. Open the interview
    e. Work on data generation
    f. Possible problems during the interview
    g. Close the interview
4. Review the interview process
B. Process collected data (2 to 4 months)
    1. Establish administrative tools
    2. Transcribe notes
    3. Control paper flow
    3. Review volume and progress
    4. Organize collected data
        a. Review the transcripts
            (1) Identify usable data
            (2) Prepare data cards or computer data base
        b. Code the data cards
    5. Select the team for the balance of the project
    6. Prepare for the analysis and interpretation
        a. Develop issue categories
III. Analysis and interpretation (3 to 5 months)
    A. Corporate history and culture
        1. Corporate culture as a reality
        2. Historical development and the shaping of a corporate culture
        3. Corporate indoctrination: passing on culture, values, assets, and liabilities
        4. A framework for analyzing corporate history and culture
    B. Planning, strategy, and structure
        1. General planning practices in the organization
        2. Strategic planning
            a. Core mission
            b. Environmental scanning
                (1) Performing the environmental scanning
            c. Scenarios and strategies
                (1) Marketing strategy
                (2) Positioning the strategic business units (SBUs)
                (3) Managing the strategic business units
            d. Strategy implementation
                (1) Transition
                (2) Problems with strategy implementation
            e. The prospects of strategic planning

3. Operational planning
   4. Organizational structure
      a. Extent to which "form follows function"
   5. Evaluation of strategic advantage
      a. Environmental threat and opportunities analysis
      b. Strategic advantage profile
  C. Organizational Resources
   1. Financial resources
      a. Goals of financial management
      b. Financial-statement analysis
      c. Common-size analysis
      d. Ratio analysis
      e. Percentage-change analysis
      f. Analysis of financial goals
   2. Technological resources
   3. Physical resources
   4. Human resources
      a. Employee-turnover patterns
      b. Turnover trend analysis
      c. Performance appraisal
      d. Management development
  D. Organizational processes
   1. Leadership and power characteristics
      a. Types of leaders
   2. Authority and power
      a. Bases of power
      b. Power, influence, and politics
         (1) Power and conflict
         (2) Management of conflict
   3. Problem-solving practices
   4. Decision-making practices
   5. Reward systems
   6. Work and productivity
      a. Assess levels of performance deficiency
         (1) Individuals
         (2) Groups
         (3) Intergroups
IV. Feedback, action planning, and evaluation
  A. Complete and deliver the diagnosis (1 to 2 months)
   1. Diagnostic conclusions
      a. Summary of significant issues and problems
      b. Indicators of unresolved issues and problems
         (1) Failure to meet goals
         (2) Drop in performance
         (3) Conflict
         (4) Inaction
   2. Present phase of organizational crisis

3. Significant organizational strengths and assets
   a. Aspects of the organization that should not be changed
4. Diagnostic recommendations
5. Present the diagnosis to management
   a. The structure of the diagnosis
      (1) The introduction
      (2) The body of the report
   b. Prepare for the presentation
   c. Deliver the presentation
      (1) Introduction
      (2) Summary presentation and discussion

B. Action planning and evaluation (3 months to 1 year)
   1. Review the diagnosis with management
      a. Handle the questions
      b. Reach consensus on major issues or problem areas
   2. Action planning
   3. Plan the organizational change and development
      a. Reach agreement on the company's core mission
      b. Determine an appropriate response to the identified environmental demands
      c. Project into the future
      d. Define the desired future state
   4. Organizational interventions
   5. Evaluate the effectiveness of the diagnosis
      a. Conduct an evaluation study

PART II
Plan and Organize the Diagnostic Project

This part covers the various steps necessary to plan and organize a diagnostic project.

Since a diagnosis is likely to demand significant time and resources, it is important to assess whether the project is appropriate in the first place. This assessment includes defining clearly your role as a diagnostician and understanding the nature of the situation to be examined, as well as acknowledging the position of the project's sponsor. Since a diagnosis is likely to examine past actions of present management, you must judge the political climate of the organization, not only to determine whether you will indeed have the independence necessary to develop an unbiased study but also to ensure some measure of support from the sponsor and other people in authority.

We then discuss how to determine implementation requirements so as to include a definition of the focus and scope of the project, the target population of respondents, and the resources required.

Finally, we consider the formal organization of the project: the establishment of a legitimate management council, the enlistment and training of a diagnostic team, and the assignment of specific responsibilities for administration, data gathering, review, and analysis.

CHAPTER 2

Preliminary Assessment and Startup

A comprehensive organizational diagnosis can be proposed, planned, and conducted in a step-by-step fashion. This chapter covers the steps necessary to assess whether a diagnosis is appropriate to the situation, and what safeguards need to be taken prior to implementation, so as to ensure proper commitment from the sponsor or management. Many of the suggested precautions at this early stage of assessment are intended for situations that involve problems. Obviously, they are less of an issue when a developmental diagnosis is involved. As a sophisticated individual, however, you should satisfy yourself that the diagnosis is indeed for developmental purposes. Corporate language today is full of euphemisms intended to conceal undesirable situations. Words and phrases such as "concerns," "unrealized goals," "need to address," "short of the objective," and "need for development" are a warning that all is not well. While you understand that even a remedial diagnosis, if properly done, ultimately will be developmental in nature because it will solve problems, this may not be the intent of the sponsor, who may only be interested in a quick fix. It is therefore important to conduct a thorough preliminary assessment, regardless of the stated intent of the people sponsoring the project.

Define Your Role as a Diagnostician

The first question to be asked is, How does a manager or human resources professional—or for that matter, anyone interested in organizational improvement—become a diagnostician or a team leader for a diagnostic project? In any number of ways. Suppose, for example, you feel that a significant change or development must be initiated for the organization to survive or so it can take advantage of opportunities for growth. As a result, you could propose a diagnosis to your company's management. Or you may be appointed by management to be a leader or a team member of a diagnostic project, by virtue of your personal qualities that management may have perceived as maturity, impartiality, technical competence, and leadership. Regardless of the reason, it is important to assess at the very beginning what you are expected to do, why, and in what manner.

Undertaking a project of the magnitude and with the implications of a diagnosis requires a clear definition of your role as leader. As project manager for such an effort, you can play many parts, all of them appropriate, depending on the circumstances.

Analyst

An analyst is anyone who has a clear understanding of the methodology being used. Specialized knowledge or experience in specific areas such as finance, planning, behavioral science, or organizational development is desirable, because the role of analyst emphasizes the analysis of data using given criteria or models. In assembling an organic diagnosis, the analyst is expected to collect the data provided by a combination of sources, which could include himself and other interviewers, and to arrange the data according to the guidelines. He or she then writes the report based on what the data disclose, and interprets what is happening in light of what seems to be accepted practice by established guidelines, models, literature, and observations. The analyst generally sticks to these resources, and refrains from extraneous comments or personal observations if they are not reflected in the accepted wisdom.

Expert or Problem Solver

This role is close to what a traditional "expert" consultant in a technical discipline does. Consultants consider themselves experts in diagnostic methodology, and may be quite learned in one or more traditional disciplines such as finance, marketing, or operations. Some consultants may be experts in organizational dynamics, particularly in the psychological aspects of leadership. The expert consultant is likely to analyze the data using a disciplined and comprehensive model, and to feed the information back to management in a measured and authoritative, almost prescriptive (i.e., "tell them what to do") manner. In this role, consultants consider themselves as contributors, and will advance their own opinions with the assumption that they are involved because of their specialized knowledge and problem-solving skills, the exercise of which may or may not be bound by existing practices and guidelines.

Even though the organic diagnosis requires a high degree of competence, its methodology is based essentially on collecting and analyzing the perceptions and opinions of the organization's own members, and it is not inherently prescriptive; as a result, it does not require an expert or problem-solver approach.

Behavioral Scientist or Technologist

This role generally is played by consultant and behavioral scientists, who are likely to use OD approaches and survey research methodology, which are then processed using strict behavioral criteria, often with computer analysis. A behavioral scientist is not likely to be prescriptive, and the output of his or her work is apt to stress the communication of data that will be the basis for management action. Even though it is desirable to have someone of this background as part of the diagnostic team, participation by a behavioral technologist is not essential to an organic diagnosis, because the diagnosis is generally conducted by an organization's own managers, who focus on the more concrete problems and issues whose resolution, it is assumed, will eliminate many behavioral and interpersonal dysfunctions.

Facilitator

The facilitator role generally is played by an external or internal consultant who goes out of his or her way not to interject personal opinion or feelings into the situation, preferring the data provided by the respondents themselves to be the primary feedback mechanism. The facilitator then works with the group to help it act on the information. He or she is also likely to use group dynamics to facilitate analysis and problem solving by the management group itself. The role of the facilitator comes into its own when the data collection and its analysis are completed. Then, the facilitator works with management to discuss the implications of the diagnosis so that they can plan appropriate action. A facilitator can also be quite effective when working with limited interventions such as team building and process consultation.

As the leader of a diagnostic project, you can act in any of these roles, and sometimes in a combination of them. The organic diagnosis does not preclude a particular role; rather, it suggests that you start as an analyst up to the point at which management decides to take action after considering the conclusions of the diagnosis, whereupon you switch to the role of the facilitator and, in some cases, to that of expert to help resolve given issues. Henceforth, for convenience's sake, we refer to these roles as simply "project manager" and, alternatively, "analyst."

Understand the Reasons for the Diagnostic Project

Diagnosis for Remedial Purposes

As we have seen, a remedial diagnosis is intended primarily for solving problems. If this seems to be the case, it is necessary to ask a few critical questions to ascertain to what extent a problem really exists, who feels compelled to do something about it, and why. You need also to take into account some less obvious factors of human behavior, which may stand in the way of solving the problem. The following questions should be answered before you proceed.

1. *Who is the client/sponsor?*
   At the outset, you must find out who the real client or sponsor of the diagnosis is. Often, the manager who gives you—an internal staff member—the approval to proceed, or who signs the contract when an outside consultant is used, is designated as the person responsible for overseeing the diagnostic team's activities. But he or she is not necessarily the person with the power to make things happen. For several reasons, you must be concerned about interacting with the person who has real authority. Reporting to an intermediate manager means having to deal with a "filter" who will often deliberately—or out of fear— insist on suppressing data that the real boss may not care to face. Also, the intermediate manager often does not have the authority to open doors that might otherwise be closed to you in your role as the diagnosis project manager. Depending on who the sponsor is, people may be cooperative or sullen, candid or evasive. Like it or not, you are associated with the sponsor. If the latter is known as a forthright, fair, reliable, and—above all—powerful individual, chances are people will receive you with the proper attitude.

   If, on the other hand, the sponsor is an unpopular manager or someone who is perceived to be political and manipulative—or even worse, powerless—then you will be seen as a tool of management and will have great difficulty getting people to open up and cooperate. You must be reasonably comfortable in your relationship with the sponsor. If such comfort is not there, it may be best to withdraw.

2. *Is there a genuine problem?*
   Though you may be asked to plan and conduct a diagnosis, such a request is not always presented "up front." The sponsor may indicate that he or she feels the time has come to study how additional data might bring about general improvements. Taken literally, this request is as it should be—the prescription for a developmental diagnosis. However, make sure that a developmental approach is indeed desired. Almost invariably, it is likely a problem exists, and that problem is the primary reason why someone with your credibility is involved or a consultant has been brought in. Whether the sponsor acknowledges the problem constitutes in itself an important piece of preliminary diagnostic data, because it indicates to what extent he or she is committed to finding a genuine solution.

3. *Is the reason for the problem elusive?*
   If management knew the cause of the problem, you can safely assume that you would not be asked to take on a diagnostic project. Chances are that many people have attempted to deal with the issue, and they either failed or did not have the know-how or resources. Watch out for situations that have obvious solutions which are not being addressed, perhaps because no one else wants to take the responsibility. Often, a consultant is brought in to look at a problem. He or she then presents perfectly obvious, and valid, recommendations necessitating unsavory

actions such as staff reductions—recommendations which absolve the sponsor from making those decisions himself. As an internal consultant or manager, you cannot afford to participate in this kind of activity.

4. *Does the sponsor really feel he or she needs help?*
   The fact that you have persuaded management or a sponsor to let you conduct a diagnosis—or have been asked to do it—does not necessarily mean that the sponsor feels he or she needs help. It may be that his or her superiors feel help is necessary or that the sponsor may be seeking confirmation of his or her own conclusions. Again, it is important to make sure you are not being manipulated into doing someone else's dirty work.

5. *Is the sponsor really looking for a solution?*
   Even though a real problem exists that is begging for a solution, be wary of subconscious motives that may direct the sponsor's behavior. The sponsor may feel inadequate, guilty, and probably angry at what he or she perceives as a personal failure to solve the problem. It is possible, then, that the sponsor may consciously or unconsciously throw obstacles in your way in an attempt to prevent your finding a solution. Failure to solve the problem, on the other hand, will result in disappointment for the manager, but it may also make him or her feel better for not having been able to deal with the problem personally. A more thorough discussion of this phenomenon is provided in Appendix 2, in the discussion of "transference."

   A sponsor often feels that because he or she has hired an expert or has asked you as a respected manager for help, the solution to the problem should be as forthcoming as if you had a magic wand. Moreover, the manager may be anxious to resume the normal work routine. Therefore, there will be a tendency to look upon a minor discovery or some minuscule progress as sufficient, thus warranting termination of the rest of the diagnosis. This is particularly true when dealing with issues of human-resources development. Whether the matter concerns performance appraisal, training, or group development, once the manager recognizes that the solution may be a long-term one, there is a tendency to succumb to short-term pressure and accept a partial solution or no solution at all.

6. *Is there sufficient "pain" to motivate change?*
   It is truly amazing how many problems people will tolerate if they fear blame or long-term solutions that require investment and effort in the present. Just as a person who afraid of the dentist will avoid having a cavity filled, and will tolerate a toothache until the pain is excruciating, a manager will suffer untold inconvenience and inefficiency as long as the cure is perceived as painful, whether it is a short-term cure or one requiring time and resources. Only when the situation becomes intolerable and the manager may find his or her own job in jeopardy, will a decision reluctantly be made to seek help.

In your role of diagnostician, Harry Levinson advises that you should approach this stage of the diagnosis much as a physician would, asking such questions as:

1. *Where is the pain?*
   Generally, this is the easiest thing to observe. The pain may be expressed in financial losses, chronic low productivity, low morale, severe interpersonal difficulties among team members, or significant uncertainty about a company's future.

2. *What is it like?*
   Depending on the nature of the problem, managers may develop psychosomatic illnesses and ulcers, workers may feel extremely harassed for more production, and executives may sense significant anxiety about the company's future. Often, a sense of inferiority is expressed when the company is compared to similar organizations that are perceived as successful. In more concrete terms, organizational pain may be exhibited as a loss of market share, financial losses, and low employee morale.

3. *How long has it been going on?*
   Finding out how long the pain has existed is a valuable piece of data, because it may help isolate conditions or events that might be the cause of the problem. If the problem did not exist prior to a certain date, then time can be saved by examining what has happened since that time to change the situation and cause the pain.

4. *What has been done about it?*
   If the pain is such that a sponsor is willing to ask you or to pay a consultant to find a solution, it can generally be assumed that attempts have been made to solve the problem. In fact, it is not unusual for a company to have tolerated a painful situation for quite some time. Probably, several proposals have been made by concerned employees and turned down by management. Reasons for these rejections may be an unequal distribution of pain, with some departments or divisions not being affected by the problem until more recently; lack of understanding of the implications of the problem, thus contributing to an underestimation of it; a feeling that the solution will cost more than the problem; or political issues such as one manager's protecting his or her turf at expense of the other managers.

   For example, at a plant manufacturing surgical adhesive tape, the Primary Department, responsible for producing the plastic adhesive rolls which are then cut to size by the Finishing Department, habitually delivered an unacceptably high percentage of defective rolls, which caused the Finishing Department to jam its machines and lose production. Since the least experienced managers and supervisors were generally assigned to Finishing, the high waste and low production was attributed to inexperience, and the plant superintendent ignored complaints about the poor quality of raw stock from the Primary Department. In fact, the Primary Department had been tolerating severe technical problems for quite some time, but failed to get engineering help because it would have meant time charges to the department. Since the Primary Department was able to pass on its problem to the Finishing Department, the pain was not sufficient for them to do something about it, and the Finishing Department could not do much about the problem either, because of its low influence in the organization. The problem was eventually solved when it became apparent that the plant's low average productivity made it uncompetitive when compared to the competition.

5. *What would a "painless" situation be like?*
Answering this question before any action is taken is important, because it provides a yardstick for success. In particular, it is critical to find out if there ever was a time when things were going as desired, and to determine what conditions would be under "normal" circumstances. For example, if the pain involves low productivity in a department, you should find out what level of productivity is considered acceptable, and whether such a level was ever attained in the past.

Diagnosis for Developmental Purposes

Even though the emphasis thus far has been on preparing to deal with organizational problems, an organizational diagnosis, as briefly discussed in Chapter 1, is most useful when its aim is to help management deal more effectively with a new or more challenging environment. In this context, the focus of the diagnosis is only partially directed toward solving problems. Management may be concerned primarily with assessing the organization in its present circumstances and with developing a forward-looking, proactive approach to change what is no longer effective, while preserving and enhancing the company's unique assets and strengths. The scope of such a diagnosis can range from a full-blown process that starts with a close examination of the organization since its founding, to a here-and-now approach that concerns itself only with the present and with what needs to be done to strengthen the organization to meet the challenges ahead.

For a remedial diagnosis, the questions that have been discussed focus on the motivation of the sponsor and other executives, and on the detection of sufficient "pain" as evidence of possible motivation for change. For a developmental diagnosis, the same questions, plus an analysis of the political environment as discussed in the following section, also apply, because management commitment is still necessary—even crucial—when planned development of an organization is contemplated. You can also assume that the desire to develop the organization carries with it a certain element of pain, or at least a desire to avoid it, possibly because someone in power has detected negative business trends that may affect the organization. On the other hand, management, especially if it has a successful track record, may indeed be looking at diagnosis as another tool that will help improve the competitiveness of the organization. Again, regardless of the reasons behind a commission for a diagnosis, you need to be clear about what the motivations of the sponsors are.

Analyze the Political Environment

If the organization's problems, challenges, and solutions are fairly clear, the issue is not so much whether a diagnosis will help but why necessary and obvious action has not already being taken. Could it be that no one wants to take responsibility for the genesis of the problem or address the solution because the issue is politically sensitive? Or is it that the staff knows what to do, but dares not contradict previous management decisions, such as the purchase of expensive and unfortunately unsuitable equipment, and thus is seeking an "outside expert" to bring the message home? In this kind of situation, it makes no sense to proceed with a diagnosis, because the solution is obvious. Rather, you should explore the reasons for the lack in communication, the evasive behavior, or possible alienation between the workers and management. You could, therefore, conduct a different diagnosis than originally intended, but with a better chance for success, provided ways are found to make management recognize what the real problem is.

To What Extent Is the Sponsor or Company Management Invested in, or Responsible for, the Way Things Are?

If management—or the sponsor himself—has been with the organization for many years, chances are it—or he—either is responsible or has participated in decisions that have led to the present state of affairs. This can be a dangerous situation for you as the leader of the diagnosis, because the pride and reputation of many managers is at stake, not to mention the possibility that management may fear being blamed for the problems. Even if management has commissioned the diagnosis, you should take care to develop data that show cause-and-effect in the context in which such decisions were originally made. Often, decisions have to be made with incomplete data or may be forced upon managers because of special circumstances. Exercise care to present causes of problems as issues that, when addressed, will probably be resolved. Blaming individuals and pointing fingers will almost certainly result in attempts by management to discredit the diagnosis, its source of data, and, ultimately, the analyst as well.

Is the Sponsor in a Position of Sufficient Authority to Legitimize the Project With Other Key Managers?

In its initial stages, a diagnosis generally elicits predictable reactions: (1) some faint hope that the study will indeed lead to solutions, (2) significant skepticism about the chances of being successful at this particular time, and (3) some measure of apprehension and fear about who might get the blame for what is or is not happening. It can be safely assumed, then, that obtaining cooperation will not be easy, unless the sponsor of the diagnosis is perceived as significant and powerful enough to enforce cooperation should he or she find it necessary to do so. Lack of cooperation is rarely overt. It is expressed in subtle and not so subtle ways, such as not showing up for interviews, having to attend to "emergencies," or being tied up with monthly financial closings. It is important to ascertain at the outset how others in the organization will perceive the project. If the sponsor is essentially a colleague and the diagnosis is for purposes of identifying problems and causes in his or her department, even though some data may need to be gathered outside that department, it is likely other managers will cooperate. However, if the scope of the diagnosis is global, affecting the whole organization, then only the top manager has sufficient authority to legitimize the project.

Who Are the Significant Players Making Up the Critical Mass? Is It Necessary to Get Them Involved as Part of the Diagnostic Team?

Many stories have been told about organizations that have commissioned expensive consulting projects and studies, only to file them away with no action taken on the recommendations. The reason often given for this consequence is that the consultants were not aware of the "uniqueness" of the organization and, as a result, failed to take certain considerations into account. Unfortunately, they add, such failure made the recommendations less valid than they could have been. The truth, in this case, is irrelevant. It could be that the company's managers were correct in rejecting the consulting report. More often, however, they may have exercised the previously discussed fear of admitting that an outsider might have a solution to a problem that could not be dealt with internally. Essentially, they are reluctant to admit failure, and they suppress a valid study that they had paid for in order to feel better about themselves. A device to overcome this potential pitfall involves using selected knowledgeable employees as part of the diagnostic team. If these employees are the right people, they will be useful in the analysis by virtue of their familiarity with the organization.

Key people at middle- and upper-management levels possess considerable influence, regardless of their formal titles or official places in the organizational chart. These people have to be identified at the outset, and an assessment needs to be made about the potential power and influence they can bring to the situation. This group of powerful people is called the "critical mass"— the critical few who can make the difference. Without them, little can be done.

Identifying the members of the critical mass is relatively easy. In a well-documented instance (see Appendix 3), the author, acting as the project manager of a major diagnostic effort, during the course of several conversations with many people asked essentially: "Who can get things done around here? Who has 'clout,' power, and influence?" He then went to the nominees and, in a subtle way, he asked them if they thought they had power. When the responses were affirmative, he considered the nominees "powerful," the logic being: "If they think he has power, and so does he, then he probably *does* have power." The net result of such an informal analysis often yields valuable dividends in forming a list of people who make up the genuine power structure of the organization.

In the same project, the author managed to persuade the managers of the critical mass to become part of the diagnostic team. Not only did this remove a potentially significant obstacle to the diagnostic effort, but it provided an opportunity for these people to better understand each other and the problems and issues facing the organization. When it was time to implement the action plans, the people who could make it happen did not have to be sold on the idea.

Does the Situation Require the Establishment of an Organizational Development Council?

As a general rule, an organizational development council (ODC) is desirable. For practical reasons, though, a mandate from the top manager may be all you can expect. However, in instances in which there are many powerful managers who may challenge the leadership, or as a sound strategy for involving the key people in decision making, establishing an ODC is generally a good idea, if it can be sold. Most successful change efforts in organizations have in common both top management commitment and an understanding of the effort. An organizational development council is a semipermanent body of company executives who are asked to play an active role in the planning, execution, and evaluation of the diagnosis, as well as in the change effort that is likely to result if the recommendations are implemented in whole or in part.

Specifically, the role of the ODC is to:

1. Stress top management's involvement in the diagnostic project
2. Act as an advisory group to the diagnosis project manager in matters of strategy for improving the chances of conducting a successful diagnosis
3. Review the conclusions of the diagnostic report and assist in setting development objectives
4. Act as a monitoring and evaluative body
5. Act as a channel of communication to the president and/or chief executive officer (if the latter is not a member of the council)

How is an organizational development council assembled? Generally, you must have the sponsor convinced that such a body would be useful to the successful execution of the diagnosis. He or she must be willing to undertake the risk of involving top power figures in a project that will be highly visible and the results of which might be critical of the present approach to business or of the council members' past decisions. The positive aspects of involving significant figures also should not be overlooked. The political realities of corporate life suggest that it is always better for people involved in risky decision making to get others involved, so that blame can be shared should something unpalatable surface. Of course, credit is also shared for successful results. Lastly, association with a change effort generally facilitates commitment of the individuals by virtue of their involvement in the diagnosis from its inception.

A simple strategy for soliciting participation by top company officers is for the sponsor, and preferably the CEO, to send a memorandum to the selected individuals. The letter should state the major goals of the project and describe the reason for seeking each person's involvement at the outset. A typical message is shown in Figure 2–1.

The sponsorship of the diagnosis now becomes a joint affair, and all key people in the organization can feel some measure of involvement in something important. A key benefit accruing from these people's participation at this level is that it facilitates cooperation from their own people.

Present a Detailed Proposal

At this point, it is prudent for you, as project manager, to prepare and submit a final proposal detailing the scope of the project. This proposal takes into account any new information you have obtained since your initial charge to

Figure 2-1. Invitation to the council.

> As you know, the Management Committee decided to initiate a significant organizational development effort to help us review where we are today and what we have to do to increase our effectiveness and profitability as a whole. For this reason, we decided to initiate a major organizational diagnosis led by John Doe, who will be relieved of his departmental responsibilities for the duration of the project. At the outset, as project manager for the diagnosis, John will be responsible for planning and conducting a broad and comprehensive review of all departments. This review will involve a systematic evaluation of organizational effectiveness; the development of a strategic plan for improvement; and the development of human resources to implement necessary changes and, more important, to lead the company in the future toward a different business environment.
>
> In order to provide the necessary guidance and management overview to this important effort, an Organizational Development Council (ODC) has been formed. You are asked to become a member of this council.
>
> The initial role of the ODC will be to review, consider, and approve the format, content, and scope of the contemplated organizational diagnosis. You will then be asked to be available for consultation throughout the study and to review the findings and recommendations when they are submitted to the council in a few months. Please join us for the initial meeting of the council, which will be scheduled shortly.

examine the feasibility of a diagnosis. It is a necessary step, primarily because the sponsor or council needs to be aware of and approve the scope of the diagnosis, as well as the budget that will go with it. The scope should define whether the diagnosis will be comprehensive—i.e., whether it is applicable to the whole organization and all its functions, so that all data provided by the respondents will be considered, or that the data will be restricted, meaning that the range of the inquiry will be limited to an issue, an area, or a department. An example of a proposal is provided in Appendix 1.1.

Obtain Final Approval to Proceed

The sponsor or ODC should be given sufficient time to review your proposal and to make comments. It is also advisable to hold one or more meetings to clarify questions. The more typical responses by ODC members are likely to be as follows:*

> "I assume the approach here is not to give the questionnaire to any persons beforehand, since they would compare notes, waste time, etc."

> "Does the interviewer have a secretary available to minimize errors? Also, will he or she help record and compile data, and review same for accuracy, thus saving time for the manager?"

> "By looking at the resources required, I estimated what the diagnostic effort would cost: 72 hours $\times$ 28 people = 53.8 workweeks or 269 work-days = \$40,350."

The last statement, a version of which is inevitable, is the final test of whether management is committed to make the diagnosis happen. It is likely that the council will attempt to cut corners, principally by reducing the scope of the study. The sponsor's role is critical in minimizing potential neutralization of the planned effort by well-meaning, cost-conscious executives who—deep down—would rather do without a diagnosis in the first place. The proof of commitment is whether management is willing to foot the bill. As project manager, you should use the deliberations as a valuable element of diagnostic data for future reference.

At this point, you should be reasonably certain that conditions in the organization will allow you to conduct and, it is hoped, successfully execute the diagnosis. Before proceeding, however, again make certain the sponsor is committed to the project and fully understands the implications of conducting such a study. Hold a meeting to discuss a full outline of the next steps and seek the sponsor's unequivocal blessing. (In fact, such wide approval is rarely given. The best that can be expected is a mandate accompanied by apprehension.)

---

*The darkened quotes that follow, and others you will find throughout the text, represent actual or typical commentary and remarks made by people involved in organizational diagnoses.

Before proceeding, it is prudent to go back to your proposal and formally agree on what essentially is a contract or documented list of expectations. This contract includes:

- *Objectives* of the diagnostic effort
- *Results* to be obtained
- *Methods* to be employed and avoided
- *Roles* of the consultant and the sponsor, clearly defined
- *Constraints* within which the effort must be conducted

Organize the Project

Establish a Political Support System

If Possible, Establish a Council

As discussed previously, it is always desirable to set up a council to sponsor the diagnosis. In practice, persuading the sponsor to establish such a body is quite difficult, unless the study encompasses the whole organization.

Enlist the Critical Mass

Again, same as with the enlistment of an ODC, it is highly desirable to identify and involve the managers who make up the critical mass, preferably as members of the diagnostic team. We have already seen how such individuals can be identified through a simple "power diagnosis." If the project gets this far, an orientation to the project and appropriate training for the managers must be ready for use.

Prior to contacting the individuals selected as data gatherers, as the project manager you should advise the candidates' managers, even if the individuals have already been approved by the organizational development council. Generally, a simple memorandum such as the one shown in Figure 2-2 should suffice.

A memorandum inviting each member of the critical mass to a preliminary meeting should also be developed. Figure 2-3 is an example.

At the preliminary meetings, the managers should receive a thorough briefing. At the outset, the purpose of the meeting should be stated, namely: (1) to discuss the scope of the diagnostic study and (2) to discuss their roles as members of the diagnostic team.

The group should be given a presentation that includes a discussion of reasons why management has decided to initiate a diagnosis and a review of the plan, including desired milestones and tasks. At this time, they should be advised that a training program will be forthcoming, in order to ensure their full understanding of what is expected.

It is quite common for such meetings to be punctuated by questions from the participants, ranging from incredulity to skepticism. Some comments will reveal a measure of anxiety. Often, such a high-powered group will not be compliant or cooperative at the outset. The only way to deal with such a situation is to be as open as possible.

One of the first questions likely to be asked is whether management is indeed behind the effort. The response should be that management is not relying on consultants, but is mobilizing valuable internal resources—i.e., the people in this room—to conduct an in-depth analysis of the organization. This is evidence of a willingness to spend considerable sums to obtain valuable help from the people in the organization who are likely to be the best available resources for feedback.

A second challenge, in the form a question, will probably show skepticism about the likely success of this effort compared to previous studies. The reply should be that, indeed, there is a significant difference. First, the study will be conducted by the company's own professionals, of which the people in the room will be key participants; the project will be difficult to ignore under such circumstances. Second, the model used for the diagnosis will allow the most thorough coverage possible; no "sacred cow" will be spared scrutiny. Moreover, the intent is not just to read the "climate" of the organization, but to analyze virtually all meaningful aspects of organizational function. Third, and most important, it will be difficult to "bury" the report, since too many people will be involved in the effort.

To the likely question indicating anxiety about participation in a project that might be perceived as controversial, your response might be that the se-

Figure 2-2. Memorandum to participant's manager.

TO: George J. Smith

FROM: Sarah Clinton

SUBJECT: Organizational Study

The Organizational Development Council has approved plans to conduct a corporate-wide organizational study. The major objective of the study is to develop information that may lead to improvement of organizational performance. The study will be conducted by a team consisting of selected managers from the operating departments. One of your subordinates, whose name appears on the list below, will be invited to participate as a member of the team. Attached is a memorandum for your signature, requesting him or her to join the organizational study team, along with relevant information about the planned study. Please advise your staff member as soon as possible. Should there be any question, please do not hesitate to advise me. Your cooperation is sincerely appreciated.

lection of the supplementary team was not random, but quite deliberately an attempt to enlist the company's best people—the people who hold genuine influence and respect, without whom it is unlikely things could get done. **"We know, and management knows, that without your participation we will fail."** This is a statement that always works, and is entirely appropriate, because it is foolish to try to deceive such people by not disclosing the real reason for their selection. Generally, people are stunned with such candor. It is possible that a recalcitrant member might suggest that the group is being manip-

Figure 2-3. Memorandum to potential team members.

TO: Janet S. Smith

FROM: Sarah Clinton

SUBJECT: Organizational Study

The Organizational Development Council, in an announcement which was sent to all employees a few days ago, advised that plans are being made to conduct a corporate-wide study, whose primary purpose is to develop information that might help improve organizational performance. The study is a company-wide activity. It will be the effort of a work-team composed of members of the corporate staff and selected key managers in the operating departments. You are asked to become a member of the study team. In making this request, we have taken into account your level in the organization, your departmental responsibilities, and your knowledge of company operations. Most important, we believe that you will see this task as an opportunity to help the company improve its operational effectiveness and ability to compete in the marketplace.

As a member of the diagnostic team, you will be asked to attend a workshop describing the diagnostic study, conduct interviews to collect data, and verify the accuracy of same. It is fully recognized that you are a key professional with great demands on your time. We are nevertheless asking for your involvement in this important task because you have exhibited the talent, enthusiasm, and dedication necessary to help lead the company toward meaningful change and development. A preliminary meeting to fully explain the details of the project has been scheduled on two alternate dates:

January 31; 10 A.M.–2 P.M.

February 2; 10 A.M.–2 P.M.

Please call my office and indicate which meeting you would prefer to attend. Attached for your review is a list of participants in this project. Should you have any questions in the interim, please do not hesitate to call.

ulated into participating. Even so, almost invariably one of the group will retort with a statement such as:

> "Can't you see he's leveling with you? Whether or not you agree with what's being planned, at least they are not trying to do it behind your back, and, believe me, it's a hell of a change from what has been done in the past!"

It is likely that a heated discussion will ensue, still punctuated by skepticism about management's intentions, particularly its commitment to change. The only way to deal with such assertions is to point out, again, that in the final analysis, management is sinking a lot of money into the project. Even the most skeptical of participants must admit that this constitutes a certain measure of commitment.

The final question generally will be whether individuals in the group can withdraw from participation in the project. The response should be that forcing anyone to participate is counterproductive and inconsistent with the objectives of the diagnosis. It should be stressed, however, that the importance of the diagnosis demands that the decision to participate be held until after the workshop. At that time, a decision not to participate will be honored as long as it is based on a clear understanding of the nature of the diagnostic project, its goals, and its demands upon individual participants. Making such a decision at that time, after all the facts about the project are known, is fair to the company and to the participants.

After such issues are addressed, you should describe the objectives of the upcoming workshop, which will enable participants to: (1) conduct diagnostic interviews with designated members of the organization for the purpose of gathering relevant data, and (2) assist in developing a diagnostic report containing feedback, analysis, interpretation, and recommendations to management.

The managers should be advised that each of them will be interviewed before any training takes place. Since they represent a key segment of the organization's leadership, it is absolutely necessary that they be interviewed before any "contamination" occurs owing to training.

Establish an Administrative System

Setting up procedures for effective management of the diagnostic process is essential. A project of this scope must address a number of technical and logistical tasks. The following are general recommendations.

Define the Final Scope of the Project

The most extensive data collection and range of inquiry is a comprehensive diagnosis. By definition, such a diagnosis involves an examination of virtually all aspects of an organization, with no defined boundaries. The scope of this type of study is essentially up to the project manager. It is assumed, of course, that management has provided such a mandate.

A comprehensive diagnosis should be designed to enable a collection of data that is focused on both strategic and operational issues. Your definition of the project should specify the range of diagnostic coverage. For instance, state whether the study is to be comprehensive or restricted, based on a specific model or conducted along the principles of the organic approach.

If the scope of the diagnosis is restricted, the areas of inquiry should be defined at the outset. These may include any or all of the following:

- Historical data relevant to present circumstances
- Corporate culture
- Structural data, including organization, policies, procedures, and communication
- Functional and operational data
- Attitudes, internal and external

In a restricted diagnosis, management may wish to specify additional areas of particular interest, such as evaluations of the competition, product development evaluations, strategic portfolio analysis, financial review, and the like.

Kinds of data. You need also to define the nature of the information that will be sought. The diagnosis might include collecting relevant data expressing (1) perceptions of a defined respondent population that may include executives, managers, employees, former employees, and consultants or (2) relatively neutral facts from researchers and outside data sources such as newspapers, publications, and commercial data bases.

Data-collection methods. Define the methods that will be used to collect the data. These methods may include:

- *Structured interviews*—questions following a prescribed series developed by the interviewing team along with management, or questions provided by a diagnostic model
- *Unstructured interviews*—nonleading questions aimed at generating the respondent's own definition of relevant problems and issues
- *Questionnaires*—paper-and-pencil instruments developed by the diagnostic team in conjunction with management or using commercial products
- *Survey-research methods*—data collection by consultants and subsequent feedback of the data to management

In defining the scope of the data collection, consider especially using strategic-issues analysis (example in Appendix 1.5), which is designed specifically to facilitate the interviewing of executives. This analysis explores how executives view strategic issues affecting the organization, and helps determine the degree of consensus among key figures around the company's core mission and principal strategic objectives.

A general interview can be administered to executives and to selected managers and employees. Special paper-and-pencil instruments are useful when management wants to collect general employee attitudes about various issues such as benefits programs. In addition, basic background information about the company—that is, documents, newspapers, books, and commercial data bases—should be reviewed to create a comprehensive data base.

The following steps generally are necessary to define the magnitude of the diagnostic effort:

1. Review the corporate organizational chart and select the various individuals to be interviewed.
2. Develop a list of representative managers and department heads who will be included in the study as members of the diagnostic team.
3. Design appropriate questionnaires to generate data about defined areas from existing and previous employees, as well as external contacts such as clients, vendors, and other meaningful sources.
4. Determine the types of records and relevant data that will need to be examined.

These steps do not necessarily have to be taken in sequential order, as long as they are addressed at some point during the diagnosis.

Define Major Task Areas

The administrative task clusters could be as follows:

Task Cluster 1

- Develop a master project checklist for the entire diagnostic effort (see Appendix 1.2).
- Update the control chart daily to document progress.
- Obtain data from the area/data managers, as necessary, to update the control chart.
- Promptly notify the area managers or the project leader of obstacles that may delay the project.
- Develop and implement a procedure or filing system for the systematic classification of completed components of the diagnosis.

Task Cluster 2

- Assure availability of needed equipment (dictaphones, recorders, tapes, typewriters or word processors, and materials).
- Obtain required clerical support.
- Coordinate work flow of clerical resources to ensure prompt transcription of taped data and other relevant documents as the diagnostic effort progresses.
- Assure that transcribed data are promptly forwarded to the appropriate area manager for validation and analysis.

Task Cluster 3

- Develop a master schedule for interviewing.
- Ascertain the interviewer's availability and time preferences.
- Set up interviews with respondents.
- Forward scheduling information to the interviewers.
- Keep track of cancelled or rescheduled meetings and arrange for new dates.
- Post schedules.

Finalize the List of Respondents

In a comprehensive diagnosis, it is desirable to select the target population so that a cross section of employees is interviewed (for example, the top management group, critical mass, managers, professionals, and clericals). The criteria used for selection of the respondent population should be consistent with the scope of the diagnosis itself. If, for example, the focus will be on how the organization interfaces with the environment on a strategic level, it would not be fruitful to involve first-line supervisors and secretaries. On the other hand, if the the focus is on the organization's relationship with the community, then a representative cross section of the employee population can provide meaningful, up-to-date data.

This is a preliminary definition of the potential respondent population. Final selection should take place after top management and the members of the diagnostic team themselves have been interviewed, because after collection of data from these groups, you might want to target the main respondent group on the basis of the issues that appear most important. For example, if the predominant theme of the executive interviews centers on operational effectiveness, you may want to increase your sample in the manufacturing operations group. If, on the other hand, the theme focuses on morale, then a broader sample may be more appropriate.

To obtain a representative sampling, it is desirable to collect data from at least 10 percent of the employees. The respondents should include:

- All executives
- All department heads
- Selected managers representative of all major functional areas
- Selected professional personnel from all relevant areas
- Selected clerical personnel from all relevant areas

Finalize Resource Requirements

There is no way to get around it; an organization-wide diagnosis is expensive. The following are general guidelines for planning resources for such an undertaking in a relatively large company:

Human resources. The administrative system will include a range of human resources. These may include:

- *A sponsor or ODC*—who should budget enough time to function in advisory, evaluative, and monitoring roles during the conduct of the study and during subsequent development and implementation of action plans
- *A project manager*—by now already appointed, a respected member of middle management who will probably work on the diagnosis full time
- *A diagnostic team*—composed of one or more members of the human resources staff, and selected line managers, members of the critical mass who will participate in data collection and some of them in analysis and interpretation

The selected line managers will also be reviewers of the diagnostic drafts, and will act as resources to the project manager when necessary, particularly when detailed data about the organization are sought. In order to anticipate potential objections to using busy managers for such an undertaking, you should acknowledge the burden that they will be asked to bear. Point out that you are fully aware that the individuals are key managers who already face great demands on their time. It is important for the sponsor and ODC to realize, however, that those individuals are the people who "make things happen" in the organization. Employing their talents, credibility, and clout at the initial stages of the diagnosis not only will facilitate the conduct of the project but will give these people a long-sought opportunity to lead the company toward meaningful change and development.

Table 2-1 provides a summary of how such human resources requirements can be quantified.

Now equate those figures with the allocation of time. For example, an equation for time use set for interviewing and preliminary processing of responses would be:

$$300 \text{ respondents} \div 30 = 10 \text{ interviews per team member}$$

Then, for each team member,

$$10 \text{ interviews} \times 2 \text{ hours per interview} = 20 \text{ hours total}$$

If you calculate that each team member needs an average of 10 hours to prepare the interview data, you have a total of 30 hours per team member. Thus,

$$30 \text{ team members} \times 30 \text{ hours each} = 900 \text{ hours}$$

Note that two hours have been allocated per interview. It is prudent to do so, because in some instances the entire two hours will be necessary. However, in practice the average interview will take one hour or less.

For core team activities, assume two people at full time for three months and four people at half time for three months. The technical review of certain data by critical-mass managers is generally 10 percent of the total time required.

Table 2-1. Personnel involved in diagnosis.

	Number of Persons
Total number of employees in the company	6,000
Number of managers/professional employees	600
Sampling—50 percent of managers/professionals	300
Diagnostic teams	
Core team members (generally will stay with the project until completion)	6
Supplementary team members (line managers/critical mass)	22
Administration team	6
Graduate students, part time (recommended)	2
Total diagnostic team members	36

Financial resources. Financial resources—in the form of an adequate budget—should be requested at this time. Sufficient detail should be provided, along with cost estimates for the following items:

1. Time of the diagnostic team members. This includes salaries of the project manager, ODC, managers of the critical mass, and the equivalent of one hour's time of each respondent at average rates.
2. Cost of data transcription, preparing drafts, and final typing.
3. Cost of office supplies and equipment such as word processors, dictating machines, typewriters, and duplicating equipment.
4. Cost of facilities used.
5. Cost of producing the report, including artwork, duplication, binding, and similar expenses.
6. Cost of research, particularly if extensive library searches are conducted, including paying graduate students for this work.

Draw Up Interview or Data-Collection Schedule

Indicate that the people selected to participate in data collection should receive orientation and appropriate training for one month. The actual interviews should be scheduled for the subsequent two months, depending more or less on the number of respondents. Data review, analysis, and interpretation should take about three months. Preparation of the diagnostic report itself should take about one month.

Assemble the Diagnostic Team

Select the Team Members

The composition of the diagnostic team is crucial. We have already mentioned that, ideally, it should be composed of an internal project manager, one or more human resources professionals, and selected line managers as members of the critical mass. The larger and more complex the scope of the diagnosis, the more representative the diagnostic team should be. For example, in one of the largest diagnostic projects (see Appendix 3), the diagnostic team included one internal project manager, six members of the Training Department, twenty-four line managers as a supplementary team, twelve members of the training department to help with processing and logistics, many clericals involved in transcription and typing, three academicians, and several graduate students. The objective, of course, is to do the job with the fewest possible people.

Assign Responsibilities

Provisions must be made for assembling, categorizing, and analyzing an enormous amount of incoming data. This can best be done by appointing individuals to perform specific administrative tasks.

Area managers. Data/area managers are responsible for seeing that all data relevant to an area or issue are properly categorized, treated, and organized. Such areas could be Performance Appraisal, Strategic Planning, Marketing, and the like. Specifically, the data/area manager, in addition to carrying out other major tasks in the diagnosis (interviewing, data analysis, and integration), should be responsible for (1) validating the data, either by checking back with the source of the information, by having a technical expert review the data, or both; (2) ascertaining the completeness of the data; and (3) organizing the data so that they will be readily available for treatment in subsequent phases of the project.

Project administrator. This appointment is necessary in order to coordinate interdependent administrative task clusters. The function is critical to the performance of the project, particularly in facilitating the various tasks in an efficient manner.

Editor(s). These should be people with appropriate writing skills to ensure the quality of the final report. They should be responsible for reviewing the diagnostic drafts for spelling and style, and for working with the authors to produce a literate final version.

Temporary research personnel. An effective, and inexpensive, way to supplement your resources is by using graduate students to perform various tasks during the diagnosis. For example, you can arrange for students to work on basic background research, particularly the section dealing with historical perspectives. By reviewing books, articles, and documents and supplementing that data with interviews of "old timers" in the company, students can focus on the development of the organization over the years, and analyze its past crises, successes, and failures to help you understand what elements molded the company into what it is today.

Other administrative considerations involving the planning and scheduling of interviews is discussed in Chapter 3.

Train the Diagnostic Team

Besides organizing the logistics of the diagnosis, your most immediate task is to train the diagnostic team in the concepts, methodology, and administrative processes of the diagnostic method.

Interview the Critical Mass

The managers in the critical mass, having been identified as the "power brokers" of the organization, naturally can be sources of important data that should not be lost. These people should be interviewed just like other employees, and the interviews should take place before the managers participate in the diagnostic training, otherwise vital data will become adulterated by a premature knowledge of the process.

These preliminary interviews are also valuable as indicators of how subsequent interviews will be perceived in the organization. It is possible that these managers may exhibit fear of involvement, cynicism about the intent of the diagnosis, and negativism about its chances of success. At this stage their feelings should be acknowledged, but there should be no effort to discuss the behavior or to change their perceptions. Only after the interviews are over and the training is under way, will it be appropriate to review those concerns and explore how their negative attitudes can be subordinated, at least temporarily, so as to interview employees on an unbiased and nonevaluative basis.

Conduct a Workshop

A workshop should then be convened off the company premises, preferably at a location devoid of after-hours amenities, in order to ensure continued evening work without regrets.

The content of the workshop should be designed so that, at the end of the training program, the participants will be able to:

1. Conduct diagnostic interviews for the purpose of collecting valid data.
2. Differentiate between the respondent's verbalized data and the interviewer's own observations.
3. Assist in the development of a diagnostic report to management.

The agenda for the program should contain the concepts behind the diagnostic model, the fundamentals of interviewing, and practice in interviewing.

Start the session by briefly reviewing the presentation previously given to the sponsor or ODC. Besides providing the participants with a general overview of what the executives have heard, you should focus on what management expects from the diagnosis. This discussion provides the team with a focus and a list of objectives.

Key points. Several key points about the diagnosis process itself need to be stressed:

1. A diagnosis is a sophisticated method of examining issues, problems, and challenges facing a company. It is also a sound, fundamental step that enables the team to take a "snapshot" of where the organization is today, so that decisions, based on valid information, can be made by management.
2. An organization-wide, systematic diagnosis helps sort out the multiple causes of problems, thus avoiding superficial or simplistic solutions.
3. A systematic diagnosis provides the basis for conclusions, plans for solutions, and carries out action plans with reasonable assurance that the real problems will, indeed, be solved using appropriate actions.
4. The diagnosis itself is only a start; it induces subsequent action that will specify the desired objectives and direction of change, predicated on addressing variables with the most potential for payoff.

It should be stressed that the diagnosis is a major intervention in its own right. A close examination of various aspects of the company reveals facts, perceptions, patterns, and phenomena that, in all probability, cannot be ignored. It is likely that certain problems can be addressed on the spot by responsible individuals who might become aware of their existence through feedback by a respondent, or from having gone through the interview process personally. A person's having to articulate opinions and perceptions to an interviewer often results in his or her thinking through the nature of issues and problems; solutions may even surface that hitherto may have gone unnoticed. Whether or not the recommendations of the diagnostic team will be accepted and implemented by management, the fact remains that some changes will occur just because someone asked a lot of questions.

Ethical guidelines. An important issue to be discussed during the training is the inevitable tendency to focus on identifying problems and their causes, and on finding ways to cure what ails the organization. Certainly, it is possible for a diagnostic team to lose sight of its major task as a data gatherer by becoming overly critical, rather than remaining as an uninvolved analyst observing the activities of people engaged in the performance of complex tasks with various degrees of success. It must be recognized that the diagnosis, and subsequent action by management, will be more effective if based on an accurate analysis of the situation and not on the biases or defenses of the decision-making respondents. A corollary is that the diagnosis itself will be more accurate and palatable to the recipients if it reflects facts and not the biases of the diagnostician.

The attitude of the diagnostic team during the process is important. It is desirable to avoid the medical approach: Something hurts, let's find what causes the pain, and let's prescribe a cure. Rather, it is preferable to use the positive approach: We're OK, healthy, but let's find out ways to be even more healthy. You should not forget that most organizations also have significant strengths and positives, and these should be at least acknowledged as a legitimate part of the diagnostic process. As project manager, you should be concerned about relatively inexperienced and eager diagnosticians losing sight of their fundamental responsibility, which is not to find fault, but to find ways to help the people in the organization do a better job by "working smarter, not harder."

Also, in spite of the frequent references to initiating change, in fact change is not the primary task of the diagnostician. The diagnostician's primary responsibility is to generate valid data that can be used by management to assess the situation and make responsible choices based on the available alternatives. You must be particularly aware that "change" is often construed to mean disruption, with some validity. Most employees probably have been affected negatively by changes such as reorganizations and takeovers; experiences such as these have made them defensive and wary of change for its own sake. People will probably remember past consulting studies that hardly benefited the company or themselves in particular.

The natural skepticism and potential opposition to any program that is likely to result in change necessitate incorporating means to overcome this expected resistance to the diagnosis. Just as important, the subsequent action plans beyond the diagnosis need to be planned just as carefully to ensure that the change effort is perceived as a positive event and not as a threat.

Certainly, the attitude of the primary diagnostic team should be unequivocally positive throughout the process, particularly since his or her attitude spills over onto the attitude of the supplementary team, which is likely to be skeptical about the project in the first place.

Practice interviewing. As soon as the group begins to interview people, this in a real sense starts the intervention activity. The way the diagnostic team approaches this first, and extremely important, step has implications for how the diagnosis itself will be received by all concerned and sets the stage for its chances of helping in organizational improvement and development.

The best way to practice interviewing is to break the participants into triads, and staff members should monitor this exercise. Each participant receives a copy of the basic questionnaire, which he or she uses as a guide for interviewing a member of the triad. The participant proceeds with asking the questions as if he or she were talking to an actual respondent. Feedback is obtained from the member of the triad not engaged in the interview at the time. Acting as an observer and as a critic of the interview, the third party makes appropriate notes, describing positive and negative aspects of the interview. Observations should be made about facial expressions, words and phrases used, as well as techniques discussed earlier in the workshop. (The interviewing process as described in Chapter 3 should be used as a guide.) The process continues until each of the triad members completes a term as interviewer. If any issues surface that were not covered during the training, appropriate notes should be made for discussion when the whole class reconvenes.

Program closure. At this stage, a critical issue needs to be addressed: should the managers, as a group or as individuals, participate as members of the diagnostic team? Remind them that they were allowed to postpone their decision until after the training program, to assure a full understanding of the project, its scope, and its implications. Now ask the participants to consider seriously their reasons for joining the project, or for not doing so. Make it clear that you will not accept "lack of time" as a valid excuse. Practically everyone in management is under extreme time pressures, and there is no question that participation in the diagnosis places an additional burden; nevertheless, the diagnosis needs to be done. Even so, no one should be forced to participate.

Managers who decide to participate will be expected to handle questions about the project constructively, whether or not they are convinced that the right thing is being done or is being done in the right way. Managers who choose not to participate should be asked to give the diagnostic effort the benefit of the doubt, at least until the project is completed. A decision need not be made on the spot, and it is appropriate for managers to indicate their decision within an appropriate period of time.

Close the session by thanking the group for its patience and hard work, and indicate that you are looking forward to working with them in this important undertaking.

PART III
Collect and Process Diagnostic Data

This part covers the critical steps of data gathering and initial processing. First, in the logistics of interviewing we explore the key administrative tasks involved with scheduling the interviews. Next, we review how a reference data base is developed. This step involves necessary background research about the organization and the interviewing of executives; these sessions include, in addition to the regular interview, a discussion of strategic issues, core mission statements, and organizational objectives.

The section on development of the main data base, which is information collected from the main respondent population, includes a thorough discussion of diagnostic interviewing techniques. Chapter 4 treats the processing of raw data into the transcripts, which then form the basis for the analysis that follows.

CHAPTER 3
Data Gathering

During the initial planning stages, you selected the main respondent groups on the basis of a "diagonal slice" of the organization, representing as many groups of employees as possible at all levels. During this process, some pressure may have been applied to restrict the inquiry below a certain level. If at all possible, however, you should insist on a complete cross section of the population in order to obtain a balanced view of the organization's issues and problems. Such a selection can be made on the basis of a computer algorithm if the resources are available.

Organize the Logistics of Interviewing

Now that you are ready to start the project, you must address the logistics of matching interviewers, executives, and employees. This is not necessarily a simple task because, in most busy organizations, people are not always available when you want them. It is therefore necessary to commence scheduling interviews as soon as possible.

Confirm the Availability of Interviewers

At the outset, make sure that the members of the diagnostic team who are to conduct the interviews are available. This is best done by sending them each a brief note such as the one shown in Figure 3-1, accompanied by a chart such as the one shown in Figure 3-2.

It is wise not to schedule more than two interviews for each, which should be the minimum requirement for every participant of the diagnostic team. The opposite will also occur; you will receive expressions of overwhelming interest by some team members who will volunteer to do more interviews after they complete their assigned ones. They will indicate that they enjoy doing the interviews and learn more about the company, their colleagues, and themselves all at once. This inevitable interest and dedication will probably surprise you, particularly since, in the early stages of the project, you will remem-

Figure 3-1. Interview scheduling letter.

> Please choose two alternative times and days for your interview and insert the information in the appropriate boxes on the accompanying chart. Indicate your first preference, and we will do everything we can to meet it. One more consideration: even though an interview should be completed in one hour or less, allow two hours, just in case. Also, it is not advisable to schedule interviews later than 2:30 P.M. unless you prefer to stay after hours. The filled-in chart should be returned within the week; the sooner your response is received, the more likely we will be able to meet your first preference.

ber how hard it was to persuade line managers to invest their valuable time in this experience.

Notify the Respondents

The employees who have been selected to participate as respondents should also be notified by memorandum, with a copy to their supervisors. A sample is shown in Figure 3-3.

Match Interviewer with Respondent

Selecting the interviewer, though it sounds easy, is in fact not a simple task. Perhaps one of the most important elements of managing the project is planning who is to interview whom in the organization. Precautions need to be taken to ensure that no interviewer reports to the same vice president or immediate manager as does the respondent.

Considerations for Matching Interviewers and Executives

By the time you reach this stage, you should already have interviewed and trained the managers of the critical mass and have recruited them as part of the diagnostic team. Now you will discover how difficult it is to select which manager should interview each high-level executive. The proven skills of an interviewer must be considered, because of the potential that exists for creating a negative impression with a powerful individual. If the diagnostic team is composed wholly or in part of middle managers, the selection of the interviewer for certain top executives could be sensitive, since some of these individuals would like an opportunity for exposure to the power elite and a chance to extend their initial contact for possible future benefit. Certainly, you can understand their desire for an opportunity to talk to influential people; however, your overriding concern must be to ensure the consistent quality of the

Data Gathering

Figure 3-2. Interviewer availability chart.

Interviewer: *Please choose two alternative times and days for each interview and write your name on the appropriate lines. You will be contacted regarding confirmation.*

MARCH 19XX

Monday	Tuesday	Wednesday	Thursday	Friday
1	2	3	4	5
8–10 _____	8–10 _____	8–10 _____	8–10 _____	8–10 _____
10–12 _____	10–12 _____	10–12 _____	10–12 _____	10–12 _____
1–3 _____	1–3 _____	1–3 _____	1–3 _____	1–3 _____
3–5 _____	3–5 _____	3–5 _____	3–5 _____	3–5 _____
8	9	10	11	12
8–10 _____	8–10 _____	8–10 _____	8–10 _____	8–10 _____
10–12 _____	10–12 _____	10–12 _____	10–12 _____	10–12 _____
1–3 _____	1–3 _____	1–3 _____	1–3 _____	1–3 _____
3–5 _____	3–5 _____	3–5 _____	3–5 _____	3–5 _____
15	16	17	18	19
8–10 _____	8–10 _____	8–10 _____	8–10 _____	8–10 _____
10–12 _____	10–12 _____	10–12 _____	10–12 _____	10–12 _____
1–3 _____	1–3 _____	1–3 _____	1–3 _____	1–3 _____
3–5 _____	3–5 _____	3–5 _____	3–5 _____	3–5 _____
22	23	24	25	26
8–10 _____	8–10 _____	8–10 _____	8–10 _____	8–10 _____
10–12 _____	10–12 _____	10–12 _____	10–12 _____	10–12 _____
1–3 _____	1–3 _____	1–3 _____	1–3 _____	1–3 _____
3–5 _____	3–5 _____	3–5 _____	3–5 _____	3–5 _____
29	30	31		
8–10 _____	8–10 _____	8–10 _____		
10–12 _____	10–12 _____	10–12 _____		
1–3 _____	1–3 _____	1–3 _____		
3–5 _____	3–5 _____	3–5 _____		

Figure 3-3. Notification to respondents.

> The company is presently undergoing an operational improvement study, a comprehensive project that will be conducted by a team comprising human resources staff and selected department heads, directors, and managers. The study involves interviews with more than one hundred employees.
>
> You are one of the individuals who have been asked to assist in the generation of information for the study, because your knowledge and experience are considered most valuable. The interviews are scheduled to take place between March 1 and 31. Your interview should last approximately two hours, and will be scheduled at your convenience. You will be contacted shortly to determine a suitable time and place for the interview. In the interim, should you have any questions, please do not hesitate to call me. Thank you for your cooperation.

interviewing; a fawning interviewer is not likely to be effective and produce valid data.

Executives, moreover, may not wish to be interviewed by a specific individual, and vice versa, for whatever reason. This issue, which can be quite sensitive, is dealt with best by developing a matrix listing the names of the executives down the left side of the paper and the names of the interviewers across the top (see Figure 3-4). Copies of the matrix can then be given to concerned interviewers, asking them to place an *X* at the conjunction of their name and that of a given executive if there is a direct or departmental relationship. An *X* should also be placed at the junction with an individual whom the team member would prefer not to interview. The same matrix can be sent to the executives for their responses. If nothing else, this process minimizes anxiety about a potentially stressful encounter that would have implications about its long-term effects on a person's career.

Schedule the Interviews

The best way to approach this task is first, to derive from the interviewer availability chart a master interviewer availability schedule (Figure 3-5) that can be used as a control system from which to schedule the interviews.

The final scheduling is then done by telephone. When talking to the respondent, discuss the following:

1. Review the purpose of the study and explain why the individual has been chosen.
2. Explain the interview process: a fellow employee will ask a series of open-ended questions, seeking input regarding the respondent's perceptions about relevant problems and issues facing the company.

Data Gathering

Figure 3-4. Executive interview selection.

Interviewer Executive	J. Howard	R. Ross	T. Ahrens	B. Rollo	F. Gens	H. Stern	T. Gatti	A. Mann	B. Furst
A. Doe			X						
B. Green				X					
C. White						X			
H. Leonard							X		
J. Arquette		X							
B. Rossi									
F. Levine		X							
K. Jones									
B. Okuyama									
G. Martin	X								
H. Fletcher					X				
A. Jenkins									
A. Greeley									X
B. Confort									
H. Burger									

Figure 3-5. Partial version of a filled-in master interviewer availability schedule.

Monday		Tuesday	
	1		2
8–10	Reynolds	8–10	Behrens
	Jackson		Mann
	Hall		
10–12	Taddeo	10–12	Jackson
	Hall		Taddeo
	Behrens		
1–3	Mann	1–3	Smith
			Hall
3–5	Reynolds	3–5	Reynolds

3. Define the expected duration of the interview: about two hours.
4. Request an upcoming date, a two-hour period, and a location to conduct the interview.
5. Remind the respondent that a confirmation announcement will be sent as soon as the interviewer is assigned.

Additional steps involved in the scheduling include:

- Checking the master interviewer availability schedule to identify primary and backup interviewers.
- Calling the primary interviewer to verify his or her availability.
- Calling the backup interviewer to ensure his or her standby status.
- Calling the respondent to confirm the interview date, time, and place, and preferably sending a written confirmation.
- Sending an interview packet and scheduling confirmation to the primary interviewer. Each interviewer packet should contain:
  — A cover sheet identifying the respondent, the place of interview, and the scheduled time.
  — A one-page statement (see Figure 3-6): the top portion of the page

consists of suggested introductory remarks, which briefly describe the diagnostic study, to be read aloud by the interviewer to the respondent; the lower portion of the page contains some guidelines for the interviewer on reinforcing in his or her remarks the confidential nature of the project in general.

— An interview booklet containing the basic questions to be asked, with sufficient paper for notes.

Figure 3-6. Sample opening statement.

"The company is conducting an operational improvement study. This study will attempt to gather information from many employees such as yourself, as a means of putting together a total picture of what needs to be done.

"My objective as an interviewer is to learn as much as I can about perceptions of the good things that are going on in the company, as well as some of the problems and challenges that you feel should be addressed.

"Before we begin the interview, let us review what brought about this study: Can you tell me your understanding of what we are about to do? [Correct any misunderstanding the employee might have.] Do you have any questions about the study? [Allow time for questions and explanations.]

"Now, let's talk about why I'm here. I will be asking questions relevant to the study. You might find my probing not easy to answer. There are no trick questions. There are no correct answers. I will repeat the questions if you desire.

"Your responses and comments will be added to information gathered from many other individuals in the company. This information will be analyzed for use in a report to senior management.

"I encourage you to be candid, and to express your feelings and opinions as openly as you can. I assure you that we will do everything possible to keep your comments confidential. However, we cannot absolutely guarantee that such confidentiality will be maintained. Therefore, you may wish to take this into consideration.

"We can take as much time as you like. Are there any questions before we start?"

[*The confidential nature of the study should be emphasized. The respondent should know that he or she will be identified only by code number, and that care will be taken to delete all references to the respondent. The respondent should also be told that the data he or she provides will be combined with similar information provided by other employees. However, as stated in the preamble, there are no absolute guarantees.*]

Interviews can be scheduled only on a tentative basis. In a company in which many people travel, it is essential to confirm the meeting shortly before it is to take place. This is particularly necessary when scheduling interviewers who are part of the supplementary team and who may not always be able to meet their commitments owing to pressing business needs. Backup interviewers should be available to step in, in order not to derail a scheduled interview.

Misunderstandings about the expected duration of the interview sometimes create difficulties. In one instance, a manager who came from a regional office was interviewed at headquarters. After an hour—approximately the middle of the interview—he had to leave because of a scheduled flight back to his office. He was under the impression that the interview would last only one hour. Even though many interviews can be completed within this time, it is important to allocate at least the median time for successful completion of such interviews. When a meeting is scheduled, the respondent should be asked to set aside up to two hours; if the interview takes less time, both parties will have gained. In the above case, the interview was not completed until two months later, and thus was fragmented and of questionable value. It was later discarded, because a diagnostic interview is most useful when it takes a "snapshot" of a person's perceptions at a particular point in time. Much can happen in a few months to change those perceptions, thus contaminating the data.

Develop a Reference Data Base

The data-collection phase is in two parts. First, you need to collect basic information about the organization through formal research, review of documents, and interviews with key executives. Then, you interview the balance of the selected population.

Perform Background Research

Even though you might have worked for the company for many years, you are not likely to have a complete understanding of all its facets. One way of getting valuable information is to collect and read much of what is on paper about the company. In the process, you will develop a better perspective of how policies, procedures, financial records, newsletters, historical documents, and the like fit together to tell a story. Unless the organization engages in regular and systematic censorship, these materials are interrelated and of collective importance to the organization.

Of special importance to you as a diagnostician is the language of these materials. Harry Levinson pays particular attention to this point, since implicit in the kinds of written materials that exist and their corresponding "language" are attitudes toward the people who are going to be governed by them and assumptions about what motivates people. These assumptions are reflected in the types of control systems employed, such as management-by-objective (MBO) programs, incentive compensation systems, vacation and sick-leave policies, and the like. Much of the time these hidden assumptions have dubious validity, and therefore must be noted, because management groups rarely examine their own assumptions and more often than not become angry when their practices do not work well, attributing their failure to the negativism of the employees.

While the collection of internal materials is going on, external data about the organization can also be developed and collected. Sources of external data might include the company's competitors, suppliers, agents, and professional associates. In comparison to internal data, external data enable you to examine how outsiders perceive the company and the impact it has on other systems.

Throughout the study, it is essential that you take a "holistic" approach, understanding the whole system in relation to the immediate interaction of a few subsystems. Therefore, a likely starting point for your study is a copy of the company's organizational chart, describing the obvious relationships and responsibilities among its employees. You must realize, however, that the organizational chart is only a beginning. The relevant data lie not only in how the organization *is* structured but in how the people *perceive* it to be structured. If possible, during the interviewing process have the respondents draw an organizational chart to illustrate how they think the business actually gets done or, at the very least, ask them to describe the relationships that are involved. You can then compare their responses to the formal chart and note the differences as representing points of influence or perhaps even power.

In carrying out the study, you will find yourself giving more time and attention to larger organizational groups, those units that have a central purpose and are particularly indispensable for attaining the company's principal goals. For example, the Research, Software Development, Manufacturing and Sales Divisions would be of primary importance to a company that produces computers. Since these areas are at the heart of the company's business, the divisions are likely to command particular attention. Do not neglect to examine smaller units, however. They generally have a meaningful purpose, and should be considered part of a whole, particularly if growth is expected.

Interview Key Management Personnel

The executives should be scheduled for two interviews. The first, called the "strategic issues" interview, is unique to this group because the issues that will be explored have to do mainly with mission and strategy. The second interview is exactly the same as that administered to the rest of the respondent population.

Part 1: The Strategic Issues Interview

Prior to the actual interview, the company's executives should be asked to complete a special questionnaire, called the Core Mission and Strategic Planning Issues Analysis (see Appendix 1.5). This questionnaire should be returned to you for review prior to the interview, and should be used as the basis of your discussion with the executives.

Core-mission statement. The interview should explore top management's perception of the company's "reason for being," as well as its understanding of present internal and external forces that aid or hinder the company from realizing its goals. Each executive should then be asked to explain his or her definition of the organization's core mission. In all likelihood, the most common response will be that the mission of the company is to make money. At this stage, you should point out that the definition of a core mission is that it provides a sense of *how* the organization makes money. What kind of business is it? What is the reason for its being? While making money is obviously a legitimate objective for a company, you should stress the difference between objectives and overall core mission. Companies operating in a "planned economy," such as in a Socialist country, may have objectives other than profit, of course. Providing jobs may supersede achieving profits. For such companies to remain viable, however, the government usually intervenes in other ways, through protectionist trade policies or the creation of state monopolies.

The next portion of the interview asks the executive to describe relevant key factors that might impact on the company's core mission five years into the future, and to suggest any "response mechanisms" that would have to be developed in order to effectively cope with those future demands and pressures.

Organizational objectives. The next portion of the interview should focus on an in-depth review of strategic issues affecting the company. This particular part of the study could benefit from participation by university faculty members. Their contribution could range from design of the questionnaire to analysis of the collected data as applied to similar organizations they may have previously studied. In most cases, professors do not charge much, if anything, and are grateful for the opportunity to conduct research in a business organization.

The clear expression of an unequivocal core-mission statement inevitably leads to a sharper definition and more coherent picture of organizational objectives, a critical ingredient in the development of strategic planning scenarios. Objectives, in the strategic sense, are those things that management wishes to achieve, such as growth by a certain percentage at certain points in time, the meeting of specified profit targets, entry into new markets, increased employee population, or introduction of new products.

As we have seen, most organizational objectives are profit oriented, or can be viewed as "subobjectives" of goals related to bottom-line results. Also, objectives are normally quantified—expressed in dollar amounts, percentages, calendar dates, and so on—and provide performance standards and a means of measuring progress toward a goal.

Ideally, the objectives emerge from the specific realities of the organization. Such goals should be less a "wish list" than a clear appraisal of obtainable benchmarks, based on such factors as the following:

- The capabilities of internal resources, strengths, and weaknesses, as derived from analysis of the financial, performance, technology, and human resources assets of the company
- The value system of top management, including perceptions of the overall core mission and attitudes toward its successful accomplishment

- The realities of the external environment, as discussed in Part IV, which include market pressures, regulatory requirements, demographic changes, economic factors, and the like

During the interview process, it is important to realize that organizational objectives are not necessarily identical with official statements. Lofty ideals such as fair employment and job security for the employees, concern for the stockholders' investment, or contributions to society do not necessarily translate into operational objectives as expressed through actual behavior.

Genuine organizational objectives nearly always focus on the survival of the company, improvement of its market position, and the constant and relentless pursuit of profitability. In the course of events, it is likely that achieving these true objectives will also result in accomplishing the idealized goals: Employment is provided, shares appreciate in value, taxes are collected, and useful products or services are made available to more people.

Part 2: The Regular Interview

The strategic-issues interview is intended solely for executives, since it deals mostly with issues affecting the future direction of the company. Now those executives should be asked exactly the same questions as the general employee population will be asked. Two considerations should be paramount. Executives and many of the senior managers are a significant source of historical data—and up-to-date information, as well. More important, however, the data provided by this group should be analyzed separately and compared with the perceptions of several responding groups in the organization to ascertain whether top leadership's perceptions correspond to the perceptions of managers and employees. Generally, some sort of dichotomy can be expected. The value of this comparison is most obvious when differences in perception are significant, indicating a possible isolation of top management from what's really happening.

Develop the Main Data Base

Following the preliminary background research and the interviews with executives and managers of the critical mass, you are ready to interview the employee population. During the training of the diagnostic team, you spent most of the time discussing the interview process and the techniques that would elicit the most valid data from the respondent. Now we look a little closer at the how the interview technique is developed.

The Process of Diagnostic Interviewing

The actual process of interviewing respondents requires skill, which can be developed through training, and sensitivity, which is somewhat less easy to develop. Part of the skill is an awareness of pitfalls that may result from a less-than-adequate interview. Even so, diagnostic interviewing is one of the most powerful methods of gathering data.

Advantages of the Interview Method

A diagnostic interview has several purposes:

1. It generates data for the study itself.
2. It clarifies the data as they are generated. A major advantage of the interview is that it allows verification of the interviewer's understanding, by providing clarification from the respondent, if necessary.
3. It enables discovery of problem areas that would not have been identified through a written questionnaire. Essentially, with a questionnaire, people respond to the questions you ask, and not to the questions you don't ask. In contrast, the probing that takes place during the interview allows the pursuit of interesting data.
4. It increases ownership of the diagnosis by involving line managers who help generate and collect data, and who may also become more committed to any changes that may be attempted in the future.
5. It provides a cathartic experience by allowing respondents to "get things off their chest." Within the bounds of the private interview, the openness of the respondent is promoted. When people feel they are being understood, they are more likely to be candid.
6. It provides contact between the interviewer and the respondent, thus establishing a rapport that is difficult to achieve with a questionnaire. This personal connection demonstrates that the respondent is important, and it facilitates the collection of meaningful data.

An incidental effect is that the respondent may better crystallize his or her own point of view during the interview than if simply surveyed through an inventory or questionnaire. Furthermore, if an employee participates in future problem-solving groups, team-building sessions, and other change interventions, he or she is more likely to see the issues as less threatening, by having discussed them with a line manager during the diagnostic interview.

Disadvantages of the Interview Method

There are, of course, some disadvantages to diagnostic interviewing:

1. Interviewing is expensive in terms of time, space, and staff. It is not unusual to spend an hour with each individual, away from the job.
2. The interviewer may lose objectivity, possibly commiserating with the respondent, or may agree or disagree and forget that the primary task is to collect data without filtering it in any way.
3. The data gathered from one respondent may not be directly compa-

rable—in terms of quality, emphasis, and accuracy—to data gathered by other means.
4. The data gathered through interviews are not easily standardized or summarized. Judgment is required to compare statements of respondents, and sometimes the data get lost in the summarizing process. For this reason, in the organic diagnostic process, a key requirement is the collection of *all* elements of data, particularly the repetitive ones.
5. The interview may constitute a potential threat to the respondent, obligating the interviewer to be sensitive to the possibility that the respondent may be doing it involuntarily.
6. In organizations in which people are not physically present in the same building at the same time, occasionally it is difficult to gain access to the respondents.

Given a choice, you will find that diagnostic interviewing is the method of choice, because its advantages far outweigh its disadvantages. Survey instruments may appear more scientific and precise, but it is difficult to avoid an element of sterility and depersonalization. Interviewing, on the other hand, is colorful and far more illustrative and anecdotal, with the added benefit of flexibility in questioning.

The Interview Procedure

As with any complex task, diagnostic interviewing follows a certain procedure: (1) Prepare the interviewer, (2) prepare the respondent, (3) open the interview, (4) work on data generation and record the interview data, (5) close the interview, and (6) transcribe the data. We begin by discussing the first two steps.

Prepare the Interviewer

The interviewer should gather some basic information about the department in which the respondent works. It is advisable, for example, to examine the organizational chart so that unnecessary questions can be avoided. Prior to the meeting, each interviewer should have received appropriate information and materials from the diagnosis administrative manager. These should have the name and location of the respondent and the scheduled time for the interview. In addition, a package with a stack of blank data cards should be made available.

Prepare the Respondent

Each respondent should receive a short memo from the administrative manager, confirming the interview. This is not a substitute for the clarification of goals by the interviewer at the beginning of the interview. The setting of the interview is also important. It should be in a quiet, private place. If this is not available at the respondent's workplace, suitable arrangements should be made in advance.

Important Considerations

An interviewer must relate to many people with individual concepts of the work environment. If, for example, the interviewer is talking to a member of the sales department, he or she must continually keep in mind that the sales environment is the dominant reality for this person. A respondent in the Manufacturing Division will have a different concept of the work environment, reflecting his or her experience. By recognizing such differences throughout the organization, the interviewer will have a better perspective on the feelings of the people being interviewed and the significance of their work in relation to the rest of the organization.

An interviewer might be viewed and treated by the respondent in many different ways:

1. As an evaluator who judges the competencies of people
2. As an unwelcome guest
3. As a hero or ally who is expected to give management or the workers the "right" point of view
4. As someone who will punish
5. As someone who can give rewards

The interviewer can achieve a measure of control over how he or she is perceived. Besides ensuring that the respondent knows as much as possible about the study, and the reasons why the input is considered valuable, the interviewer is responsible for setting the tone at the beginning of the interview. He or she must be reassuring and supportive in the relationship to the respondent and to others referred to in the discussion. This should help the interviewer relate better to a particular organizational setting or workplace.

It is important to guard against making casual, indiscreet remarks to the respondent. The latter may try to obtain some reaction from the interviewer that would indicate his or her feelings on certain issues. Occasionally, the interviewer may unwittingly begin a conversation by mentioning what he or she has already observed in discussions with other people. The content of such remarks and the tone conveyed can very easily influence what is discussed and what is subsequently learned. Of particular concern are evaluative statements or judgments about other people and other organizational units. These kinds of comments should be avoided at all costs.

Open the Interview

If the interviwer and the respondent have not met before, it is desirable that they exchange some information about each other.

Part of the interviewing process involves explaining the purpose of the diagnosis and making the respondent as comfortable as possible under the circumstances. In most cases, it is helpful for all interviewers to go through a prepared statement. Figure 3-6 shows a single sheet that can be used as a guide. After addressing any remaining questions, the interview can begin.

Work on Data Generation

In diagnostic interviewing, four primary sets of verbal techniques are generally used: leading, probing, understanding, and supporting.

The first category, leading questions, generally include such questions as:

1. How long have you worked for the company?
2. Can you describe in a few words where you fit in the organization and what the major responsibilities are of your job?
3. As a person with significant responsibilities, you must have insights which might help improve the organization. We would like you to share your observations and opinions with us, by describing what you consider are the major issues that the company has to address today.
4. Are there any significant problems in your area which are cause for concern? What are they, and do you have suggestions as to what can be done to deal with them?
5. What do you consider the most significant assets or strengths of the company at this stage?

The intent of these seemingly easy questions is to encourage the employee to share his or her perceptions about the organization—its positives and negatives—while at the same time enabling communication of potential solutions that may have gone undetected by management. It is important that the questions be explored rather than simply asked. The respondent may not interpret them in the same way as the interviewer has intended them. For common understanding to be experienced, therefore, it is critical that the questions be phrased in a nonthreatening manner and that they be checked for understanding.

The employee may start by responding cryptically and noncommittally, such as **"I don't think that we are experiencing anything that's uncommon in the industry today."** Leaving such a statement without probing further might encourage the employee to later respond in a yes or no fashion, which generally is not very productive.

The most useful function of an interviewer is to ask probing questions, to ensure that the response has been understood and to elicit further elaboration. Follow-up questions such as: **"Can you tell me more about this?" "Are you aware of what the other companies are doing?"** and **"Have they found a solution to the problem?"** set the stage for more open communication and minimize the tendency to oversimplify and exaggerate. Another useful probing technique is to ask for examples of what the person means, again in an attempt to get away from the generic and the unfocused and move toward the specific and the useful.

It is important not to make these questions loaded, in the sense that they imply a particular acceptable response. An example of this is called the binary question, as in **"Do problems come up?"** This is likely to elicit a yes or no response, and it shuts off discussion rather than opens it up. A better way to ask the same question is, **"What happens when problems come up?"**

Another variation of the probing question is the follow-up lead. This kind of question starts with asking for elaboration on a comment in a general area by generating a number of increasingly specific questions to explore the details of an issue. An example of this is, **"How closely are things scheduled, and why?"** These leads, of course, must be timed to the responsiveness of the person.

A further variation on the probing question is the cue or exploration lead. Respondents often emit signals to the effect that there is a particular thing they would like to talk about. These clues should be picked up and explored if they appear to be relevant to the objectives of the interview: **"You seem to want to discuss relocation policies in more detail. . . ."** In fact, the pacing and direction of the interview should largely be responsive to the clues—verbal and nonverbal—that the respondent gives out.

The continuation lead is yet another kind of probing question: **"Can you tell me why you think we still don't have an effective performance appraisal system?"** This kind of question is intended to get the respondent to continue talking about a particular point of view, a topic or issue that he or she is explaining. Closely related to this is the amplification lead: **"You indicated that for some reason the company has not been receptive to ideas for diversification. Can you be more specific?"** Here, the interviewer occasionally asks the respondent to provide more information on a particular topic by explaining and further amplifying the issue being discussed.

The last kind of probe is the testing question: **"You indicated that, in your opinion, the company has not been successful in new-product introductions, yet from the information I have, it appears that of the last five introductions, at least three are doing very well in the marketplace. Perhaps you can clarify it for me?"** Occasionally, the interviewer might confront the person about certain assumptions that he or she is making.

The third major category of diagnostic questions are employed to assure understanding. A restatement is simply a repetition, in word-for-word fashion, of the statement that the respondent has just made: **"Let me repeat what you have just said to make sure I have it right."** A paraphrase is similar, with the difference that the statement is summarized in the interviewer's own words: **"Is it fair to say that, in conclusion, you feel that the company has done a reasonably good job of R & D, particularly in relation to its competition?"** Reflection is a technique whereby the interviewer plays back to the respondent the feelings that he or she believes are being experienced: **"I gather, then, that you don't feel the budgeting process is fair to departments which are in a support role."** Reflection of feelings can be a powerful technique for communicating to the respondent that he or she is being understood. Summarization is advised, because it helps the interviewer integrate the sets of data from the person being interviewed in the form of brief summaries. This creates a climate of understanding and produces a greater respect for the interviewer.

The fourth major category of diagnostic questions are supportive. Sharing is one of these. Sometimes, the respondent needs some support in order to continue a discussion: **"I know what you mean when you talk about excessive business travel. In my previous job, I was on the road 60 percent of the time, and it was rough."** If the respondent can share an experience, point of view, or attitude briefly, it will indicate that the respondent is not the only person in the world who has the problems or concerns being discussed.

Another kind of supportive question is consoling. Although it is sometimes ridiculous for the interviewer to say, **"I know how you feel,"** such a statement can often serve as a means of indicating that the interviewer wants the respondent to feel better. Consoling or sharing one's concern for the other person can be effective when the person being interviewed is uncomfortable about having expressed feelings to a relative stranger.

The last kind of supportive question expresses caring. Interviewing is not a mechanical, impersonal activity, and sometimes it helps for the interviewer to say whatever caring he feels about the person and the situation being explored during the interview: **"I feel that talking about the closing of the Toronto office is painful to you. Perhaps we can go to something else."** This is largely a matter of style, but it is important to consider that the data are no better than the perceptions of the relationship formed by the two persons engaged in the interview.

This discussion is meant primarily to illustrate various interviewing techniques, but it must be cautioned that many lines of questioning, while valid in certain circumstances, generally are not appropriate to organic diagnosis, owing to the premium it places on unadulterated and unforced data from the respondents. A preferred method of interviewing, consistent with the organic approach, cautions the interviewer from becoming involved in the situation as it affects the respondent. Since the data are to be used as is, even if some of the facts contradict what the respondent says, it is important to minimize interpretation by the data gatherer. For this reason, stress letting the respondent communicate what he or she desires—in his or her own words and recorded as closely as possible to the real utterances—with a minimum of coloration by the interviewer; this is essential to the integrity of the approach.

The organic diagnosis is merely a reflection of what people feel. Probing is necessary to understand what is being said. Doing more, especially sharing the respondent's perceptions and values, may contaminate the process by creating an issue where there isn't one, by unwittingly suppressing valuable data, or by not recording the data verbatim.

Possible Problems During the Interview

Providing a list of techniques may give the impression that all will go well if such instructions are followed. In reality, problems do occur during an interview. Let us review the most common.

It is not unusual for the respondent to be hostile, frustrated, pessimistic, or defensive. Unless dealt with, such feelings and behaviors make the interview difficult. There is absolutely no sense in proceeding until such feelings are explored in order to legitimize them. The interviewer should be careful not to give the respondent the impression that such feelings are unacceptable. The significant fact is that such feelings are there, and they become part of the data. In any case, denial of such feelings can result in increased tension and possible distortion of interview data.

A second problem occurs when the respondent attempts to turn the tables on the interviewer and begin interviewing instead. This can be frustrating unless the interviewer develops a constructive response, which in this case is a tactful reminder of the objectives of the interview.

A third problem occurs when the interviewer experiences some pressure to violate the confidentiality of previous interviews. The respondent may ask questions such as: "**What have you heard thus far?**" Needless to say, the interviewer must avoid disclosing any confidential information, and point out to the respondent that the information he or she provides will be treated in confidence also.

There is a possibility that you will encounter denial, lying, and other deceptions by respondents. It is important not to confront the speaker with the suspicion that he or she may not be telling the truth. Make a mental note to verify certain facts. In any case, observing that the respondent is not telling the truth is in itself a significant piece of diagnostic data.

Close the Interview

It is often difficult to end an interview, particularly if the respondent is highly verbal. There are, however, a number of techniques that can help close an interview constructively. The first is summarizing; the second is restating the objectives of the interview; the third is explaining the next steps in the diagnostic process; and the fourth is standing up, thanking the respondent, and walking out. However, before charging though any of these, the interviewer should ask whether the respondent has any further data to provide or whether there are any other questions. The interviewer should then clarify and discuss any parts of the interview data that might be unclear or incomplete. He or she should again assure the respondent that the data will be kept in confidence, and express personal appreciation that the respondent has been helpful. The interviewer has the primary responsibility for ending the interview in a comfortable, businesslike way.

Review the Interview Process

Upon completion of a few interviews, it is advisable to discuss with the diagnostic team how the process seems to work and the general nature of the collected data. This sharing will help other members of the team gain a better understanding of the process, thus increasing their confidence.

Begin the meeting by having each member of the team briefly describe the interviews he or she has conducted up to that point, noting any difficulties or specific questions that might not have worked out well during the interviews. If a respondent allowed the interviewer to use a tape recorder, problems attributed to its use should be shared. For example, during an actual interview, in which the analyst tried to record the entire session, the discussion was frank and open. At one point, however, the respondent asked to turn off the recorder for a few minutes. In fact, the respondent gradually became nervous about having his every word taped, and the machine was not turned on again. Fortunately, the analyst was taking written notes simultaneously with the taping, and he continued to write for the remainder of the interview. In this case the conclusion of the analyst was that by taping the discussion, the interviewer actually created more work for himself, because he would have a tendency to relax, knowing that everything was being recorded. This meant that if the interviewer spent one hour interviewing, he would have to spend more than one additional hour listening to the tape and transposing workable notes from it.

In another instance, upon reviewing her notes, an interviewer felt that a tape-recorded interview had not been quite complete, and she asked for another meeting with the respondent. She brought the recorded tape with her to help the manager review what was said. The manager was so startled to hear his own comments that he gained a new perspective on his attitude toward his job, and realized that he found it more convenient to complain than to take positive action about several problem areas that were within his ability to address. He also realized that he had a tendency to let his colleagues struggle, lacking information that he possessed but did not always volunteer. He later stated that holding data close to his chest unconsciously gave him a sense of informal power. He asked to have several sessions with a human resources professional to discuss how he could deal with such instances in a positive manner. In any case, the second round of this interview lasted over two hours. To avoid such additional time investment, endeavor to collect all data from a respondent on the first try.

An interviewer may express frustration with the instances when it is obvious a respondent is not being candid or not telling everything, or diluting the facts to evade certain issues or avoid controversial topics. The respondent may also be talking to someone who relates something that the interviewer knows is not true. This creates a difficult problem for an interviewer, who must force him or herself to enter the interview with an open mind, only to hear the respondent paint a glorious, troublefree scenario of work in the organization. It is possible that probing questions and requests for clarifications may be to no avail, which is particularly frustrating if the respondent is someone who could be particularly helpful because of his or her position and experience. If it is not possible to get the person to change, it does not make much sense to use data that are obviously of little value. During the discussion, the interviewer might recommend shelving the interview results, although if such evasion is replicated by several individuals, the behavior should be used as a piece of diagnostic data that may have import when examining the organizational culture, trust, and openness.

CHAPTER 4
Process Collected Data

Once the interviewing process has started, you must address the tasks associated with handling notes, turning them into transcripts, and preparing the material so it can be transformed into a usable data base.

Establish Administrative Tools

Be ready to handle the data as it is transcribed and forwarded to you. The following are some of the administrative tools you should have available.

- *Data recording guide*—Given to the interviewers beforehand, this is a list of the steps to be taken after completion of the interview to develop usable transcripts (see Appendix 1.4).
- *Weekly interview control log*—A listing, by day, of the individual to be interviewed, the time and place of the interview, and the interviewer's name.
- *Equipment control log*—Some interviewers may prefer to dictate the results of the interview on tape for transcription, rather than use a secretary (see Appendix 1.6). You should maintain an inventory of available machines with their serial numbers and an erasable notation for the names of the people using them.
- *Transcription control log*—After an interviewer has dictated a tape, the tape should be logged in and assigned its own control number, which usually consist of the interviewer's initials followed by a number indicating the sequence of the interview (see Appendix 1.7). For instance, HT-2 represents a tape of the second interview conducted by a person with those initials. Following the coding and listing on the control form, the tapes should be sent in a confidential envelope to the transcription center for typing. The log helps you keep track of the date the tape is submitted, the date the transcript is finished, the date it is sent back to the interviewer for proofing and correcting, and the date the finished, proofed transcript is returned to the project office.

Transcribe Notes

The best time to transcribe collected data is immediately after the interview. The longer the transcription of data is delayed, the more likely it will reflect inaccuracies, because even the best notetaker forgets details a few days after an interview.

It is likely that the form and comprehensiveness of collected notes will vary, depending on the skill of the interviewer. The interviewer should make every effort to record data in usable form, with a minimum of interpretive "contamination." As with any report, there is tendency for the interviewer to introduce his or her own biases or assumptions, particularly if there is a need to have the data conform to his or her own concept of logic.

We have already seen in the section on interviewing techniques that the issue is not whether the interviewer agrees with the data provided by the respondent. The objective is to collect intelligible data that reflect the perspective of the respondent in his or her own words, with his or her own emphasis. Interpretation by the interviewer should be minimal. Even inaccuracies, if they are recorded, provide data about the level of information available to the respondent. It is particularly inappropriate for an interviewer to fill in apparent gaps with his or her own input.

The most time-effective way of transcribing data is for the interviewer to select meaningful elements of data and transfer each sentence to a file card. Another method is to dictate the information onto tape and arrange to have it typed as a transcript, which can later be analyzed. In some organizations with computer capability, data can be keyed directly into a microcomputer, using a word-processing program with word-search capability. If you prefer to have transcripts typed first, they can later be scanned into a computer for processing, as you would any other document. Word processing enables the user to search for key sentences and to sort and reorganize text at will. In most cases, however, nonclerical professionals are not sufficiently trained or willing to use such equipment; thus file cards generally are the most practical approach.

Control Paper Flow

As soon as the interviews start, be ready for the floodgates to open, not only in terms of activity level but also in sheer volume of paper. The interoffice mail delivery will probably need a heavy-duty cart to deliver transcripts up to four times a day. You may want to establish a temporary transcription center on your premises, or arrange for confidentiality with the supervisor of the typing pool or word-processing services. Either way, you will be receiving first-draft transcripts, which have to be logged in and sent for proofing and correction to the people who dictated them. The interviewers will then return the corrected materials to you, along with the original notes. If you used strategic-issues surveys, or any other supplementary paper-and-pencil instruments, most of these will already have come in, but depending on the schedule, a few will trickle in later. If you are not prepared for the volume of paper coming in, you will risk being overwhelmed. Moreover, since much of the material is confidential in nature, special steps should be taken to guarantee its safekeeping. You may need to obtain a secure room and order file cabinets. Requests should be made to all diagnostic team members to clear their desks of the material they are working on at the end of the day, and secure it. As we have already seen, very detailed logs are needed to keep track of every bit of information being used.

Review Volume and Progress

At some point toward the end of the data-collection phase, you will have to take stock of where you are. This will include determining:

1. How many interviews have been conducted, and by whom
2. How many have been transcribed, edited, corrected, and ready for coding
3. How many strategic-issues surveys have been completed and returned How many follow-up interviews were done and recorded on tape, and how many of those transcribed
4. If paper-and-pencil instruments are used, how many of the questionnaires have been returned and processed on the computer

You might still have a number of executives who were unable to take time to be interviewed, and a few stragglers from remote offices who still need to be interviewed. The question that inevitably comes up is, "Did we miss anyone?" You will find that your team members will have no difficulty in suggesting names of other people who could provide meaningful data. At this point, however, you should be more concerned about how much is enough data. You will probably already be awash in transcripts and data. Avoid overkill if you can.

Organize Collected Data

The process of organizing the collected data is in many ways the most critical part of the diagnostic effort.

Review the Transcripts

This part of the diagnosis is perhaps the most laborious. For this reason, you should pay particular attention to making sure people do not take the easy way out and discard valid data merely because handling it becomes tedious. Each interviewer should process his or her own transcripts as follows:

Identify Usable Data

Using the transcripts themselves (preferably a copy, since it is a good idea to keep a master safely filed away), the interviewer's initial task is to separate the "garbage" from the facts. Each transcript should be scrutinized, and each sentence providing a meaningful element of data should be circled or underlined.

Prepare Data Cards or Computer Data Base

The actual transfer of data from an interviewer's notes or transcripts to cards is relatively simple. The interviewer should select *each and every* usable statement that was provided by the respondent and consider it a piece of data. Each usable element of data should be cut from the transcript and glued to a card. Alternatively, this transfer can be done by working directly on a word processor. In this way, the portions of the transcript that are not usable can be deleted, and sentences that are retained as data elements can be separated as paragraphs.

Each statement should be written or selected so that it can stand on its own as a meaningful element of data. The following are some examples:

> "People have problems because of the organizational structure."

> "The fractionalization that has existed for many years has not been corrected by the new structure."

> "The problem is at the management level. Each vice president has his own tribe, and the tribesmen work for the tribe, forgetting about the company as a whole."

> "We shouldn't kid ourselves about our ability to make money. Any fool can make money in a good market."

> "People come here to learn the business; then they leave."

> "The company has not trained anyone for the last seven years."

> "We still run into areas where departments are reluctant to promote someone simply because the department hasn't given consideration to replacing that person."

> "The purchasing procedures require contract-type signatures from vendors, who are not always willing to do it. Most of this is unneccessary paperwork, which gets in the way."

> "We are spread out over six locations in town. This makes it tough to coordinate."

> "The adoption of the matrix system has dealt a dramatic blow to managers used to a relatively straightforward organization."

> "The Project Management System has created a great amount of conflict ever since it was established, because it cannot clearly define responsibilities."

Particular attention must be paid to apparently conflicting statements to see if they make sense in their overall context.

The end result of the transcription process is a significant number of data cards. At this stage, it is best to avoid categorizing the cards, because doing so will encourage the transcriber to avoid picking up repeated or similar statements. As noted earlier, repetition of a particular point by many individuals is indicative of the relative importance of an issue, and that importance can only be reflected in how many times the same concern is raised.

Code the Data Cards

Once the laborious process of transferring the data elements is completed, you and the other interviewers will be faced with stacks of cards that need to be sorted and coded. This process is essential to all further work, because it helps arrange the data in a meaningful pattern.

Each of the data cards should be examined for content and assigned a preliminary code or subject. For example,

> "People have problems because of the organizational structure."

Initially, this statement could be classified as Organization.

> "The problem is at the management level. Each vice president has his own tribe, and the tribesmen work for the tribe, forgetting about the company as a whole."

This could be also coded as Organization. You may, on the other hand, classify this as Structure.

> "People come here to learn the business; then they leave."

This can be coded as Turnover.

> "We have a unique opportunity to move from manufacturing components such as memory boards to making complete microcomputers, because we have the technology and the extra capacity to do so."

This can be coded in a number of ways, to include Technology, Capacity, Opportunity, and even Diversification.

> "Our unique asset is a loyal and well-trained employee population with high morale, because the company is employee owned and most of us have some say in what's going on. If we decide to move in a certain direction, you can count on all of us to work as a team to get us there."

This can be coded as Morale, Cohesion, Teamwork, or Commitment.

This is just an initial rough classification of data elements. You will find yourself adding topics as you go. Cards can be labeled Morale, Resources, Strategy, and so on. Once the entire data base is completed, the cards should be roughly organized into related areas for further processing. This coding should be done by the interviewer himself, if possible. If this is not feasible, it can still be done by another member of the diagnostic team, provided the usual precautions are taken to ensure proper processing. In any case, the coding should be done by someone with at least a one-hour block of time available. You—or whoever else does it—will need this amount of time to compose your thoughts to do an effective job.

Now that all the data cards have been assigned a general topic, you are ready to work on a higher level of detail and assign appropriate subcategories. What should these be? Simply let the data itself do the selection. The following are examples of how previously mentioned statements can be categorized:

- "People have problems because of the organizational structure." Initially, this statement was classified as Organization. After looking at many more statements in this area, you will probably have to go back to this data card and add subcategories such as Organization/Structure/Problems.
- "The problem is at the management level. Each vice president has his own tribe, and the tribesmen work for the tribe, forgetting about the company as a whole." This could be coded as Organization/Structure/Conflict/Intergroup.
- "We shouldn't kid ourselves about our ability to make money. Any fool can make money in a good market." This kind of comment can be tough to classify. Here's a try: Finance/Income/Prospects.
- "People come here to learn the business; then they leave." This can be easily classified as Personnel/Turnover.
- "The company has not trained anyone for the last seven years." This could be coded simply as Personnel/Training/Frequency. However, since the comment implies a consequence of not training, it could be classified as Personnel/Turnover/Causes/Lack of Training. In such a case, you can justify using the data element in both areas.
- "We still run into areas where departments are reluctant to promote someone simply because the department hasn't given consideration to replacing that person." This comment is another example of multiple concerns. It could be coded as Personnel/Policies/Promotion or Personnel/Replacement Planning. When in doubt, use the

data element in both places. Don't over-interpret, however. You could infer that such an oversight could cause people to leave, with some justification, and be tempted to code this Personnel/Turnover. However, the statement doesn't say that.
- **"The purchasing procedures require contract-type signatures from vendors, who are not always willing to do it. Most of this is unnecessary paperwork, which gets in the way."** This could be coded as Procedures/Unneccessary or Procedures/Purchasing, or even Paperwork/Procedures.
- **"We are spread out over six locations in town. This makes it tough to coordinate."** This could be coded as Locations/Convenience or Communications/Problems/Location.
- **"The Project Management System has created a great amount of conflict ever since it was established, because it cannot clearly define responsibilities."** This could be coded as Organization/Projects/Problems or Conflict/Organizational.

The point is that there are no hard-and-fast rules of coding data. It is literally a function of how you see it. Your way of classifying is just as valid as any other person's, as long as consistency is maintained. When in doubt, do not hesitate to replicate the data element and use it elsewhere. It may be preferable to do so, rather than create more than four subject levels.

Select the Team for the Balance of the Project

When most of the data are collected, recorded, and transferred to data cards, you are ready for the most challenging part of the diagnosis: analysis and interpretation.

It is important when reaching this stage to keep in mind that, ideally, the fewer people involved in the analysis, the more coherent and accessible the results. There is also a potentially significant reduction in the time required to complete the task. This particular aspect of the project should be restricted to relatively few individuals, for no other reason than that more than six people get in each other's way. This point offers an opportunity for the reluctant members of the team to bail out and let the "survivors" worry about what to do with the mass of data, which is now waiting to be worked on. Of course, you can also expect the converse, in that some converts would like to participate in this new stage of the project.

At this point, you must attend to some housekeeping chores. First, you need to thank the interviewers for their contributions to the study thus far. A memo such as the one shown in Figure 4-1, with copies to the individuals' bosses, is in order.

Following your solicitation for further contributions to the project, you can expect the majority of interviewers to elect not to participate in the analysis and interpretation. Those who remain are not likely to number more than

Figure 4-1. Sample "thank-you" memo.

> The structured interviews for the operational improvement study have been completed. The achievement of this objective was made possible by the cooperation exhibited by each of you. Since everyone stayed involved, we were able to do the job by averaging three interviews each. A high degree of interest and conscientiousness is reflected in the top-quality data that were collected.
>
> The second phase of the study involves the analysis and interpretation process. Some of you have expressed an interest in this activity. If you should like to participate, please call for details.
>
> Please accept my sincere thanks for your contribution and support.

six, but they will have a genuine interest in seeing the project through. In any case, the rest of the team is not completely off the hook. They should be asked to review the various sections of the diagnosis as it is completed, and to comment as necessary.

Prepare for the Analysis and Interpretation

When all the cards are properly coded and arranged by general topic, the real job of analysis begins. This portion of the study requires a high degree of concentration and care, and it is wise for the team to reserve a quiet facility out of the office to avoid the inevitable interruptions at the workplace. The initial session should aim to do the following:

1. Examine the amount and quality of data collected and preliminarily arrange the topic/issue categories.
2. Analyze the data to assess the impact of main issues and areas of concern.
3. Develop a structure for the report to management.
4. If necessary, identify additional areas of inquiry.

The participants should be reminded to bring to the workshop all the materials they will need.

The few days of work that start the analysis and interpretation phase of the diagnosis are crucial. People will be very much aware that processing a mountain of data is not an easy task, and they will be anxious about their chances for success. As the project manager, at the end of each review session, you should bring home a stack of data cards and sift through them several times to get a preliminary idea of where the data lead. Don't be surprised if, after doing this, you are no better off than before. You may have difficulty detecting particular trends, other than the predictable perception that the company is facing problems in a number of areas. Don't be alarmed if, after two days, you haven't reached any meaningful conclusions. At this stage, to paraphrase Harry Levinson, you are merely "immersing" yourself in the data, "wallowing" in it, soaking up as much of it as you can until you are able to detect a trend or structure that gives meaning to the amorphous mass of diverse information, opinions, and perceptions. Recognize that the other members of the team will experience the same results initially, and that it is important for the leader to demonstrate confidence throughout the process.

Once your team is gathered, open the meeting by stating that the next few days will constitute an intensive "immersion" process, where all of you will "wallow in" and "soak up" the data.

Develop Issue Categories

At this stage of the diagnosis, you are dealing essentially with a giant research project. Initial sorting of data should produce several stacks of cards that roughly fit into a general category. As mentioned earlier, the categories themselves are developed as the data become available. For example, the first data card may indicate a complaint about the organizational chart, hence it can be placed initially in a category called Organizational Structure. A second card may express concerns about the fact that the company does not seem interested in planning for the future. A tentative categorization for this may be Long-range Planning. As patterns and areas of emphasis and concern emerge, the initial categories may proliferate, until there are several dozen areas that need to be addressed.

The next step involves consolidation of topics. For example, initial categories having to do with Long-range Planning, Organizational Mission, Unpreparedness, and the like could be consolidated under the umbrella category of Strategic Planning. The important consideration is that the data dictate the categories that seem to matter to the respondents. Furthermore, a separate set of subcategories will probably offer the respondents' suggestions about how such concerns and problems can be solved. From this point on, the focus should be on further refinement of the sorting process, until a meaningful structure has developed for writing the diagnostic report itself.

Again, the data dictate both the areas to be dealt with and the relative emphasis. The data naturally flow from the respondents to the data cards, to the categories, to the possible solutions in a natural, organic way that is not forced, as it would be through a preordained "model" that is likely to act as a filter, favoring certain kinds of data that may or may not be useful.

The massive amount of data can be best processed by assigning designated area managers to work with defined topics. For example, you may wish to work with the temporary researchers on the topic Historical Development of the Organization; someone else may handle Organizational Structure, and so on. This division of responsibility does not mean that persons with primary responsibility for one section should be the only ones working on that section. All of you should review each other's work as a minimum, and contribute as necessary. However, the person assigned the particular section should be responsible for ensuring completion of the designated work.

Quality control at the outset, starting with a review of the coding on each data card, will pay dividends in the end. The following predictable problems can be minimized through an awareness of their inevitability:

- *Similar elements of data being placed in different major categories.* For example, a simple item such as Performance Appraisal could be placed under Rewards, Relationships, Evaluation, Appraisal, Feedback, and Development, depending on how the coder perceives the issue.
- *Lack of compartmentalization.* Within a particular category, dozens of issues are listed, none of them in order or grouped coherently, and there is a failure to separate positive and negative aspects of given issues.

It is imperative to start by reviewing each data card and agreeing on how it should be coded. Initially, this is a slow and tedious process. It will not take long, however, for the team to comprehend the various categories as they are developed and refined, and progress will soon become evident. This front-end work to properly categorize the data is essential. Failure to do so will cost innumerable additional hours of processing.

PART IV
Analysis and Interpretation

Now that the data have been collected, sorted, categorized, and coded, you are ready to attempt an interpretation of what you have. The final result of your work will be the diagnostic document itself. Working within a general structure, the members of your team will develop assigned sections on their own. Those sections will then be reviewed by other members of the team, and eventually combined into one overall document. During this process, a reconciliation of two kinds of data—objective information and the perceptions of the respondents—takes place. If perceptions are in conflict with hard evidence, such discrepancies should be noted—not discounted—because the behavior of people is based primarily on the strength of their perceptions.

This portion of the project can be considered a tremendous chore or an exhilarating experience; more than likely, it will be the latter. You will at last have a handle on every aspect of the project, and will have formulated clear ideas on how to write a report that is constructive and provides enough insight to make it truly worthwhile for management. Now you will concentrate on the analysis of issues and problems in Corporate History and Culture (Chapter 5); Planning, Strategy and Structure (Chapter 6); Organizational Resources (Chapter 7), and Organizational Processes (Chapter 8).

Your work should lead to the development of conclusions that summarize the major areas of concern as well as the issues that need to be dealt with in the near future. You will then be in a position to present the diagnosis to representatives of management, discuss it with them, then work toward the development of action plans designed to address the problems and prepare strategies for long-term development of the company.

CHAPTER 5
Corporate History and Culture

Each organization is dominated by its own unique history. This section of the diagnosis is primarily concerned with understanding your company's history and culture—how the organization has developed over the years and how such development affects its present way of doing things. A company's culture is deeply set in its historical experience, and through the years it evolves and defines the "personality" and "climate" of the organization. Culture thus affects the behavior of the company's employees, particularly those in its leadership and, by implication, the extent to which the system is successful in dealing with its environment.

Corporate Culture as a Reality

The assumption in much of the current literature is that adherence to corporate culture is desirable; in fact, this assertion has been disputed by critics of the corporate establishment, who deplore what they perceive as a lack of humanistic values or social conscience, which allegedly results in a relentless effort to satisfy institutionalized greed. In the diagnosis, such controversy is irrelevant, because the corporate culture—whether "good" or "bad"—is a reality. You only want to know what it is, because it provides a good initial profile of what the company is all about: where it comes from, how it evolved, how its people think and act, and how they are "socialized" into a system with its own characteristics. We can then assess whether the company's culture is an asset or a liability, because the norms and behavior it encourages figure prominently in the willingness of its leadership to accept feedback and to change the way it is doing things, should such changes be necessary.

Often we think of a company as an entity with a concrete substance, a mind and will of its own, possessing a personality and values that are often transferred to willing subjects, its employees. In fact, organizations literally don't have values or purposes; the people within the system do.[1] It is important, therefore, to be constantly aware that you are dealing with people and not with an abstract concept of an organization. Certainly, this organization is made up of individuals in a *system,* which has properties and an ability to change itself to cope with the environment. This concept of a system is important, because it implies that interventions or changes to one part of the system will affect other parts.[2]

In order to have a system, it is not necessary to insist on absolute homogeneity in its people's attitudes, values, and behavior. Harry Levinson points out that "organizations are composed of interdependent groups having different immediate goals, different ways of working, different formal training and even different personality types within them."[3] Even so, he adds, an organization can be viewed as a system of interrelated subsystems. Moreover, it is also a component of much larger systems such as an industry and a community, which it affects and is affected by in turn. All of these factors define a total environment for an organization. Thus it can indeed be stated that most organizations do exhibit values, a culture, and personalities of their own, even accounting for internal variations. Organizations and their subsystems tend to develop their own autonomy and their own internal norms—shared beliefs or values that become behavioral settings for the people who work within them. These internal norms shape their thoughts, aspirations, and feelings about themselves, their work, and the organization to which they belong.[4]

Historical Development and the Shaping of a Corporate Culture

The portion of the diagnosis that examines historical development asks questions such as: "What led the company to be the way it is today?" "How did the company adapt?" "What crises molded the company into what it is today?" The study of past practices often provides valuable insight, because it gives an explanation of how an organization's characteristic adaptive patterns have led to present problem-solving behavior.[5]

Since a company has a developmental course that begins at its inception, the practices, values, and behavior of its management—both routinely and under stress—often manifest the underlying assumptions of the company's founders. Such influence has continuity into the present, because successive generations of managers adopted those values and reinforce their managerial approach as a result of using them, often successfully, to deal with past crises. Statements such as, **"The reason why we did not get into that market is that we were not willing to be dishonest—that is, to pay bribes or kickbacks"** and **"We want the customer to get value for his dollar,"** are evidence of long-held values and beliefs that have been carried through to the present.

Of course, adherence to traditional ways of doing things can also have a negative effect on organizations. Since much of the management behavior in organizations, both positive and negative, can be traced to past practices that were successful in their day, often the traditional approaches to doing business go unquestioned, even though the organization may be facing a different environment and set of variables.[6] Statements such as, **"We have our own way of doing things"** and **"We have never allowed outsiders to tell us what to do,"** are indicative of a tendency to foreclose on nontraditional options.

To a certain extent, corporate culture is quite similar to national culture, because it also has its roots in the past—in the organization's history, legends, heroes and villains, achievements and disasters, recoveries, hardships, contributions, and successes. All of this constitutes a Jungian "collective unconscious," which is manifested in the present-day values of the organization: **"The ghost of the old organization is still with us. . . . It still maintains a grip on how we do things."**

The influence of a company's history on its present way of doing things is not always considered when managers and consultants search for ways to improve organizational effectiveness. In fact, most examinations of a company's background are limited to past years' financial performance. Many consultants and organizational specialists seem to have a bias toward the here-and-now, the problems facing an organization today and how they may affect its future goals and objectives. Serious examination is rarely made of *why* a business organization (i.e., the people within it) behaves in a certain way and how it got where it is today. Interventions to improve the organization, with their focus exclusively on the present and future, often ignore the true complexity of large systems by saying in effect that neither the lifetimes that people spend in an organization nor their collective learning through generations of past experiences mean much, and neither do the organization's past achievements and its self-image, as expressed through its values and traditions.

Yet it is obvious that the most powerful manifestations of corporate culture, hence its likelihood to respond to stimuli for change, revolve around an understanding of the organization's heritage. On its long-term record: **"Ours is a company with a glorious history—a history of superlative engineering performance."** On its ancient legends: **"We were the first to venture into the South American primordial forest to drill for oil."** On its folklore about particularly colorful or powerful early managers or founders of the business and their values, ideas, and eccentricities: **"The 'Old Man' once threw a broom through a plate-glass window, broke it, and said that henceforth he expected to have all windows cleaned so they would look like this."** On myths, mostly relating to ancient glories and legendary accomplishments: **"We like to tell 'war stories' about ancient successes." "We put that rig up in the middle of an ocean storm in the North Sea, and it worked!"** Its slogans: **"We are the Cadillac of the industry."**

Organizational culture, and the norms that have evolved from it, to a great extent are part of a company's problem, and inversely are also its solution. This means that the present behavior of an organization can only be explained in terms of how the company has dealt with past crises, thus developing a characteristic problem-solving behavior through its natural process of adaptation.

Corporate Indoctrination: Passing on Culture, Values, Assets, and Liabilities

Just as society systematically engages in social control through education, and in many cases through religion, so does a corporation continue the "socialization" process by carefully selecting employees who are likely to conform to its norms and value system. "**It's important to get them when they are young to make them understand that this is the way we do it.**" To this end, most companies have elaborate indoctrination and training programs that are designed to weed out the "undesirables" and speed up the process of socialization. "**You are not doing your job unless you work hard and stay late.**"

Corporate culture is to a great extent internalized by its longer-term employees and is systematically passed on to new employees. This transfer process transfers desirable characteristics: "**This is a desirable company to work for, and is known for the manner in which it treats its employees**" or "**We encourage creativity and innovation.**"

Occasionally, however, it can perpetuate a narrow perspective:

> "As a place to work, the company is improving, but we are still facing an uphill fight because of the past attitudes and philosophies of the organization. We are still deeply seated in tradition, backward thinking, with too much emphasis on administrative details without regard to overall objectives."

> "We are still locked in the old ways that no longer make us competitive in the marketplace."

> "The company gives people the impression that 'Father knows best.'"

> "If you treat people like kindergarteners, they will act like kindergarteners."

> "Emotionally, this is a depressing place to work. It is a place where it is difficult to get encouragement, direction, support, and recognition."

> "Negative feedback is never direct; it comes to you in a roundabout way; your reputation can get tarnished without your being given a chance to defend yourself."

In some extreme cases, denial of obvious facts is encouraged: "**It may be so, but we don't say it here.**" The tobacco industry, for example, has been criticized for pressuring its employees to state that data about the dangers of smoking are inconclusive, and to encourage smoking among them to prove the point.

A culture that sets taboos on discussion of certain facts, or establishes boundaries on how far it will allow people to look at environmental realities, may restrict consideration of the very alternatives the organization needs to deal with issues critical to its long-term survival: "**Don't rock the boat.**" "**Not invented here.**" "**The general atmosphere prevents initiative, innovation, and motivation.**" "**One mistake and you're out.**" This situation is evident when an organization's managers are unable to resolve severe business problems, seem to have run out of solutions, and start blaming tough times or an unfavorable environment:

"The higher you go, the more defensive people become."

"We spend a lot of time and energy protecting areas of jurisdiction. It is so bad that in some departments it borders on paranoia."

"Sure we are not making money.... How can we, with this kind of competition from the foreigners?"

A Framework for Analyzing Corporate History and Culture

The concept of growth stages of an organization, as developed by Gordon Lippitt and Warren Schmidt, is often used as a framework for tracing the historical development of a company and how that development has affected its culture. This view adds detail to Harry Levinson's argument that organizations have stages of potential growth in their life cycles, and that they experience crises and situations demanding certain management and organizational responses that are indispensable if the company is to achieve its next stage of growth.

This model of growth, closely related to the organic change concept, stresses the need for:

- Reality assessment within the organization, with respect to its present state
- Identification of the key issues or concerns that the organization is now facing
- Planned efforts to confront the situation with those activities or actions that will help achieve growth for the people, the process, and the organization

According to Lippitt and Schmidt, the continuum of an organization's life encompasses three developmental stages: birth, youth, and maturity (see Table 5-1). Some organizations succeed in reaching higher stages of development than others; however, organizations also tend to decline because of internal mismanagement or drastic changes in the external environment. The objective of organizational renewal is to handle the key issues of development in such a way as to achieve higher stages progressively and to preclude a decline toward a lower age. Renewal may occur at any time in the growth cycle.[7]

Lippitt and Schmidt also point out that it is important to realize that crises do not always occur in consecutive order; a company may find itself facing a past crisis all over again. For example, new competition, declining markets, and other developments may repeatedly thrust a mature organization or one of its subsystems into a survival confrontation. It will experience crises and situations demanding certain management and organizational responses that are indispensable if the organization is to achieve its next stage of growth. As we have discussed, such actions must address the present reality,

Table 5-1. Stages of organizational growth.

Developmental Stage	Critical Concern	Key Issue	Consequences If Concern Is Not Met
Birth	1. To create a new organization	What to risk	Frustration and inaction
			Death of organization
	2. To survive as a viable system	What to sacrifice	Further subsidy by "faith" capital
Youth	3. To gain stability	How to organize	Reactive, crisis-dominated organization
	4. To gain reputation and develop pride	How to review and evaluate	Opportunistic rather than self-directing attitudes and policies
			Difficulty in attracting good personnel and clients
			Inappropriate, overly aggressive, and distorted image building
Maturity	5. To achieve uniqueness and adaptability	Whether and how to change	Unnecessarily defensive or competitive attitudes; diffusion of energy
	6. To contribute to society	Whether and how to share	Loss of most creative personnel
			Possible lack of public respect and appreciation
			Bankruptcy or profit loss

Source: Reprinted by permission of the *Harvard Business Review.* An exhibit from "Crises in a Developing Organization" by Gordon L. Lippitt and Warren H. Schmidt (November/December 1967). Copyright © 1967 by the President and Fellows of Harvard College; all rights reserved.

and should not be patterned on successful past behaviors unless the situation is quite similar.

By tracing the continuum of an organization's life through the three developmental stages, you gain a better understanding of where the company is and to what extent flexibility exists to plan and implement the changes that a diagnosis will almost certainly identify as necessary.

A key positive developmental phase is one that reflects growth or greater sophistication, maturity, stability, or access to personnel or financial resources. A negative developmental phase is a type of organizational aging or failure. Evidence of such a phase might be a decline in profitability because products become obsolete, declining membership, or lower quality of job applicants by virtue of uncontrollable external events.[8]

A diagnosis that provides a meaningful analysis of historical development, and shows how the culture developed over the years to affect the way people think and behave in the company, is a valuable contribution to management. Moreover, such background will help you assess to what extent the company and its management set limits on its freedom of choice, not necessarily because of concrete impediments to appropriate action, but owing to artificial constraints and a narrow focus that has been self-imposed over the years.

Such knowledge is important also because it affects the nature of the recommendations developed by the diagnostic team. Some perfectly sensible and necessary action, such as the phasing out of a marginally profitable product, may be out of the question because that product might have been the first item produced by the company and is closely linked with its identity. On the other hand, a company may indeed break such a bond with its past and move itself into a completely different business environment. This is exactly what happened to the Singer Company, which divested itself of the venerable sewing-machine business to go into advanced electronics. If the people in an organization are unwilling to transform it into something that no longer has a link to its past, then they must make choices about restricting their options.

Regardless of the potential attitudes of the people in the organization, the diagnostic team must take the time to define the history and culture of the organization, because this background sets the stage for careful consideration of the more contemporary issues that will be discussed in the diagnostic report. Appendix 3 provides an example of a historical and cultural analysis used as an introduction to a major diagnosis.

CHAPTER 6
Planning, Strategy, and Structure

This section of a diagnosis examines the business environment and the external factors that the organization must deal with. These external factors include stockholders, customers, competitors, the government, and the financial community. With this information, you will be able to look at the company's stated mission in relation to its environment and assess the adequacy of its strategy and structure.

The majority of this data come from the strategic-issues interviews with top executives. Their responses should be analyzed in the context of whether there is, as a group, a common concept of the company's "reason for being." Planning issues can also be examined by establishing Mission, Strategy, Objectives, and Goals as major topics that take into account not only the comments of executives, but also the perceptions of other managers and relevant research data obtained from records and other objective sources, as necessary.

General Planning Practices in the Organization

The ability to plan a company's future path realistically and effectively is a key factor in ensuring the organization's competitive position. Not only must you address long-term planning within a strategic framework, but you must also do an effective job of addressing intermediate plans, in order to proceed systematically from the present to a point in the future that has been defined as a meaningful strategic objective. Do not forget that you must also attend to short-term operational planning. Moreover, all planning systems in the organization should be integrated to ensure uniform progress toward corporate goals. Complaints about lack of planning, conflicting planning systems, or overbearing planning often indicate a failure to either design or use a fundamental management tool: "Planning is strictly short term." "We only address financial planning; everything else takes a back seat." "What planning?" In some extreme cases, the absence of meaningful plans places the organization at the mercy of its environment, thus denying management its opportunity to influence, or at least react systematically to, anticipated market changes, new-product introductions, and competitive pressures.

Strategic Planning

Strategic planning is primarily concerned with the long-term welfare of the company. It involves a combination of data collection and analysis of the business environment and the organization itself, in order to assess potential future scenarios that the company will have to deal with. This up-front analysis allows for the development of strategies and specific action plans that can specify exactly how the company will organize itself and muster its resources in the near term and proximate future to ensure its long-term survival and success.

Core Mission

Before reviewing data about the company's business environment, you must understand the thinking of top management in regard to what it considers the business of the company. A review of the diagnostic data might reveal that the organization's mission, strategies, and goals are often nebulous to the majority of the employees or are a closely guarded secret at the highest levels of management. Yet clarity of mission and commitment to its fulfillment are considered major determinants of an organization's—and its employees'—ability to deal effectively with its environment.

Many executives may point out that the core mission is to make a profit: **"Ultimately, the mission of any company is to make money. How you make that money depends on what you can do."** Yet it is not so. Profit is a given, a prerequisite for survival. The profit objective by itself, however, will not give insight into which portion of the market to concentrate in and which product is compatible with the organization's unique competence. The core mission of an organization, as defined by Richard Beckhard and Reubin Harris,[1] is nothing less than its *raison d'être,* its "reason for being."

The core mission should be as explicit and sharply defined as possible, but it is more important that it reflect what the organization is trying to accomplish in the long-range future. For example, the O. M. Scott Company reportedly spent a year deciding between two definitions of its core mission: The first was "to make fertilizers"; the second was "to keep lawns green." Product diversification would not be consistent with fertilizer production alone, Scott's traditional business. The company decided to go with the latter definition, in spite of the significant added resources it would require, because a broader product line aimed at "keeping lawns green" ultimately would be better for the organization.

Certainly, a vaguely formulated mission or goal is a prescription for confusion. General, nebulous goals such as "maximizing profits," "improving customer satisfaction," "maximizing quality," or "improving efficiency and minimizing costs" are not very helpful to the person who might be charged with meeting those goals. Vague goals leave significant room for interpretation. The end result is that the person might compromise quality to minimize costs, because that is what he or she thought was important, whereas management's intent was to improve quality to compete with foreign products.

The explicit definition and recognition of the core mission as a driving force in strategic planning is important because decisions based on departmental or parochial "goals and objectives" may be at variance with the core mission. When all planning and decision making, including resource allocation, are based on the same core mission, the company is less likely to suffer from conflicting policies or programs that are out of step with the overall strategic plan.

Goals and objectives are not necessarily the same as—or always consistent with—the core mission. Goals are often functional or departmental, or are based on a relatively narrow view of the organization's future. For example, one group in the company may be making decisions as though the future lies in domestic products, while another group might see the future in international operations. Such situations present great potential for wasted effort, inefficiently deployed resources, and lack of cooperation.[2]

In order to be helpful, the strategies, goals, and objectives have to be sufficiently detailed to provide meaningful guidance for the implementers. For example, a bank's strategy may have as a primary objective "increasing retail-banking efficiency and reducing personnel costs while maintaining customer satisfaction." If not properly detailed, these may seem like conflicting goals. If proper thought is given to implementation, however, such a combination can be dealt with effectively. In this instance, the bank decided that its objective could be reached through increased computerization, involving installation of cash machines that process a variety of transactions and consumer-banking services through a customer's personal computer. Managers recognized that these objectives could not be reached overnight, owing to the general resistance of the average banking customers to computerized services. So the bank included in its action plans a campaign to educate customers about the benefits of computerized banking, stressing its convenience, flexibility, security, and time efficiency and assuring them that a live person would always be available if needed. The bank ran ads in newspapers, sent promotional literature to customers' homes, set up demonstration stations at all of its branches, and made available PC service at very attractive rates, which included access to various information services. As a result, the bank's customers are becoming used to cash machines, PC banking is proliferating, and the bank is able to run its retail branches with fewer people and, in some cases, close some branches altogether.

In an organization with significant resources, it is possible to have multiple core missions, because they can be achieved by sufficiently differentiated subunits. This is the case with large companies such as General Electric, which is heavily involved in areas ranging from heavy equipment and aerospace to consumer products.

Despite its importance, a clearly written, unequivocal core-mission statement does not exist in many firms, or has not been effectively communicated. Part of the diagnostic process is to determine if such communication has taken place and to help clarify what the company's core-mission statement is and should be in the future.

Environmental Scanning

In theory, plans could be based on inward analysis alone: "**We should do what we are best able to do, what makes the greatest profit, or what we can do with our technology and resources at hand.**" In fact, the business environment does not change in readily predictable ways, with obvious effects on the organization:

> "To some extent, this generation of managers is out of luck. Our predecessors could count on a stable market where we were one of the few players. Now, with the introduction of microcomputers, every Tom, Dick, and Harry is chipping away at our turf, and eroding not only our market share, but also our profit margins. This forces us to fundamentally rethink the nature of our business."

Today's managers, in effect, must spend ever more time trying to anticipate what will happen in the troublesome, difficult, largely uncomfortable external environment, the totality of outside factors that may or may not affect the future of the company.

Since a company concerned about its future is very much involved with how it will be affected by the environment, its people are likely to spend considerable resources on formal and informal environmental scanning, a data-gathering effort that continuously attempts to identify trends and changes, and isolate and track those changes that are likely to make a difference. Depending on the organization, the changes that could have an impact range from the fluctuating petroleum reserves in a foreign nation (and that nation's political climate) to increases or decreases in the regional fertility rate among twenty- to twenty-four-year-old women. Some trends are relatively easy to project, such as demographic age distributions based on the existing population; others defy analysis because they depend on a complex of other factors, such as political attitudes toward government-supported day care. Almost all are beyond the control of the organization, even though they will have a profound effect on its future. Generally, companies should identify and track the following environmental factors, as a minimum:

- *Economic trends*—such as projected inflation rates, cost of raw materials, energy costs, productivity rates, interest rates, and other domestic or international economic factors impacting on the organization.
- *Regulatory requirements*—including government regulation applying to specific industries, laws affecting treatment of workers by employers, and government programs affecting the quality and quantity of the labor force.
- *Technical developments*—such as the impact of new products and services; technology affecting employment, jobs, and markets; and new skills requirements.

- *Competitors' actions*—including international competitors, new companies, diversifying organizations, and firms exiting the marketplace. A formal program of competitor analysis can be employed. This program involves assessing each competitor's resource commitments and overall expenditures in terms of their impact on the market; recognizing the relative strengths and weaknesses of both the competitor and your company, from the perspective of the market; profiling the track records and personalities of the competitor's key decision-makers to determine their likely responses to your company's moves; and developing the basis for cost and pricing strategies that aim directly at the competitor's vulnerabilities.
- *Availability of human resources*—particularly the supply of skilled workers from the educational system.

Concurrent with the general environmental scanning, the Marketing Division is usually responsible for preparing an analysis of where the company stands in the marketplace, including trends and development affecting its market share.

As discussed in the sections that follow, the nomenclature and analytical framework for examining the external environment can vary enormously. The terms used inside the organization, however, should be consistent, and the outline for examining environmental conditions must be relevant to the organization's strategic planning needs.

Performing the Environmental Scanning

For a diagnosis, the first question to ask is whether the company is engaging in environmental scanning as an integral part of its strategic planning. If the answer is affirmative, the job of defining the company's environment essentially is done, unless you feel that supplementary information is necessary. On the other hand, if information about the relevant aspects of the business environment is sketchy or not available, then the question is who should undertake the process of environmental scanning, particularly if this is the first time such an activity is attempted. In one sense, it is convenient for the diagnostic team to do it. This would minimize any "contamination" of the data by people with vested interests. In reality, however, it is not easy for a diagnostic team to perform a reasonably complete analysis of a company's outside environment, because much of the research involves specialized knowledge and skills that the diagnostic team may not possess. For practical reasons, then, this task of environmental scanning is better performed by a group of diagnostic team members supplemented by academicians, graduate students, and various staff members with the specialized skills required.

Ideally, whether scanning occurs as a regular part of the strategic-planning process or as a special activity of the diagnostic process, the human-resources function should participate, primarily because it needs to provide an assessment of data and trends relating specifically to human resources. Corporate Planning and Marketing Planning Divisions should have the perspective and capabilities necessary to structure the overall scanning process. Responsibility for the initial framework, including determining which aspects of the environment deserve the most attention because they are the most critical to the organization's future, might thus repose with the corporate and marketing planners, although input from other staff managers and operational planners is essential.

A review of the current strategic-planning process in the company should highlight the key environmental trends affecting business plans, enabling an examination of how these factors are integrated with internal data to develop scenarios upon which alternative strategic plans are based. Thus, the overall perspective for environmental scanning, whether already established or as a feature of the diagnostic study, should be corporate, although participation by departments with specific kinds of expertise—legal, financial, human resources, and line organizations and subsidiaries—is essential.

If this is a new task, by involving the people who would in any case be responsible for performing the environmental scanning, the diagnosis in effect initiates the process, which in itself is a significant contributor to an organization's ability to deal better with environmental challenges.

Scenarios and Strategies

In your review, you should identify whether the data collected during the environmental-scanning process is sufficient for developing economic and environmental scenarios—ranging from optimistic to pessimistic—to deal with the state of the economy, expected regulatory impacts, technological changes, and other variables. The research should also involve assimilation of current market data reflecting existing market conditions as well as new market trends. This analysis should help a company's leadership and its planning group to anticipate future environmental challenges to the organization and to plan appropriate action.

Next, review the process that leads to the design of initial response strategies, actions that the company could take to cope with the given scenarios.

You should then review whether the planners have made an impact analysis for each of the preliminary strategies:

> **"Our problem is not so much our ability to create meaningful scenarios—we have been reasonably accurate in the past. We are even good at developing strategies which make sense in each circumstance, except that we can't put them into action because our parent company won't let us have the budgets to fund some of these necessary programs."**

Indeed, in practice not all of the previously developed strategies will be feasible for implementation, primarily because the company, for whatever reasons, may not be able to generate enough financial and human resources to meet some of the requirements. Those strategies that are not feasible to pursue should have been discarded. Of the remaining scenarios and strategies, the variance (the difference between resource demand and availability) should determine the strategy most realistic for the company to implement. Obviously, the choice of optimum scenario and strategy should be made by top management.

In order to protect the organization from unforeseen changes in the economy, at least two scenarios and strategies should be selected and maintained. This procedure facilitates the development of a corporate data base for operational and long-range planning. The planning consists of resource-demand forecasts for the most likely scenario and strategy. It also includes alternative scenarios and strategies that would serve as contingency plans, and would normally not be used for operational planning unless a radical change in conditions made it necessary to do so.

Marketing Strategy

Market planning is integral to the development and implementation of strategy. Management recognizes that its product needs to be sold, the markets defined, the competitors analyzed. You are likely to hear comments such as: **"We need an edge over the competition." "We need to do better than the competition because our share of the market is too small."**

Marketing is a discipline of its own, and a thorough discussion of proper marketing techniques is beyond the scope of this book. As a diagnostician, however, you should have enough knowledge to assess whether this vital aspect of company operations is handled adequately. The material that follows is not intended as a primer on marketing, but as a general guide for what to look for in order to assess the marketing process in the company and to determine if there are adequate links between strategic planning and correspondent marketing strategies.

Contemporary marketing stresses the importance of the customer and how essential it is to meet the needs of the marketplace, rather than expect the market to accept your company's product, no matter how good. To use an old analogy, you can't sell ice-makers to Eskimos: **"We need to substantially improve our customer relations." "We need to examine how we, as a company, treat client contacts in general, especially at the executive level, even though such contacts are not necessarily related to today's sales."** Owing to changes in markets, many organizations have sharply redefined and broadened the definition of the businesses they are in, in order to be more responsive to their customers. For example, railroads no longer see themselves in the train business, but in the transportation business; computer companies are in the information business; and integrated companies with subsidiaries such as airlines, hotels, and auto-rental agencies see themselves in the travel business.

Strategic moves from the competition generally are followed closely, and elicit responses in kind. Once the viability of the personal computer was established by IBM, even the skeptics and nay-sayers in mainframe and minicomputer businesses had to scramble to come up with their own compatible versions of the little machines that one day may become so powerful as to make larger computers obsolete. Banks are moving to cope with the explosion of financial services offered by brokerage firms and mutual funds, which have proved adept at capturing huge deposits from low-yielding saving accounts with regulated interest rates.

Much effort is spent assessing the risks and consequences of executive decisions about which markets to enter and which to avoid: **"Are we doing anything to position ourselves for the expected surge in market demand a year from now?" "The opportunities are there, along with the risks. We have to assess the down side before we move."** When executives make strategic decisions, often they haven't enough information, or else they have too much. The art and science of divining market trends, getting everyone to agree to the likelihood of those trends, and deciding on which alternative to choose is anything but easy: **"Some of the foreign markets we are counting on may not be realized. How do we plan to deal with this?"**

Once a marketing decision has been made, you might want to examine whether the company has a structure enabling it to exercise its talents and use its limited resources in that given marketplace. Many organizations establish strategic business units (SBUs)—divisions or subsidiaries that focus on a particular market segment. Hence an electronics manufacturer may have several SBUs: consumer electronics (stereo components), instrument controls systems for aircraft and ships; and defense electronics and weapons systems control.

Positioning the Strategic Business Units

A common method of establishing and positioning strategic business units according to market served was developed by the Boston Consulting Group.[3] The portfolio analysis that they promoted essentially involved categorizing the various businesses of an organization according to the environment in which they operate (see Figure 6-1), as follows:

- *Competitive strength*—which can be high, medium, or low as compared to other companies capable of providing the same services or products
- *Business/market attractiveness*—in terms of size, potential profitability, growth prospects, ease of entry, and similar factors; these are also categorized as high, medium, and low

If this categorization has not already been done by the marketing people, you should be aware that the selection of strategy depends on where an SBU falls on the grid.

Low/low market attractiveness. A unit that falls into both low market-attractiveness and low competitive-strength categories is a candidate for a <u>harvest</u> or <u>divest</u> strategy. If this unit is producing a mature product that sells itself and requires little additional development, then the emphasis is on achieving the highest possible manufacturing effective to minimize production costs and maximize profits. Since investment is minimized, the company is in

Figure 6-1. SBU strategy selection.

	Competitive Strength		
Business/Market Attractiveness	High	Medium	Low
High	Invest and grow		
Medium		Earn and protect	
Low			Harvest or divest

essence "harvesting" all it can from this "cash cow," so that it can use the money to invest in promising new ventures. If the unit is likely to continue in a low/low market, it may become a candidate for divestiture. The company would then prune product lines, free up capacity to accommodate production of other SBUs' products sharing the sales force, and prepare the unit for sale. This is essentially the strategy followed by Primerica, formerly American Can Corporation, which divested itself of all manufacturing operations in order to become a financial services conglomerate.

Medium/medium market attractiveness. A unit in the medium/medium categories has an earn/protect status, whereby it endeavors to maintain its market share, optimize profit margins, differentiate products, segment markets, and increase efficiency.

High/high market attractiveness. A unit in a high/high quadrant is a "star," or a candidate for significant investment by the company, because it is expected to achieve substantial growth. This SBU endeavors to improve its market share, even if it means "buying" that greater portion through aggressive pricing; develops new products; increases its manufacturing capacity; and expands the sales force and distribution system.

What can go wrong with this? Management can make crucial errors in defining a business unit by considering what it does and not what the market demands. For example, a manufacturer of auto carburetors may be very efficient, but it will become gradually obsolete because today's automobiles are increasingly using fuel-injection systems. By defining the unit's core mission as "making carburetors," the SBU limits itself to that, no matter how good the product. If, on the other hand, the core mission is defined as "making fuel-delivery systems for automobiles," then the SBU ensures a future for itself. By definition, it will have to stay abreast of fuel-delivery technology, which includes computerized systems and perhaps even battery-driven methods. Rather than being a "cash cow," this unit can be reclassified as an earn/protect or even an invest/grow. Obviously, an SBU's positioning on the strategic grid has significant implications for the approach to investment, marketing, and human resources it will require to run the show. Part of the usefulness of a diagnosis is in examining how your company addresses this area and noting any potential opportunities for improvement.

Managing the Strategic Business Units

The selection of managers to run a strategic business unit is considered important to the unit's success, and in your review you should pay particular attention to the match between people and their positions. A "cash cow" is better managed by efficiency-minded, productivity-oriented managers whose main emphasis is on minimizing expense and investment and maximizing profits. At the other extreme, managers of a startup operation in a new and promising environment are likely to be conceptual, creative, and sales and product-development oriented.

Strategy Implementation

Transition

To properly deal with an uncertain future, you should review whether the company has a clearly stated strategy that sets appropriate goals and objectives to be reached at certain points in the future. At the same time, there should be a recognition that a vast gulf, full of obstacles, exists between the present and those various milestones:

> "There is no question that we know what our long-term objectives are, and what we have to do to get there. This means that we have to do a lot of work, because we can't ignore the fact that people expect us to make money today, so we have to mind the

store. Just the same, somehow, we have to find the time and resources to transform ourselves, over a period of five years, into a company which will be quite different."

A CEO must be primarily concerned with ensuring the long-term survival of the company. Since the most constant reality facing an organization in today's environment is that of continuing change, intermediate change plans are essential.

The implication is that the higher in the hierarchy a manager is, the more he or she should spend time on future planning. This may explain the growing importance of strategic planning among sophisticated organizations. It may also give some insight into why the leadership must have an explicit core mission and be in agreement with it.

Problems With Strategy Implementation

The complaint you may hear often during the diagnosis process is that grandiose strategic plans have a tendency to fall apart upon implementation: **"We do have a strategic plan, but it doesn't tell us how to implement it."** In fact, it is true that it is easier to develop impressive plans than to make them work in real life. A comprehensive diagnosis should explore the most common troubles with strategy implementation:

Communication of mission and strategy. Having a clear mission statement and proper goals and objectives per se will not guarantee successful implementation of the strategy: **"Everybody knows we have strategic plans; trouble is, few know what they are."** The worst thing management can do is to regard such information as top secret, something to which only the key executives are privy. Certainly, the need for confidentiality is legitimate in today's competitive environment. However, there needs to be a measure of confidence in the ability of the critical mass, the managers who have to implement the strategies, to make judicious use of the information. A company is not a military organization. Even though the typical organization is essentially authoritarian, its members are more effective when they understand not only the objectives but the relevant information that goes with them. This information may include the reasons for a particular strategy, potential threats or opportunities it attempts to address, available resources, and milestones for progress. Only an adequately informed middle management group, in concert with top management and its strategic perspective, can be expected to minimize conflicting goals and wasted efforts, in the pursuit of a common objective.

Preparation and training of managers. Strategic plans are implemented by line managers, not strategic planners or staff specialists, no matter how competent these individuals may be. Yet, the best-laid plans can fail if the people charged with their implementation are not equipped to handle them: **"We have ambitious plans, and then we find out it will take years to get the right people to implement them, because we have not taken the time to develop our own."** This concern is particularly acute when the company is trying to implement plans for diversification in areas it knows relatively little about. An organization that has been successful in the past, by virtue of the technological excellence that sold itself, will find it rough to suddenly become more market-oriented, because it may have not developed an aggressive, responsive sales force: "**We probably have the products in this market, but we don't know how to sell them to a public who doesn't know the difference.**" A switch from selling computers to industrial customers to selling microcomputers to the retail market involves a complete re-orientation. Without significant preparation, an oil company, no matter how successful, cannot expect to profitably run a newly acquired department-store chain. In some cases, the cultural gap is too wide, with predictably poor results. The conclusion is that a company concerned about the proper implementation of strategy must take stock of what managers it has; if they are found wanting, it must initiate programs to address those deficiencies. Appendix 3 illustrates how one organization attempted to upgrade the skills of its management in order to implement an ambitious diversification program.

The Prospects of Strategic Planning

Since problems with strategy formulation and implementation are far more common than many are willing to admit, there has been a tendency in the literature to dismiss strategic planning as moribund or passé. You may also hear skeptical comments from the respondents:

> "**Strategic planning is of questionable value, in my observation. It involves a lot of paper which is prepared to please the bosses, then we go on about our business.**"
>
> "**Few of the so-called strategic plans were realized, primarily because things change too fast.**"
>
> "**I question the effort we put in strategic planning, because in the clothing business we can't see six months ahead, let alone years.**"

In fact, a more subtle situation exists. Daniel Gray points out that if strategic planning does a vanishing act in the future it will be because, wherever it is done, the people engaged in the process either get better at it and show positive results, or they are unsuccessful. "If you do it poorly, either you drop out or you rattle around in its mechanics; if you do it well, you evolve beyond strategic planning to strategic management."[4]

The problem is that strategic planning is often seen as a separate discipline of a distinct management function, whereas if it is to work it really is a way of life—an integral part of a top manager's repertory of skills. In this context, strategic planning is an instrument into which all other control systems—budgeting, information, compensation, organization—can be integrated. In any case, strategic planning is a process that is here to stay. A comprehensive survey of strategic planning in the United States reports the following:

- Most companies surveyed remain firmly committed to strategic planning, even though 87 percent report feelings of disappointment and frustration with their systems.
- Of those showing disappointments, 59 percent attribute their discontent mainly to difficulties encountered in the implementation of the plans.
- When multibusiness executives compared their experiences, 67 percent traced their implemention problems to the design of their systems and the way they managed them.[5]

Most strategic-planning failures have been implementation failures. If this has happened in your company, it is no reason to abandon the process. It is an opportunity to find the reason for the failure, and fix the problem.

In any case, the reasons for the implementation failures are no mystery. An awareness of what they are can help the strategic-planning process get back on track. For example, a company cannot find its way through rough waters by using only financial goals and controls. Certainly such considerations are important, even vital, but they are essentially post-factum evaluations of bottom-line results. Financial goals per se are more constraints and boundaries than means of dealing effectively with changes in the business environment.

Operational Planning

A proper strategic plan should clearly differentiate between future planning and day-to-day operations, because running a factory is fundamentally different from running the company itself. Someone must mind the store today, hence the necessity for short-term operational planning.

Operational planning, in most cases, is unique to each organization. The end result, however, is the same: identification of the kinds and number of people necessary to do the work scheduled in the immediate future, as well as definition of the necessary raw materials and machines. Mostly, line managers are good at this task: "**We may be unsure about what to do next year, but if they give us something to do now, we can plan it successfully to the last nail.**" In complex operational planning, analytical tools such as computerized "what-if" analyses of various alternatives enable an organization to examine the various conditions that may affect the accuracy of resource forecasts, and help it reach a point of optimization.

"What-if" capability enables on-line analysis and supplementary displays of operational plans by department detail and summary; projects by department; project summaries; generic project reports; location reports, and others, as necessary. In addition, it updates and displays reports showing changes in project mix, project data, departmental location assignments, and similar alterations.

The "what-if" capabilities are also helpful to individual departments for their own internal planning and in examining staffing and other resource alternatives. Departments then have a tool that facilitates the development of departmental operating plans.

This analytical work helps in the formulation of official resource-demand forecasts. These forecasts list the resource demand expected from active workload (short-term forecast), scheduled workload (intermediate forecast), and potential workload (long-term forecast). The operational planning system should also be able to forecast resource requirements for miscellaneous projects, overhead work, and business-development efforts.

As a general rule, an organizational diagnosis does not explore operational planning to any significant degree, because it is rarely a problem. Such a scrutiny is justified only if there are sufficient complaints from the respondents.

Organizational Structure

In order to successfully execute its mission, plans, and objectives, an organization must establish a structure that reflects what is to be done, by whom, and how. This structure should show both depth (sufficient management control, appropriate levels of staffing, and defined interrelationships among units, enabling it to fulfill most of what is required) and efficiency (delegation of sufficient authority and autonomy within the units to enable decision making at the appropriate levels, without unnecessary layers of management and corporate control).

Extent to Which "Form Follows Function"

Much importance has been given in management literature to structure as a vehicle for organizational control and effectiveness. Certainly an adequate structure is important, particularly when organizations grow in size. In effect, a bureaucracy is necessary to manage the day-to-day operations. A good structure can help an organization's managers do their job. On the other hand, a poor structure can severely hinder even the most capable people:

> "A significant number of managers see the present organizational structure as the source and the cause of many of the problems currently experienced by the company."
>
> "People have problems because we are not structured properly."
>
> "Structure gets in the way of people."

In extreme cases, an archaic structure that is maintained for a variety of reasons—cronyism, the old timer's network, an original owner unwilling to delegate—can result in overstaffing and discouragement of young and energetic managers: "**In the seventies, extra levels in the organization were created to accommodate valuable employees who were not qualified to be VPs.**"

A properly designed organization reflects the classic theory of design, "Form follows function." In a business sense, the form of the organization follows the official function, defined by the organization's mission, plans, and goals. Some criteria used to examine this theory include:

- How well the organizational structure facilitates the accomplishment of the tasks that need to be performed
- To what extent the organization utilizes people to do the job, and how well these people are matched to the job requirements
- To what extent reward systems reinforce the desired behavior on the part of the employees
- How information and decision processes are used to facilitate work

During a diagnosis, executives often indicate a need to change the organizational chart frequently: "**In the last three years, the company revised and published its corporate organizational chart six times. At this very moment, a new chart is being printed.**" A developmental process is generally discernible in a number of revisions, but fragmentation is often present in reporting relationships, in authority, in communication, and in decision making:

> "**The organization's fragmentation makes it difficult to analyze, make decisions, communicate decisions, and carry them out.**"
>
> "**The organization is very complicated; the lines of responsibility and authority are poorly defined.**"

The presumption is that structure can alleviate such disparities. However, the implication is that increased complexity of the organization sometimes makes the formal organizational chart and structure less useful in describing actual responsibilities and interactions.

The underlying issues that managers focus on are, "What is the rationale for the company's present authority structure?" and "Why aren't middle managers involved in decisions concerning reorganization?" The indication is that revisions are often viewed as arbitrary and inconsistent with operating needs.

The implementation of a matrix organization is often a case in point: "**The matrix organization is difficult, but necessary.**" The fundamental factors that contribute to predictable difficulties in establishing this form of organization are:

1. Insufficient preparation by the organization to understand and accept the system: **"The reason we have difficulty working under a matrix organization is that most of our people have not been prepared to manage in an environment that demands a tolerance of ambiguity. In essence, it demands a higher level of managerial competence."**
2. Insufficient number of individuals qualified to manage it: **"Sure, the matrix makes sense for us at this time; trouble is, we don't have enough people capable of operating in such an environment. Most of us have grown up being told what to do. The matrix demands that you think for yourself, make decisions, and negotiate roles."**
3. General role conflict and ambiguity for managers resulting from a highly complex structure: **"The adoption of the matrix organization was a traumatic experience for the company; we still haven't fully managed to operate effectively in this fashion."**

Since a matrix organization brings individuals together in new and varied ways that are not reflected in the formal organizational chart, managers often require further clarification of how the company is growing and operating as a system, rather than as a structure. Management may need to deemphasize the structure and hierarchy for control in order to achieve an organic system that allows continued readjustment of individual tasks through an integrated network of communication, authority, and control.

One note of caution: Organizational structure is a very convenient scapegoat to explain a variety of ills, but it is not necessarily the reason why things don't work. Suggesting reorganization, for whatever reason, in essence prescribes the initiation of serious and generally disruptive change for up to two years, with the accompanying trauma to the people in the organization. Reorganization should be the last alternative suggested to management, because not only is it the most serious intervention for an organization, but it also rarely solves significant problems, the resolution of which almost always lies elsewhere.

Evaluation of Strategic Advantage

As a general rule, your evaluation of an organization and its positioning versus its business environment relies on background research and the feedback you receive from respondents. If the company's executives are oriented toward quantification, you may want to provide them with the results of an exercise that does indeed provide some quantification of the business environment, particularly whether the environment is perceived as favorable or threatening along a continuum. The two analyses that follow can help summarize how people in the organization perceive the situation. This is not a strictly scientific approach; rather it is a pragmatic, practical exercise that is easily understood by the respondents.

Environmental Threat and Opportunities Analysis

This instrument asks the respondent to assign points to each of several questions about the business environment that the company is facing. The scale ranges from 1 to 5, with 1 point indicating that the company is strongly positioned to deal with the environment on a given area or issue, to 5 points indicating that the company is facing a serious threat to its environment. The points are then totaled and divided by the maximum threat, that is, the highest number of points possible. For example, in Table 6-1, the respondent has indicated responses that total 60 points. The maximum threat would be 75, since there are 15 questions with a maximum of 5 points each. So 60 is divided by 75, and the result (60 ÷ 75 = .80) indicates that the company is facing an environment that is quite threatening: 80 percent of the worst possible situation. What do you do with this? Merely use it as a supplementary element of

Table 6-1. Environmental threat and opportunities analysis.

	Weight				
	Positive			Negative	
	1	2	3	4	5
General environmental factors					
Government restriction, regulations, or constraints					5
Consumer loyalty and volatility					5
Projected changes in the overall economy and how such changes are likely to affect the company			3		
Projected changes in consumer spending power				4	
Demographic changes in customer base			3		
Supply factors					
Availability of raw materials				4	
Price of raw materials				4	
Number of available suppliers		2			
Technological changes affecting raw material supplies		2			
Market factors					
Demand for new products				4	
Pricing structure					5
Demand for product(s)				4	
Consumer preferences					5
New competition			3		
Product life cycle		2			
Subtotal		6	9	20	25
Total	60 points				

Minimum Threat Maximum Threat   Score: 60 ÷ 75 = 80%
15 _____ 30 _____ 45 _____ 60 _____ 75

Planning, Strategy, and Structure

data to corroborate other feedback you may have received from the respondents.

Strategic Advantage Profile

This instrument is designed to evaluate various operational variables in the company, and how such variables contribute to making the company competitive in its environment (see Table 6-2). The scale again ranges from 1 to 5, with 5 points indicating the best possible status of a given variable and 1 point showing extreme inadequacy.

You will note that a few variables have been divided into subcategories, which are not rated; these subcategories are designed to show that there can be different factors to consider in determining the weight of a single variable.

In the example shown in Table 6-2, the respondents have given a total of 129 points. Compared to the maximum possible points (230), we reach a conclusion that the company's strategic advantage is about 56 percent of what it could be (129 ÷ 230 = .56). Again, these data should be reviewed within the context of other data in the diagnosis.

You may wish to work with the sponsor or ODC to develop similar instruments incorporating variables that may be most appropriate to your company or industry. The approach is relatively simple, and the results are almost invariably worth examination.

Table 6-2. Strategic advantage profile.

	Weight				
	Positive			Negative	
	5	4	3	2	1
Financial conditions					
Cost of capital				2	
Effectiveness of capital structure (flexibility in raising additional capital as needed)				2	
Relations with stockholders and/or parent company			3		
Tax conditions			3		
Barriers to new entry because of amount of required resources				2	
Effective financial planning, working capital, and capital budgeting				2	
Effective systems for cost accounting, budget and profit planning, and auditing procedures		4			
Subtotal		4	6	8	
Total for financial conditions	18 points				

Positive   Negative   Score: 18 ÷ 35 = 51%
35_____28_____21_____14_____7

(Continued)

Table 6-2 (Continued)

	Weight				
	Positive			Negative	
	5	4	3	2	1
Marketing					
Total market share				2	
Market research system				2	
Product or service mix				2	
Quality of products or services		4			
Product or service leadership		4			
Phase of product or service life cycle				2	
Channels of distribution or service delivery				2	
Geographic coverage (domestic)		4			
Geographic coverage (international)				2	
Pricing of products and services				2	
Effectiveness of sales force				2	
Client base (narrow or broad)				2	
Advertising				2	
Marketing promotion		4			
Service after purchase		4			
Subtotal		20		20	

Total for marketing   40 points

Positive   Negative   Score: 40 ÷ 75 = 53%
75_____60_____45_____30_____15

	Weight				
	Positive			Negative	
	5	4	3	2	1
Operations					
Raw materials cost					1
Raw materials availability			3		
Inventory control systems			3		
Facilities (adequacy, overutilized, under-utilized)				2	
Integration of operations			3		
Management information systems			3		
Equipment and machinery			3		
Location of facilities				2	
Operations procedures		4			

	Weight				
	Positive			Negative	
	5	4	3	2	1
Design					
Scheduling					
Production					
Quality control					
Total cost of operations as compared to competitors		4			
Research and development		4			
Legal protection or patents for products, processes, and similar trade secrets			3		
Subtotal		12	18	4	1

Total for operations 35 points

Positive 60_____48_____36_____24_____12 Negative

Score: 35 ÷ 60 = 58%

	Weight				
	Positive			Negative	
	5	4	3	2	1
Personnel and Management					
Quality managers			3		
Quality employees		4			
Relations with unions			3		
Employee relations policies		4			
Staffing					
Appraisal					
Training and development					
Compensation and benefits					
Corporate image and prestige		4			
Organizational structure		4			
Size relative to industry				2	
Strategic planning system				2	
Record in reaching past objectives		4			
Influence with government regulatory bodies				2	
Management succession planning				2	
Teamwork in management				2	
Subtotal		20	6	10	

Total for personnel and management 36 points

Positive 60_____48_____36_____24_____12 Negative

Score: 36 ÷ 60 = 60%

(Continued)

Table 6-2 (Continued)

Summary of strategic advantage profile.			
	Maximum	*Score*	*Percent Significance*
Financial conditions	35	18	51%
Marketing	75	40	53%
Operations	60	35	58%
Personnel and management	60	36	60%
	230	129	56%
	Total	Total	Total Score ÷ Total Maximum

Source: Adapted from William F. Glueck, *Business Policy: Strategy Formation and Management Action,* copyright 1972, McGraw-Hill. Used by permission.

CHAPTER 7
Organizational Resources

Organizational resources generally are indicative of a company's size, status in the business community, and profitability. Just having the resources, however, does not mean they are being used efficiently, or that they may be the proper resources in the first place. In a diagnosis, you are primarily interested in whether the organizational resources are adequate in relation to the demands of the company's strategic and operational plans.

The fact that a company may not have certain types of resources available at a given time does not necessarily mean it will be unable to meet the demands of a given strategy. Implementation of plans and strategies is still possible if the organization can obtain such resources by exchanging one kind for another. For example, a corporation may have significant funds available, but not enough executives with marketing experience. Both are resources, and spending one of them (funds) will bring in the other needed resource (additional executives).

Other kinds of resources are less obvious. For example, if significant additional funds are needed to build a new plant, a corporation could obtain them by issuing stock or establishing larger credit lines with its banks. As long as such options are available to management, you can say that it has adequate resources to do what it takes to implement its plans. On the other hand, if the company is already highly leveraged, it might not be able to raise additional financial resources, and its options will be limited.

An examination of the company's resources should include:

- *Financial resources*—which may dictate the level of overall resources available for implementation of strategies
- *Human resources*—in terms of both quantity and quality of employees presently in the organization: the number of people, an evaluation of their skills and talents, and their ability to adapt to future needs
- *Technological resources*—including research and development considerations, such as knowledge of new and developing technologies that could drastically change the organization's capabilities, costs, and markets

- *Physical assets*—such as plant, equipment, buildings, natural resources, and oil and gas reserves

Each of these areas deserves special attention, and is treated in this chapter.

Financial Resources

The current financial status of the organization, is, of course, one of the most important "resource" factors to evaluate. If, for example, changing technology requires a vast investment for capital improvement, and funding is unavailable or unobtainable because of a weak financial position, this condition is a critical consideration in assessing the company's current capability.

Even though an organization's financial health is important to its survival, often it turns out to be a rather abstract issue for most employees, mostly because it is a matter generally handled at the highest levels of management and, in some cases, what actually is going on is clouded in secrecy.

A review of an organization's financial health normally is not part of a developmental diagnosis, mainly because this kind of financial analysis is often performed as a matter of course during annual audits and reviews by security analysts. Even so, if time and resources allow, there is sufficient reason to take a hard look at the official financial statements and shareholders' reports. It is no secret that often the numbers represented in such reports are embellished and sweetened by deliberately optimistic comments and are accompanied by photographs of well-tailored executives, happy employees, and impressive facilities—all are superficialities that don't tell the whole story. A comprehensive diagnosis need not retrace the steps of accountants and auditors; rather, you are mostly interested in examining management's approach to setting and reaching its financial objectives, because the process may or may not result in actions that lead to a company's long-term financial health.

This portion of the diagnosis must be made by people with the appropriate background and experience. Most line managers with budget responsibility can do a good job in this area. It is prudent, however, to have a specialist—perhaps a financial consultant or a professor of finance at a local university—join the team.

If, as project manager, you plan to include an analysis of financial resources in the diagnosis but are not a specialist in this field, you should know some basic information. The traditional point of departure for evaluating a profit-making enterprise has been the development of financial criteria reflecting bottom-line results. Because management's performance is usually measured by profits, it is not surprising that financial results are the leading indicators of effectiveness, often to the exclusion of many other meaningful factors.

This pressure to produce ever-increasing profits is not necessarily compatible with the long-range viability of the organization. For example, stockholders and the financial community closely monitor a public company's quarterly results, and they exhibit little enthusiasm for major capital expenditures—such as plant upgrading and research—that could enhance future operations or the ability to compete. Comments such as the following are indicative of possible concerns:

> "Getting the company to spend any money on capital improvements or new and more efficient equipment is like pulling teeth."

> "For the last three years, instead of retaining whatever little profit we made to buy much-needed equipment, we paid it out in dividends to keep the price of the stock up. This may satisfy the investors, but they don't realize that the company is getting weaker every year."

If such expenditures reduce current dividends, the battle lines are drawn. Thus, it is not surprising that managers seeking high marks from shareholders focus on short-term financial results most of the time.

Most organizations begin both the annual and long-range planning processes in the same way: by focusing on the return on investment (ROI) and on the profit margin they wish to attain. In some cases, the ROI will be "given," as it is for regulated utilities in the United States; at other times, when the organization is a subsidiary or is controlled by a conglomerate, ROI and profit margins are dictated by the parent organization.

Financial assumptions to be reviewed in a diagnosis also include a range of other costs of doing business and factors relating to those costs, such as inflation. Overhead costs, both fixed and variable, must be understood in relation to the organizational needs they support: facilities, management, research, and the development of human resources, among others.

Generally, these assumptions lead to decisions about resource allocation that fundamentally influence the nature of a company's approach to business. Just as recognizing the importance of the information-gathering process may at first be difficult for nonfinancial people, so too the importance of understanding the company's financial policies—the goals of the company's financial management plan and its implications—cannot be overstated. Often, strategies necessary for successful change may be impossible to implement because financial policies to fund them either are not developed or are based on inappropriate goals and criteria. "**Sure, they ask us to develop strategic plans, then tell us there isn't any money to implement them. But they don't mind throwing the traditional huge parties for large clients, for questionable returns.**"

Goals of Financial Management

Although the goals and priorities of financial management differ among organizations, in general the main goals are profitability, liquidity, and solvency.

Profitability goals are to earn the highest return possible for resources used or capital employed, consistent with management's desire and ability to bear risk. Liquidity goals are to have sufficient cash to meet short-term needs. Solvency goals involve having sufficient cash and cash resources available at times when long-term obligations and claims such as bonds and pensions become due.

Financial management encompasses such questions as:

- Scorekeeping—"How well are we doing?"
- Attention directing—"Which problems need to e examined?"
- Problem solving—"Which is the best way of getting something done?"

The types of decisions that come under the heading of financial management include new investments, R & D expenditures, account balances, replacement decisions, cash flows, mergers and acquisitions, and resource allocation.

The major dilemma is one of enjoying increased profitability while reducing risk. Unfortunately, the concepts of profitability and risk are diametrically opposed.

Financial-Statement Analysis

This is the process of understanding and interpreting the financial and nonfinancial condition of an organization. It is useful in identifying the strengths and weaknesses of a firm and aids in developing future strategic plans. Generally, financial statement analysis consists of three types: (1) common-size analysis, (2) ratio analysis, and (3) percentage-change analysis.

In each case, ratios and percentages are developed that are usually compared to some standard (such as the budget, last year's results, industry norms, or competition), as follows:

- Comparison of company data: to industry norms, to the previous year's data, to the budget
- Comparison to company data of competitors
- Comparison to industry data on other industries

Common-Size Analysis

This analysis expresses each expense on the income statement as a percentage of total revenues compared to each asset, liability, or equity account on the balance sheet.

Ratio Analysis

This analysis utilizes the data from all four financial statements and provides a broader perspective of the firm's financial condition. Typically, ratio analysis helps answer four key questions:

Organizational Resources

- How profitable is the organization?
- Can the organization meet its short-term obligations?
- To what extent is the firm financed by debt?
- Is management utilizing the company's assets effectively?

Percentage-Change Analysis

This analysis allows you to track changes in income statements or balance-sheet accounts from one reporting period to the next. It is useful in diagnosing key problem areas relative to specific accounts.*

Analysis of Financial Goals

If the diagnosis has a mandate to delve into the more significant aspects of an organization's financial health, and particularly its financial goal-setting process, increasingly sophisticated analyses can be conducted. Central to this more sophisticated analysis is the fact that financial criteria are not necessarily equally valid for all organizations or, for that matter, for the same organization at different stages of its development. For example, an emphasis on superior return on investment may be appropriate in a new-product market, in which a company has a proprietary position. As the inevitable competition erodes that position, however, it becomes necessary to provide additional funding to enhance the product or develop new ones in order to maintain or enhance market share, even if it results in a declining ROI for a period of time.

Certain considerations are important during a financial diagnosis:

1. There are no absolute financial priorities; they change as the economic and competitive environments change.
2. Mature companies stress multiple financial goals based on the mix of objectives it is pursuing at a particular time.
3. Companies are limited at the outset regarding what financial goals they can attain, and they tailor their strategies accordingly.
4. Financial goals are not easy to set because of differing opinions among the company's managers regarding the relative merits of programs and goals requiring funding.
5. Internal competition for scarce resources creates power struggles among individuals who attempt to promote their particular vision of what should be done. Often, the programs that get funded are not necessarily the ones with the most merit, but those represented by the most powerful or persuasive individuals.
6. Financial goals cannot be changed unilaterally without affecting the whole system.
7. Although financial goals appear objective and precise, because of the above factors, they are in fact relative, changeable, and unstable. Their

---

*For a succinct reference on financial ratios, see Erich A. Helfert, *Techniques of Financial Analysis* (Homewood, Ill.: Richard D. Irwin, 1982).

validity can only be ascertained in light of the strategies the company is trying to implement.
8. Most managers are ambivalent about the financial goal-setting process. They are concerned with their own constituency and agendas, and have difficulty accepting the resource-competition system as a legitimate political compromise among conflicting and competing priorities.[1]

The reality in setting financial goals is that you are dealing with an essential compromise between desirable programs requiring funding and the resources available to management: "**It is a fact that most plans requiring funding have merit. It is also a fact that we don't have the resources to fund all of them. So we have to make a choice, and the manager who gets turned down is understandably upset.**" The programs that get funded are the ones that are considered vital to the company's future by significant power figures and executives with better-developed powers of persuasion:

"Budget time means spending an inordinate amount of time dressing up your presentation, buying a new suit, getting a haircut, and putting on a show for a jury who will chew you up regardless of the merits of your plan, because they have already allocated the dough to the 'golden boys' for their questionable pet projects."

Obviously, such comments may have some validity; on the other hand, they may just apply to a few disappointed managers. In any case, whether the right decision is made depends on the outcome, which unfortunately is discernible only at some time in the future.

Another reality, particularly for large firms, is that multiple financial goals are a necessity. Therefore, in a diagnosis you should try to find evidence of a corporate-mission statement that, among other things, enumerates all the critical goals the company is trying to reach. These may be either of the following:

- Investment-intensive goals such as:
    - Targeting certain product lines for rapid product development
    - Achieving a specific rank in the industry
    - Achieving a certain market share
    - Achieving a certain rate of growth in volume of operations
    - Establishing a balanced portfolio of strategic business units (SBUs)
    - Expanding overseas

- Goals focusing on sources of investment funds such as:
    - Target return on investment
    - Rate of profit growth
    - Proportion of retained earnings
    - Minimized cyclicality of earnings

— Maximum debt levels
— Minimum bond ratings

In practice, the company must deal with the interaction in the flow of funds, which, in most cases, will reveal that all the financial goals cannot be met. Often, the financial plans, goals, and objectives developed for the benefit of financial analysts, banks, and stockholders are full of contradictory goals. In practice, these may not be realistic, because invariably they mask predictable trade-offs between the desired growth rate and the return on investment (and the many subsets in this category, such as return on net assets, and so on). Accelerated growth is a desirable goal in some cases, but it often requires accelerated up-front investment, increased short-term costs, and possible reduction of profit margins in order to gain market share.[2]

The savvy diagnostician needs also to take into account that financial decisions made by management are not always consistent with what's best for the company. Rather, they are sometimes dictated by the political realities imposed by the financial markets. For example, from a strategic sense, it would be desirable for a company to fund the construction of a new plant or the purchase of a subsidiary with complementary technology by reducing dividend payments for a couple of years, rather than by issuing additional stock or incurring more debt. However, reducing the dividend almost certainly upsets the stockholders, and causes the manipulators on Wall Street to induce a drop in the stock price. Certainly, the appalling maneuvers related to leveraged buyouts and other questionable tactics used by corporate raiders show that speculation in the financial markets is alive and well. Wall Street's proponents claim that such actions force management to do a better job because of the increased pressure to generate larger profits for the stockholders. On the other hand, it cannot be denied that the management of many substantial companies is forced to spend significant time, energy, and money on defensive maneuvers to avert takeovers. Certainly, "poison pills" such as expensive "golden parachutes" for the top management of a vulnerable company are not always in the best interests of the corporation. For example, in 1987 the chairman of the Allegis Corporation proposed a "refinancing plan" whereby the company would borrow $3 billion just to pay out a special dividend, thus burdening the corporation with significant—and unnecessary—debt in order to make the firm a less desirable candidate for takeover. Such a tactic cannot possibly be regarded as sound financial action. It literally ignores the fact that dividends should be paid out of profits. The same kind of maneuver is seen when a company's management uses funds desperately needed for operations or investment for growth to pay the dividends, in an attempt to obfuscate the real performance for the quarter or year and to maintain the stock price as high as possible.

How can the financial section of a diagnosis help with the development of a company? Primarily by highlighting the discrepancies among the strategic plans, the company's financial needs, and the ability of the organization to generate sufficient funds to meet those needs. Just as important, the analysis can help establish realistic goals, which may lead to more modest achievements, but with a better chance of success.

We have already mentioned that the financial portion of a diagnosis should be performed by experts. Since the diagnostic team should be assembled with the scope of the analysis in mind, a diagnosis for developmental purposes should have a project team composed of people with appropriate technical skills; thus it makes sense to include respected employees with a solid financial background and a knowledge of the company's financial situation. In this case, however, we can make a strong argument that a consultant or academician should also be included, because in dealing with financial analysis, there is a need not only for genuine expertise, but also for detached impartiality—someone not beholden to management's dreams, which may or may not be realizable. The intent, certainly, is to examine financial goals with the attitude of a devil's advocate. Likewise, outside experts, not encumbered by an organization's norms and parochial perspectives, may be able to provide insights, data, and methods that can make ambitious financial goals possible after all.

Technological Resources

Successful technology-based organizations such as IBM have extensive technological assets that are protected by patents. However, even for organizations that may be at the leading edge of their field, keeping pace with technological change is of critical importance. The pace of technological change in today's Information Age is such that no organization can afford complacency, lest it lose its place at the leading edge and eventually relinquish its markets or profitability to more innovative firms.

In recent decades, examples abound of companies that failed to maintain their technological leadership and paid dearly for "business as usual." Respondents are generally aware of the company's posture, and their comments may indicate significant concern:

> "There are too many examples of our having stayed with older techniques because they are more predictable."

> "We wait too long to get into the things our competitors do. As a result, they are better known to the customers than we are."

> "We don't invest in research to any significant degree."

National Cash Register, for one, had to write off a $139 million loss in the early 1970s because it was unsuccessful in shifting from electromechanical to electronic designs. Similarly, companies including General Electric, Sylvania, and RCA experienced significant financial losses by staying with vacuum-tube technology at a time when transistors were revolutionizing the electronics industry.

Being aware of technological developments, and assessing their impact on the company's viability in the long run, does not necessarily dictate corporate strategy. Some companies may not feel threatened by an upstart producing a technologically advanced product at a higher market price, and they may decide that their best strategy, at least for the moment, is to hold their price advantage:

> "Sometimes we don't jump to implement new technology because it is more sensible to let the competition work out the bugs."

> "Being a technological leader can be expensive. Sometimes it is more sensible to follow than to lead, because you let the other guy make the investment."

They may be right, at least until it becomes necessary for them to make a move, and then it may be too late. In other instances, companies that do innovate are not able to exploit their advantage in a timely manner: "**The company has been responsible for major technological innovations in the field. Unfortunately, we don't move fast enough to take market advantage as fast as the Japanese do.**"

Strategies for adapting to pioneering technological developments vary. Some developments may become available through royalty arrangements; others might be acquired through patent purchases or a buyout of the pioneering company itself. Reverse engineering of a competitor's product is particularly popular with manufacturers of microcomputers, which traditionally produce functional duplicates of IBM's personal computers.

Market conditions can also affect decisions about technology. In some cases, holding on to an obsolete technology can be appropriate if the organization is clear about its objectives. For example, hi-fi buffs who consider themselves "audio purists" continue to buy expensive stereo equipment that uses vacuum tubes. General Electric, one of the few companies that has kept on making vacuum tubes, initially lost money by continuing to manufacture the product, but eventually turned this part of the business around. As time passed, tube production became a cash cow for GE, compared to more contemporary solid-state technology requiring investment capital. A similar approach has paid off for several Brazilian companies, which continued manufacturing spare parts for antique autos and selling them worldwide.

Whatever the strategy adopted in response to technological change, such decisions can have an enormous impact on the existing organization. Significant R & D expenses and capital investment may be required, specially skilled personnel for jobs that did not previously exist may now be needed, new forms of organization may be necessary, and the entire focus of the firm—its reason for being—may be shifted. In some cases, technological change may require closing obsolete plants and underutilized facilities and laying off a significant part of the existing work force. In addition, technological change is one of the factors impinging upon the analysis of the adequacy of a company's human resources: "**Do we have the people needed to compete in the new technological environment?**"

While a diagnosis may not do much more than explain the present state of technological awareness and development in the company, such a description is valuable because it helps to assess the extent to which the organization is competitive in its chosen area of operation, in both the short and long term. It also helps to determine any necessary budgetary adjustments in research and development, particularly if a redirection of strategy is in order. For example, in the microcomputer business, many manufacturers of IBM-compatible machines have produced clones that are able to use the same software and possess essentially the same functional characteristics. Many of these companies design the machines from readily available components from many sources and have them assembled in Asia. Their strategy clearly is to conform to the market leader as closely as possible, because departing from the established standard presents risks. On the other hand, companies such as Compaq Computer Corporation and the mail-order house Dell Computer Corporation with its PC Limited line have invested in innovation while maintaining compatibility with the IBM PC standard. In 1986, Compaq was the first to introduce a significantly faster machine based on the newly developed Intel 80386 chip, and it took a risk by assuming that IBM would sooner or later have to follow suit. Even though PC Limited also offers an 80386-based machine, its general product line stayed with the tried-and-true technology, focusing on producing relatively inexpensive but well-made machines.

But in 1987, IBM upset the applecart by introducing a significant new generation of machines, called the PS-2 line, which have significantly different operating characteristics. Thus far, Compaq, probably concerned with protecting its investment in the 80386 machine, insists that its product is still better and that it will stick to its technology and product line. It is likely, however, that Compaq will have to work toward eventual compliance with the new IBM machine standards.

Another major competitor in the field, AST Research, entered the market in late 1987 by introducing an 80386-based computer that in essence plays it safe, being capable of operating under both standards. This is a typical example of how technological developments "leap frog" even the most innovative firms, thus forcing everyone to do one better or perish. On the reactive strategy side, market-savvy and flexible companies such as PC Limited are likely to continue matching the market leader on a product-for-product basis. Many of the other clone-makers will probably trail the leaders.

From a diagnostic point of view, it is immaterial whether a company is a technological innovator or follower. Its success depends on a clear formulation of strategy, based on appropriately articulated policies and objectives. A comprehensive diagnosis should be able to assess to what degree these policies and objectives are congruous, in light of the company's position in the marketplace.

Physical Resources

Physical assets such as buildings, real estate, oil reserves, and equipment are important from the perspective of top management, but less so from the vantage point of the average employee, who takes such matters for granted unless the work environment is substandard: **"Our basic manufacturing plant is aging, and becoming less competitive, especially when compared with foreign producers." "Some of our offices are located in areas too far from major airports."**

An organization's physical assets are important to the extent that they form an asset base and determine to what extent the company's capital structure is, particularly if it has a heavy investment in industrial-production facilities: **"We have no physical assets of any kind. The space is rented, and the office equipment is leased. This gives us flexibility."** The age and condition of office space are important if they create an environment that is substandard and deleterious to employee performance: **"Moving the corporate offices to a suburban location has helped create a better working environment for the employees."** This is an area of relatively little importance in a diagnosis, primarily because no new data are likely to be added to what management already knows.

Human Resources

"We have to preserve our good people—they are a fragile resource." The internal availability of human resources within the company—people's number, skills, qualifications, ability to learn, potential, turnover, and other characteristics relevant to business operations—is critical to the essential viability of an organization.

Of all assets, human resources are the most widely misunderstood. It is a truism that American management sees people as costs rather than as resources. Yet there is hardly anything in organizational life, good or bad, that cannot be traced back to people. Moreover, few managers realize the major investment that companies make when they hire a person. The cost is much more than the direct dollars associated with getting the person on board. When benefits and continuing salary for years are counted, and a pension added on top of that, the average employee is a million-dollar asset or liability.

Typically, most top-level managers assume that "we have plenty of time to get the people," develop needed managers and workers, train specialists, or fulfill other human resources requirements.

In high-tech industries in particular, weak or nonexistent information about the ability of the existing work force to carry out the company's plans can have serious strategic consequences.

Personnel costs now account for nearly 50 percent of all operating costs in the average U.S. firm, and any significant escalation in these costs—for added training or for higher pay and benefits to lure experienced people from other firms—can have a major impact on the financial strength of the organization.

Changing skills requirements and the advance of technology are among the factors causing many companies to reevaluate past assumptions about human resources availability: **"We seem to have experienced a serious degradation of expertise in technical ability across the board."** Large engineering and construction organizations, for example, traditionally maintained lean organizations. As new projects increased demand for people, pirating employees from competitors rather than internal development became the rule. But as a nationwide expansion of projects—coupled with a relative lag in the supply of engineers and technicians from the nation's schools—tightened this market, these firms began experiencing a general scarcity of people, with a corresponding industry-wide escalation of salaries.

The impact of technology can have the opposite effect, of course. If large numbers of existing employees are likely to be displaced by new technology and changing operations, the company should begin to plan for downsizing. Strategies for dealing with redundant employees range from abrupt plant closings and massive layoffs to long-range retraining, relocation, early retirement, and similar gradual measures. Yet a company can deal constructively with such issues if it endeavors to determine, on a continuous basis, how technology will evolve, which jobs will become obsolete, how soon that will happen, and what new skills will be required.

Employee-Turnover Patterns

Employee turnover is often seen more as an annoyance than a serious and very costly problem. Yet attracting and retaining qualified personnel is a vital factor in remaining competitive, and it can possibly be a most critical issue to deal with. Without properly qualified personnel, an organization cannot hope to have an even distribution of technical capabilities, nor implement an effective strategic or operational plan, nor be competitive in the marketplace. Typical comments indicative of problems in this area are as follows:

> "We are having trouble hiring people recently, and the reason is that our competitors are paying higher wages. . . . The three- and four-year period of service employee is the most unstable in this regard. They get their experience and then they are gone. . . . Yet the personnel department tells us we have competitive salaries."

> "We have a problem of turnover; money is really not the problem. We are doing something that is turning the people off, so they leave."

> "There are not enough opportunities for job mobility available for many employees. We have not moved our people around horizontally, and I think it's an area that should be pursued. . . . It would help us in the total operation to understand the concerns of other parts of the company better. At one time we did have this with the management trainees coming in, but we let it fall by the wayside."

> "Department heads are hoarding their good people for fear of losing them to another department."

The turnover rate, of course, should not be so low that the organization becomes inbred and stale. At the same time, it should be recognized that excessive turnover is far more expensive than people realize. In terms of what it takes to replace a person, once you add up the lost time to reach productivity, agency costs, interviewing costs, administrative expenses, and the like, the true impact of avoidable employee losses is staggering. Yet few organizations emphasize turnover control as a performance-evaluation item for its managers. Part of the reason why turnover is difficult for management to deal with in terms other than platitudes is that it lacks complete understanding of turnover's real impact on the organization. To properly analyze this area, it is necessary to collect statistical data in addition to the perceptions of individuals. A brief technical analysis such as the following can be eye-opening.

Turnover Trend Analysis

Historical data about turnover patterns in the company can be charted on a personal computer with easy-to-use software.

Figure 7-1 provides, in a single picture, valuable information about a company's rates of turnover during a six-year period, broken down by major employee classifications.

However, simple head count can be deceiving. Turnover involves not only a raw count of employee losses, but also a composite picture of employee movement in an organization. For example, Table 7-1 displays how a detailed analysis of turnover in a company's Design Engineering Division reveals facts that are generally glossed over.

For example, in the Mechanical Division, a regular staffing report bragged that over a period of ten months, owing to workload demands, the staff increased by 18 employees, bringing the total population from 592 to 610, or 3 percent growth. A closer examination of the personnel flow in this division revealed that the division manager did indeed state a fact, but failed to tell the whole story. Once the personnel movement is traced, it can be seen that during this period 201 employees were hired and 174 were terminated. There were also 9 transfers in and 18 out to other departments. Once all the numbers are reconciled, the effective rate of turnover turns out to be not 3 percent but 68 percent! It can be reasonably argued that for most of the ten months, at least 60 percent of the employees were not fully productive, mainly because they were in transit. As a matter of fact, once the entire division's personnel flow is analyzed, it can be logically assumed that most employees were fully utilized only half the time. The implications for cost and productivity are self-evident.

Further inquiry into turnover patterns can provide extraordinary insights into the impact of personnel losses on a company's bottom line. Using the same data, you can create a graph that projects how many people the company will need to recruit in order to meet the requirements of its long-range plans (see Figure 7-2). It is shocking to some people to realize that such hiring projections

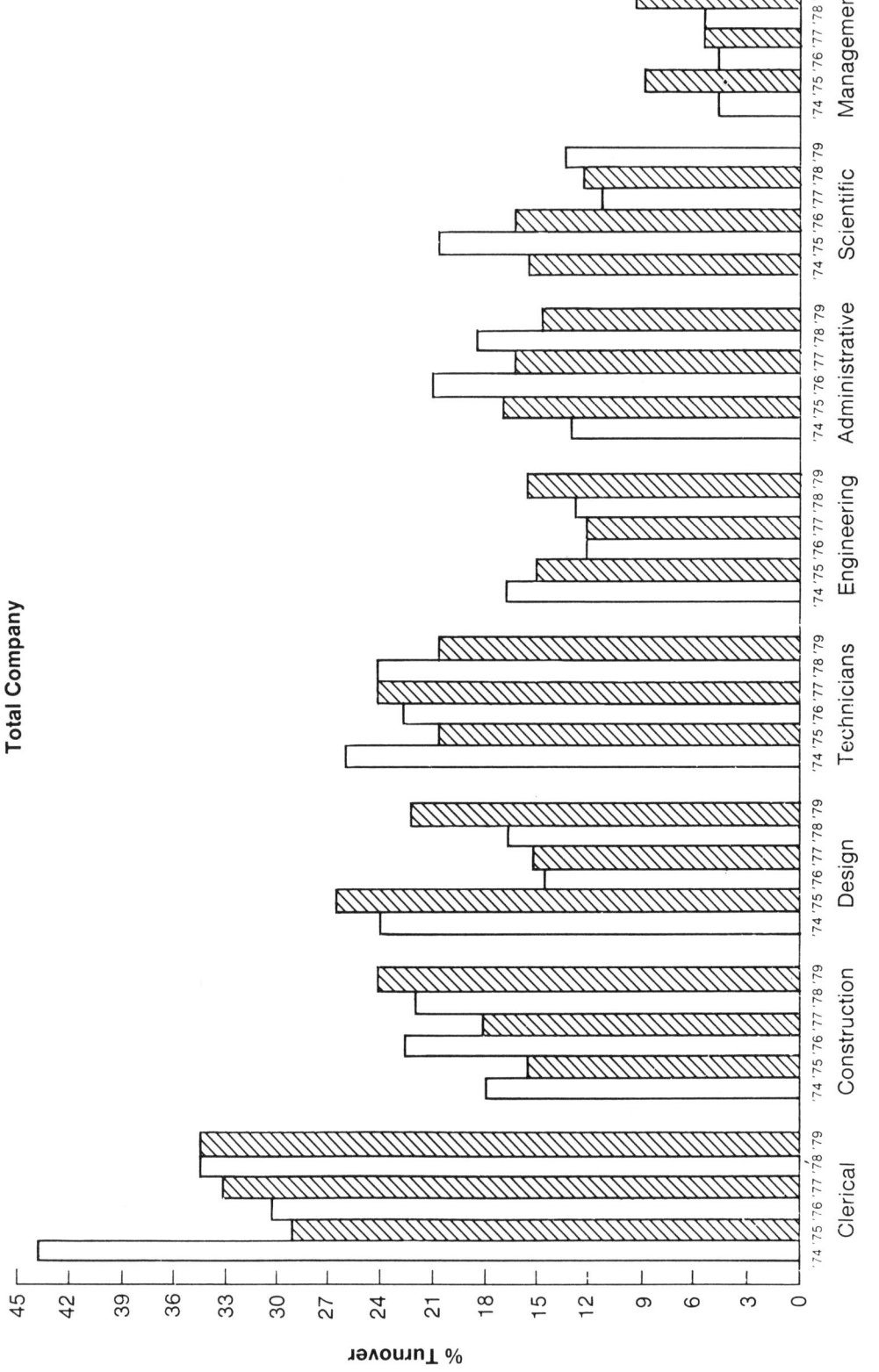

Figure 7-1. Six-year turnover analysis.

Table 7-1. Design engineering personnel changes and percent of growth—
January to October.

Discipline		Staff Total Jan.	Staff Total Oct.	Change	% Growth	Jan. to Oct. Hires & Terminations		Transfers In	Transfers Out	Total % Personnel Changes
Mechanical	(E)	592	610	+18	+3.0	201	174	9	18	68
	(D)	297	274	−23	−7.7	34	51	–	6	31
Electrical	(E)	113	121	+8	+7.1	35	17	–	10	55
	(D)	156	157	+1	+.6	33	28	–	4	42
Civil	(E)	126	127	+1	+.8	12	12	4	3	25
	(D)	377	339	−38	+10.1	25	58	–	5	23
I & C	(E)	107	124	+17	+15.9	36	16	3	6	57
	(D)	132	127	−5	−3.8	23	30	2	–	42
Projects	(E)	85	87	+2	+2.4	13	13	8	6	47
	(D)	52	52	0	0	7	4	–	3	27
Sub-totals	(E)	1023	1069	+46	+4.5	297	232	24	43	58
	(D)	1014	949	−65	−6.4	122	171	2	18	31
Totals		2037	2018	−19	−.9	419	403	26	61	45

Key:
E = engineers
D = designers

are insignificant when compared to the number of people who have to be recruited just to make up for regular turnover losses.

If the raw numbers on employee losses are multiplied by what it costs to replace each person—which can range from $2,000 to $15,000 if employment agencies are used—you can develop a graph to place the matter in total perspective (see Figure 7-3).

Once the turnover trend is extrapolated into the future and the cost implications are clearly displayed, the true magnitude of high turnover becomes evident. Conversely, the analysis presents obvious opportunities for justifying the implementation of programs designed to reduce the turnover rate based on ROI, which can generate significant savings for the company.

Performance Appraisal

An effective and comprehensive employee evaluation program, conducted through appropriate instruments, enables a careful and realistic appraisal of the strengths and weaknesses of employees throughout the company. Moreover, it provides for a meaningful performance review and feedback conference for each employee, so that potential as well as performance can be addressed.

Performance appraisal is a critical concern to most managers because of its inherent difficulty and the general lack of employee preparation and training, which do not help them do a better job. But perhaps even more critical is

Figure 7-2. Hires for growth and turnover.

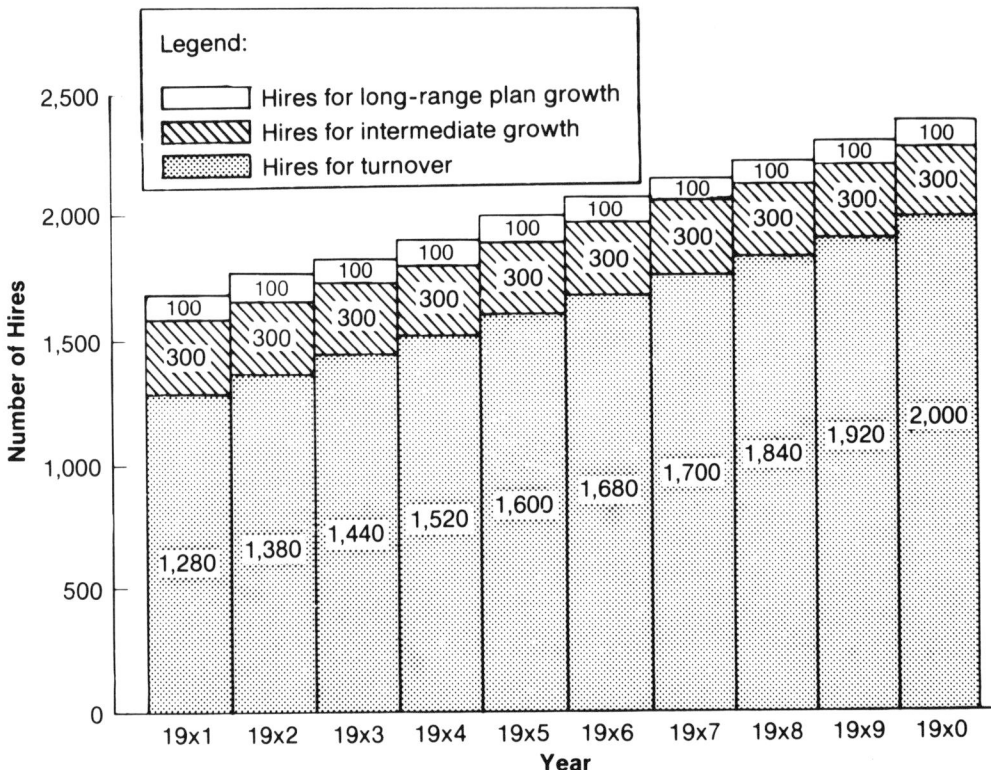

the attitude of the rank-and-file toward appraisal: "**I have had no real direction for three years, but I am called in once a year for a chewing out.**"

It is not unusual for people to complain about substantial inadequacies in the current performance-appraisal program:

> "**The evaluation process is 'an activity trap.' The company only rewards people for being busy, and not for accomplishing things.**"

> "**People are consistently evaluated only on strict adherence to or compliance with details, rather than on accomplishment.**"

Often, performance-appraisal programs are perfunctory, superficial, judgmental, indirect, negative, destructive, or irrelevant: "**I am never told whether I am doing a fair or good job, but always told of problem areas.**" "**There is no recognition for good work; only condemnation for mistakes.**"

Organizational Resources

Figure 7-3. Cost of employee replacement (8 percent annual inflation).

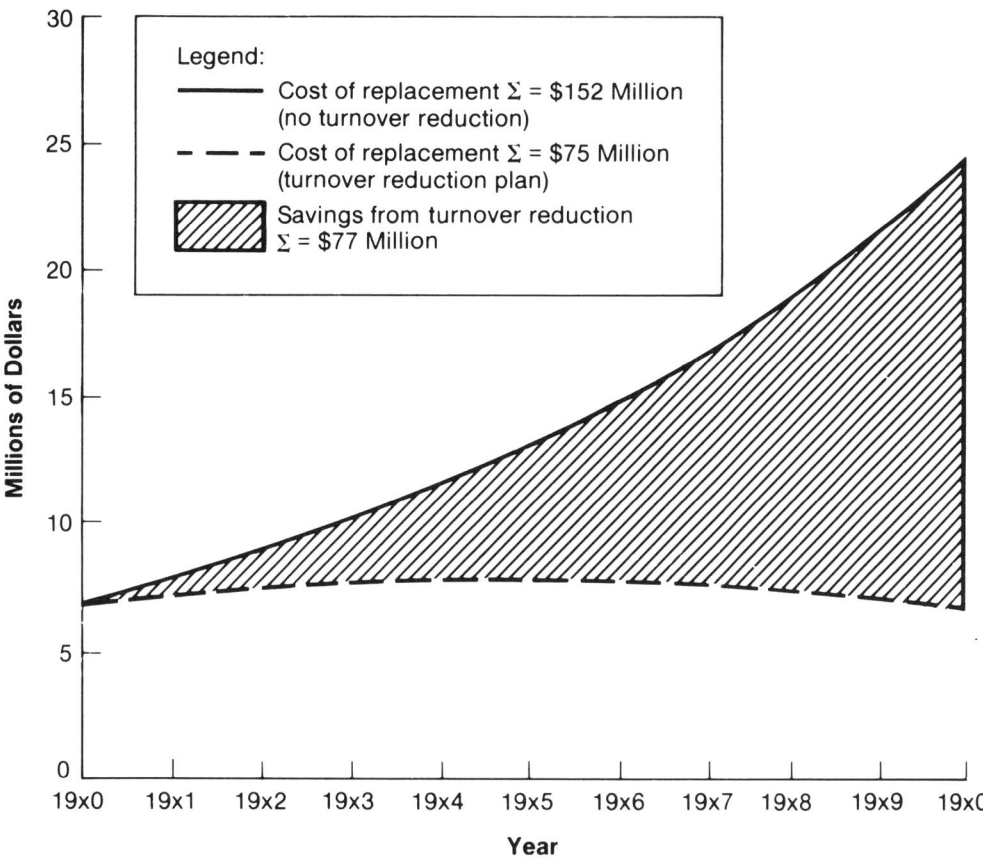

The tendency is for managers to defer or avoid appraisal sessions with subordinates: "I go by the amount of complaints I get, because I have never had a face-to-face conversation with my boss regarding my performance." "I assume that the best appraisal of performance I get is reflected on my paycheck."

For the most part, follow-up is viewed as cumbersome and thus neglected. Factors contributing to the problem often are:

- Lack of recognition of the dual purpose of appraisals: feedback for performance improvement and for employee development
- Lack of training for the supervisors and managers charged with implementation of the program
- Feelings of awkwardness in face-to-face communications of feedback, owing to unpreparedness

- Lack of uniform standards against which to evaluate performance
- Undocumented observations of employee productivity and behavior
- Overuse of emotion-laden data

The result is a general deprivation of constructive feedback, clouded performance accountabilities, and vague expectations for subordinates at all levels. Often in actual practice, managers judge performance directly or indirectly in such a way that it creates distance and is potentially destructive to their relationship with subordinates: **"Performance plans and review are, by and large, a paper exercise." "I've been rated for a multitude of things, and I still don't know what standards are used to judge my performance."**

Theoretically, managers should sustain constructive, nonpunitive environments in which subordinates can exercise increasing self-direction and professional growth. However, few if any genuine role models are available in organizations. There are no easy answers. Appraisal is an inherently difficult process because, in spite of voluminous literature, procedures, guidelines, and training programs, it ultimately depends on the subjective evaluation of a busy manager about the performance of another human being. The result often is more indicative of each player's negotiating skill and force of personality than a true reflection of accomplishment. The best that can be done is to design and implement evaluation programs tailored to the organization, its functions, and the behaviors it seeks to evaluate. Even then, implementation will be imperfect and fraught with pitfalls.

Management Development

In order to manage an organization that is subject to continuing environmental change, it is necessary to spend considerable time and resources planning and developing strategies for how the firm should cope with, and preferably capitalize on, future challenges. Crucial to this effort is the concurrent development of financial and human resources necessary to implement those plans and strategies. The concern with planning for future generations of managers has led to the establishment of programs within industry that, under the generic label of "management development," attempt to address the problem in a variety of ways.

It is generally accepted that management development in industry has evolved into a process that enables:

- Definition of key managerial positions and most likely critical incumbencies at the various levels of management
- Setting of criteria for succession planning
- Identification of managers with potential for growth, who may be suitable candidates for positions of leadership in the future
- Design of individualized career paths and corresponding development plans that include training, developmental experiences, and programmed rotation if necessary

- Establishment of a feedback mechanism on progress achieved, thus enabling corrections to the development process and, if necessary, to the candidate pool itself

In practice, many companies fail to adequately address the development of its future leadership: **"Lack of attention to management development is why we are fighting fires today."** Comments such as this are not unusual and generally indicate that today it is more important than ever to identify and develop managers with the appropriate education and experience; they must, however, also possess critical attributes such as intellect and leadership, as well as an ability to anticipate trends and future conditions likely to affect the organization: **"We are now large enough to be able to develop personnel by moving them laterally through several areas of the company in order to develop managers with a broader perspective."**

In order to be effective, top-level managers must be able to conceptualize what needs to be done for both the short and long term, plan accordingly, and execute those plans successfully. The contemporary manager must have a broad understanding of the disparate elements of a complex organization, and how the company fits within the industry and the economy. Just as important, he or she must be conscious of the impact of personal capabilities and limitations in any given situation.

Management-development techniques have been useful in helping shape replacements for key managers in many organizations. However, such development approaches are susceptible to significant limitations and shortcomings, particularly in today's rapidly changing environment, because for the most part there is a tendency to develop future managers based on executive role models who have been successful *in the past,* under different business conditions:

> **"There is too much 'line breeding' within the company. It is analogous to what is done with horses; trouble is, there are unknown deficiencies in our bloodline. We keep breeding these deficiencies back into the system."**

Certainly, the past behavior and skills of successful managers in an organization should be studied, and desirable traits and characteristics should be perpetuated in a future generation of organizational leaders. At the same time, care must be taken to ensure that future managers develop in such a way that they are capable of managing an organization that in all likelihood will be operating in a different environment, necessitating an understanding of different markets, competitors, product mixes, and societal trends.

To be truly effective, management development must be focused on the organization's long-range strategic plan. There isn't much that can be done about managers presently on board. Most of the return on investment in management development will occur if a new generation of managers has indeed been brought up with the future needs of the organization as their developmental objective. Appendix 3 describes such a program.

CHAPTER 8
Organizational Processes

By the time you reach this part of your analysis, you will have an understanding of the company's historical development, its culture, how it formulates and implements strategy, and what resources it has available to implement its objectives. This chapter focuses on important organizational processes that have to do with the way the company's leadership and employees interact, make decisions, solve problems, and manage conflict. A clear definition of the predominant behavior of the people in an organization provides a base for planning necessary changes, which can then be addressed through training and personnel changes, if necessary.

Leadership and Power Characteristics

Throughout history, leaders have been the primary force behind change and development. Their influence has been both positive and negative, leading to splendid achievements for society and to appalling calamities such as the Holocaust and the Russian purges, which even today tax the comprehension of civilized people. On a smaller scale, leaders in business can be both positive and negative forces, often both at the same time. A leader can be an executive who is the sole proprietor of a company, or one of many executives in a public corporation. The leader's behavior can range from that of a ruthless autocrat to a democratic team builder: **"In this organization we have invented a new style—MBPYWA (management by pushing your weight around)."** People may be afraid of a leader, or be fiercely loyal, or even harbor both feelings concurrently. A business leader can simultaneously be highly regarded for his or her vision, which may have led the company toward market domination and prosperity, and also criticized for the methods employed to reach those goals. Yet more important than the process a leader uses to achieve results is the fundamental impact that a single person at the top can have on the general welfare of an organization. One competent leader can lead a sleepy and insignificant company to market dominance. The converse is also true. An inadequate leader can, during his or her tenure, create enough damage to jeopardize the very existence of the organization.

Most of the management literature in Western society stresses the value of participative management, primarily because most people want to have their contribution acknowledged: "**Some middle managers feel isolated from top management.**" "**Corporate officers have an attitude of superiority when dealing with regional offices.**" Such democratic ideals, however, don't take away from the fact that leadership is a necessity, and that even in a participative situation, a leader is a leader. People need and want leadership. As much as people may resent an overbearing leader, they dislike the absence of leadership even more: "**Who is 'Management?' Why isn't there agreement on what course the company should take?**"

The impact of leaders on business organizations is fundamental; for this reason, the study of leadership has fascinated scholars for many years, and it is not surprising that a significant percentage of management training has focused on "leadership development," even though the jury is still out on whether leaders are born or made.

No matter; a diagnosis is neutral. On the subject of leadership, you are primarily concerned with describing how leadership is exercised in a company; whether certain leadership practices and styles are appropriate to the situation; and whether it is advisable, or even possible, to change the approach to leadership.

The following discussion suggests a general framework for assessing the nature of leadership in a company. It is by no means comprehensive; rather, it provides a pragmatic guide for focusing on existing leadership style and practice—how leaders acquire and use power to achieve their objectives, and the effect that has on problem solving and management of conflict in the organization.

Types of Leaders

Abraham Zaleznik and Manfred F. R. Kets de Vries[1] point out that leaders generally fall into one of three categories:

- *Proactive leaders.* These are people who look at the future, who have a long-range perspective, a sense of where the organization is in time and space. Proactive leaders tend to be turned on by ideas, concepts, and creativity. They are open to the environment, and need to make their visions come true.
- *Homeostatic leaders.* People who fit this mold are tribal leaders and come in two kinds: the benign, paternal type and the "SOB" variety. Their main thrust is the maintenance of the status quo: the past is the guide. Homeostatic leaders react to the symptoms and fail to see the whole picture. They are equivalent to the little Dutch boy plugging the hole in the dam with his finger. Homeostatic leaders invariably undermine a proactive number-two subordinate.

- *Mediative leaders*. Mediative leaders have the capacity to deal with a number of constituencies. In the transition from homeostatic to proactive leadership, there is a need for mediative leadership.

Part of your evaluation at this point is to find out who the leaders in the company are, and which of the above descriptions they fit. This identification is particularly important in a situation involving organizational change, because bureaucracies cannot be unilaterally changed from the top, from the inside, or for that matter from the outside. The only condition under which they can be changed is when there is a combination of all three forces: pressure from the top, the inside, and the outside. In order to make things happen, all three types of leader are needed.

Authority and Power

One of the reasons why leadership and power characteristics in an organization are a source of intense scrutiny during a diagnosis is that the organizational charts often describe only authority. In most cases, they do not accurately portray power relationships: **"Don't get fooled by vice president titles. In this bank, all you have to do to be a VP is to breathe."**

As we have seen, particularly because of my emphasis on identifying and working with the critical mass, considerable power is wielded by people whose position in an organizational chart may indicate otherwise: **"Sure, I am not a VP, but I am one of the few people in the company who can run this department, and since I make 20 percent of the bottom line, I carry a lot of weight."** The study of power in an organization is important, because it is necessary to identify who is in a position to get things done. Power is a very important variable in any change effort, since things get done mostly through influence and interpersonal skills. You probably have already done your power diagnosis at the outset of planning the diagnosis, because you needed to identify the critical mass. Now you are just formalizing the results of that effort.

How people exercise power and influence others often is a reflection of corporate culture, and whether it condones or frowns on the outward manifestation of power:

> **"I don't have to throw my weight around; people know that it is not healthy to get on my bad side."**

> **"We have a code here that courtesy toward each other is paramount. As a matter of fact, we are all on a first-name basis. The higher you go in the organization, the more suave and congenial people act. Such manners don't necessarily imply democracy. Powerful people are still powerful. They just don't need to remind you; the size of their office will."**

In fact, regardless of how they are expressed, power and influence are always there—and necessarily so. The only question is to what extent they are used appropriately.

Bases of Power

Another important element of the diagnosis is an understanding of how powerful people in the organization manifest their power. There is nothing wrong with power, because it is necessary to get things done. What you are looking for are indications of the predominant means of acquiring and exercising that power in the company, particularly because people will tailor their behavior accordingly. Power is a relative term, but the conditions that enable its exercise can be identified, as follows:

- *Coercion* uses fear to create power. A manager high in coercive power is seen as inducing compliance because failure to comply will lead to punishment such as undesirable work assignments, reprimands, or dismissal.
- *Influence* gives someone power based on the person's "connections" with influential or important persons inside or outside the organization. A manager high in connection power induces compliance from others because they aim at gaining favor or avoiding disfavor with the powerful connections.
- *Expertise* gives a person power, because he or she possesses skill and knowledge which, through respect, influence others. A manager high in expert power is seen as possessing the expertise to facilitate the work behavior of others. This respect leads to compliance with his or her wishes.
- *Information* gives the holder power based on the possession of or access to information perceived as valuable to others. This power base influences others because they need this information or want to be "in on things."
- *Position* carries with it legitimate power, based on where a person is on the organizational chart. Normally, the higher the position, the greater the legitimate power tends to be. A manager high in legitimate power induces compliance or influences others because they feel the power is justified, by virtue of his or her position in the organization.
- *Interpersonal skills* often endow a person with power, or at least influence. A manager who is accessible, pleasant, and has a sense of humor is generally liked and admired by others. This liking for, admiration of, and identification with the person makes him or her a leader, and enables that person to influence others.
- *Resources* invariably endow power on a person who can control them. This power is based on an ability to provide rewards for other people. They believe that their compliance will lead to positive incentives such as higher pay, promotion, or recognition.[2]

Power, Influence, and Politics

Ian C. MacMillan[3] provides an elegant summary of what power, influence, and political capability in organizations are, and how they are evidenced and exercised. He breaks them down as:

1. *Power over an opponent*—the capacity to restructure a situation in such a way as to get another to act as the originator desires
2. *Power in a situation*—the capacity to restructure the situation in such a way as to get others to act as the originator desires

Power, therefore, is situationally determined. Moreover, power is a capacity—that is, you do not need to have power to use it. Influence, on the other hand, is the capacity to restructure the perceptions of others so as to get them to act as desired. Political capability is the sum of the power and influence of an individual.

MacMillan then focuses on authority as legitimized political capability—that is, legitimized power and influence:

> To the extent that an organization allows a person to induce, coerce, persuade, and obligate others, that person has legitimate power and influence and hence legitimate formal authority.
>
> To the extent that people in the organization who are being induced, coerced, persuaded, and obligated by an individual feel that these actions are legitimate, the individual has legitimate power and influence, and hence legitimate informal authority.
>
> The actual authority of a person in a situation is really his/her informal authority in the situation. This informal authority can be greater or smaller than the formal authority conferred on the person by the organization.[4]

MacMillan points out that the basis of power rests in the ability to restructure situations, thus a power resource must be *applicable* to the situation. Moreover, the more alternatives a person has in a situation relative to his or her opponents, the more power he or she has.

Another simple way of identifying power in an organization is to follow the previously mentioned recommendation by Richard Beckhard: Find out who sees whom as possessing power; if they think he has power, and he thinks he does, he generally does.

Power and Conflict

For a comprehensive diagnosis, the data often indicate a schism between top and middle management. This is evidenced by any of the following:

1. Top management's dissatisfaction with middle management's ability and/or willingness to implement decisions and follow directives in a timely and effective manner.

2. Middle management's feeling of dependence upon top management's actions.
3. Middle management's perception of a lack of aggressive leadership in the recent past.
4. Middle management's complaints about having to deal with authoritarian top management.
5. Middle management's perception that the "room at the top" is split into several tribal factions, each vying for its own turf and dominance at the expense of the organization.
6. Middle management's perception that the top leadership is not committed to the decision it makes or to the directives it gives.

It is not unusual to find that middle management often does not seem to acknowledge much responsibility, willingness, or capability to help top management deal with difficult corporate problems. Middle management is a group that often seems to be primarily concerned with performing day-to-day production tasks. Any interface with the business environment outside the company is generally perceived by this group as the responsibility of the company's officers. Where there is evidence of this attitude, it can be attributed to the corporate culture and to management's sheltering the rest of the organization from activities extraneous to the immediate performance of production work. Certainly, this encourages the development of superb technical and production skills, by allowing the company's professionals to address their tasks with single-minded devotion and enthusiasm. However, this practice does not facilitate the development of generalists with a broader business orientation.

It is also interesting to note that even though the respondents may be less than enthusiastic about a management style which they generally characterize as authoritarian, in fact it often turns out that that they welcome a firm, unified leadership and direction. It is important to note that envisioned corporate leadership is not axiomatic with authoritarianism; rather, it merely suggests that top management often misses out on the benefit of high-quality input from other members of the organization, when such input is necessary to solve a problem or to determine the potential effects of a new strategy or plan. Failure to obtain this input also explains why implementation of management decisions sometimes is considered an elective matter by managers with the power to put them into effect.

Management of Conflict

Conflict is manifested in many ways. In some cases overt hostility among individuals can be observed: "**It seems that every time you turn around, someone is blaming someone else.**" Often warring camps are established between departments: "**We don't have departments, we have feudal kingdoms that wage war on each other.**" If left unmanaged, conflict absorbs energy that should be channeled toward work: "**We spend more time writing CYA memos than working on getting things done.**" The other side of the conflict is that it encourages a closer examination of what people do, and it may lead to better preparation and problem solving by creating a balance of power: "**Giving a presentation or making a proposal is an invitation to getting into a den of lions without a whip. On the other hand, it forces you to do the best possible job.**"

Conflict must be managed, not suppressed. Certainly, conflict in an organization should not be ignored. There are many ways to deal with conflict:

Forcing. Making people work together or cooperate with each other involves wielding managerial authority. It also places the conflicting parties in a position of making peace, at least on the surface, because the alternatives are made less pleasant by management. This means is rarely effective.

Smoothing the differences. Smoothing over is frequently used in a paternal way. Unfortunately, it does not resolve the underlying issues; it merely postpones further conflict.

Avoidance. Avoiding conflict is a time-honored method of ignoring the problem, hoping that it will go away, which it rarely does.

Bargaining. This involves negotiating concessions both ways to meet the needs of the parties in conflict. Like most compromises, both sides come away dissatisfied, and the best alternative to a problem may not be selected.

Confrontation. This approach addresses the conflict for what it is: a dysfunctional result of opposing interests and views. By not ignoring its existence, by acknowledging that both parties can suffer if the conflict is not resolved, it is possible to address the issue constructively. The various team-building techniques described in Chapter 11 are examples of confronting conflict by surfacing them through a diagnosis, and working through the issues with the help of a facilitator, if necessary.

Problem-Solving Practices

As a general rule, most managers have access to a plethora of analytical tools that help with problem solving, ranging from identification of machine failure to diagnosis of significant manufacturing problems and interdepartmental conflicts. The issue here is not so much the ability of managers to fix operational and interpersonal problems, but their willingness to do so in all circumstances.

Problem solving can be impromptu or disciplined, intuitive or systematic: "**The officers spend too much time putting out fires.**" It is also affected by the organizational culture, and whether it rewards or punishes open communication and dealing with facts: "**Management is interested in cute solutions. We really don't get into the guts of problems and recognize them for what they are. We go after quacks instead of seeing specialists.**" Problem solving is particularly difficult in an environment where the norm is telling management what they want to hear, rather than the truth. But perhaps the major impediment to addressing problems caused by a changing business environment is an organization's past successful track record: "**We seem to have an orientation that everything we do is right until proven otherwise, whereas it should be the opposite.**" If, in its history, an organization has developed a problem-handling behavior that has worked, and if the nature of the problems it has dealt with have been similar, then a certain complacency will set in, giving management the belief that they have been able to deal with problems in the past, thus it is reasonable to assume that they will be able to continue doing so in the future. Without perceived pressures to act, many problems are treated in the abstract, rather than as situations that need to be dealt with:

> "Sometimes we are unable, at the top-management level, to separate significant issues and problems from less important ones."

> "A lot of top-management meetings seem to indulge in idle discussion rather than problem solving."

Decision-Making Practices

Problem solving, when successful, leads to decision making. Again, there are many techniques to facilitate decision making, but they do not necessarily take into account the realities of political life in organizations, nor are they intended to. There are many instances in which a perfectly sensible solution is not implemented, or is implemented poorly.

"**Top management is often so inundated with trivia that it cannot make informed decisions.**" "**Too many decisions are made at too high a level of management.**" Decision making can be centralized or decentralized, authoritarian or participative, perceptions or data-based: "**We need to break the business into rational components, assign responsible people to them, and allow them to make decisions.**" In order to be effective, decision making must be based on the best possible analysis of the facts: "**I don't mind someone saying 'I don't know,' but I don't like buck-passers. I don't like people who are afraid to make a decision.**" When facts are not available, someone still has to make a decision. When the environment suggests action, by definition it encourages judicious risk taking. On the other hand, if risk is avoided owing to an inordinate fear of failure, managers soon learn that they are better off letting someone else make the decisions. In some cases, decision making will be by consensus and committee; this diffuses responsibility and, if the decision is wrong, it will diffuse blame, too.

> "We have a tendency to operate like a partnership. Every 'partner' has a right to make a decision about any aspect of the operation, whether or not he has the expertise to make that decision."

Since everyone is involved, there is a tendency to rationalize failure and to minimize evaluation for the failure. In extreme cases, it leads to a denial that problems exist, because dealing with them would be a unilateral and unrewarded action.

Reward Systems

Since power is also the ability to give or withhold rewards and punishments, the reward system constitutes a critical variable. Almost invariably, respondents have something to say about the dichotomy between the public language of an organization—i.e., **"pay for performance"** or **"taking care of the good people"**—and what actually happens when human interaction and political maneuvering are taken into account: **"There are still some departments that are reluctant to promote a person simply because they haven't given consideration to replacing him."** A major focus of inquiry usually centers on whether rewards are inconsistent or whimsical:

> "The classification system and the pay scales are a problem. When a guy is not doing his job well, he still gets a raise because the salary scale keeps moving up. According to procedures, you *have* to give him a raise if he is below minimum."

This may have implications on people's motivations and consequent performance. Since, as psychologist B. F. Skinner has pointed out, power is more efficient when rewards are associated with it, an inquiry into this area can provide significant insights.

The bestowing of rewards in an organization often shapes the very behavior of its people. People act according to their perception of what behavior is rewarded, and if such rewards are not appropriate, they may engage in behavior that is counterproductive to others: **"The doctrine here is survival of the fittest. As a result, people look out for number one, and only work as a team if they have absolutely no choice."** In extreme cases, the individual may do things because they will be noticed, rather than doing things because they should be done. To a great extent, rewards are associated with a powerful figure in the organization. As a result, this attracts people who are loyal to an executive, since they feel such an association will be beneficial to their career: **"Some people manage to move up the organization not because they are more competent, but because they aligned themselves with the 'power brokers.'"** Compensation is often an issue but rarely the solution, because the economic realities of most organizations make it difficult to compensate its best performers at a level that is significantly higher than their peers. Most salary-administration policies are too rigid to allow for much differentiation. The wise manager, therefore, should use other forms of reward, such as promotions, interesting assignments, increased autonomy, and outward recognition as a more realistic motivator.

Work and Productivity

All of the previous influences—the organization's mission, its management and leadership style, its planning and structure—influence employees' approach to task accomplishment. The results can be measured in terms of efficiency of production, deadlines met, quotas reached: "**There is a concern with our basic competitiveness in relation to cost.**" In nonproduction environments, work and productivity are measured in terms of applied creativity, development of new processes and products, and new discoveries.

In strategic terms, performance—customarily measured in terms of productivity—is a demanding subject of analysis in most organizations. Care should be taken not to confuse performance with profitability—a financial factor—because an organization may be profitable while productivity declines or while its share of a rapidly expanding market is shrinking.

In operational terms, the issues in this area generally revolve around the adequacy of productivity and the level of quality: "**Our product is apparently a good product. However, we need to achieve the same results more economically.**" As a general rule, such issues cannot be resolved easily, without an examination of what caused an unsatisfactory performance, especially if the deficiency is perceived to exist throughout the organization.

> "We need to do a better job of getting our money's worth out of our employees, and reward the people who produce."

> "The evidence of poor productivity in general should be of major concern."

> "What are we doing to improve our productivity?"

> "What it takes today in terms of work hours to do our work is astonishing. Some of this can be explained in terms of more stringent regulations and new standards, but it doesn't tell the whole story in regard to our net loss in productivity."

Assessing Levels of Performance Deficiency

Individuals

The logical, and convenient, place to look when performance or productivity is deficient is at the individual who may be responsible for the problem. In fact, organizational problems are seldom due to the actions of a particular individual, with the possible exception of people at the higher levels of management. It is relatively easy to find out if a department has had different levels of performance under varying department heads. A differential in performance may be indicative of the level of leadership and skill exhibited by the person responsible for the overall effectiveness of the unit. Marked differences in organizational performance following a change in management may show a positive or negative impact of leadership, provided little else has changed. On the other hand, if many variables such as authorized budgets, available personnel, product demand, and level of organizational and staff support have changed to a significant degree, then the change in performance may be due to those factors, and not the sole responsibility of the manager.

At the highest level of management, however, there seems to be less tolerance of environmental constraints and challenges to explain organizational nonperformance. In Chapter 1, we mentioned Elliott Jaques, who has done significant work in the area of managerial capacity and intellectual development of managers as they age and gain experience. Jaques leads us to conclude that a manager at the appropriate level of capability should be able to anticipate environmental changes and other threats or opportunities, and be able to plan and successfully execute strategies that will lead the organization to growth rather than decline.

In most cases, the problem is not due to a deficiency of skill or a need for training. In performance analysis, a common diagnostic technique used in training-needs analysis (see Appendix 2), one of the first questions asked is, "Did the individual or the organization perform satisfactorily in the past?" If the answer is yes, then you must look elsewhere for the cause of the problem, because poor performance is often the symptom, not the cause of a problem: **"The lack of communication regarding assignments beyond the present project an employee is working on often causes people to drag their feet instead of completing the work."**

An old saying in training is that if the student has failed to learn, the teacher has failed to teach. To some extent, if the employee fails to perform, and that may be true of several employees in a given unit, the manager has failed to manage or the system has not allowed the establishment of an environment that encourages a high level of performance.

Groups

Organizational problems attributed to a single group in the company could exist. In some case, the effects of an ill-performing group can drag the rest of the organization down to quite unfavorable financial results. However, care must be taken to distinguish organizational groups that may deliberately be investing money and other resources in a developmental mode, such as a research or product-development group. In some cases, management may decide to "buy into" a business by providing products and services at a loss, in order to undercut the competition; in this instance, the goals may well justify the up-front expenses. Alas, an ill-performing group may be quite successful in its financial results. Of course if these results are at the expenses of everyone else, then there may be something to look at.

Intergroups

Conflict or poor interaction among two or more groups in an organization may indeed result in significant problems for the entire company, especially when there are divergencies in goals and the means used to reach those goals. The end result may be management by what is politically expedient, rather than management in the interests of the whole organization.

Productivity problems generally are the manifestation of greater problems that lie deeper within the organization and will require you to search for solutions at their source. To do this, you need the various organizational processes previously discussed, particularly policies, procedures, planning, and supervision.

PART V
Feedback, Action Planning, and Evaluation

This part explains how to develop diagnostic conclusions from the mass of data that has been accumulated and analyzed. At this stage, you are preparing a summary of significant issues and problems, and the effect that a lack of resolution of these matters has on the organization.

Much of the diagnosis focuses on handling problem areas. It is just as important, however, to identify significant organization strengths and assets, and to specify what aspects of the organization should not be changed.

The development of recommendations and the presentation of the diagnosis to management must exhibit special care. The balance of this part of the book provides concrete advice on how to approach management in such a way that defensiveness is minimized.

We then focus on action planning and evaluation. The main issue here is, Now that you have a diagnosis, what do you do with it? Obviously, once presented to management, a diagnosis should encourage action at several levels. Part of the work will be making an assessment of what the diagnosis implies. Management must then reach consensus on what the issues of import are, and take necessary steps to address them. This results in actions that help solve relatively proximate operational problems as well as long-range strategic issues. We then review various types of interventions that can be helpful.

Ultimately, a diagnosis must produce results in order to be successful. The remainder of this part reviews how to perform an evaluation study.

CHAPTER 9

Complete and Deliver the Diagnosis

Diagnostic Conclusions

Summary of Significant Issues and Problems

Up to now, you have engaged essentially in a description of what's going on, why, where, and who or what is being affected. Now you must examine your material in its totality, and based on the evidence you have, isolate the major problems and issues facing the organization.

You should be realistic about the number of items that can reasonably be addressed at any one time. In particular, avoid presenting management with a huge laundry list of problems, which may appear overwhelming in its totality. Isolate the truly significant problems and issues, and prepare summaries that describe their nature and extent. This does not mean that minor problems should be ignored, because in actual practice many such problems are subsets of larger, more fundamental unresolved issues. Your main task is to decide which major issues merit management's time and attention. You can then reasonably expect that subordinate problems will be resolved in due course by appropriate levels of managers in the organization. Also, you should accept the fact that not all problems will be dealt with, owing to time and resource limitations. Do not feel frustrated if much of the work you have done in several problem areas cannot be addressed at all. After all, you had to lay out all the data in order to judge which problems are indeed significant.

Indicators of Unresolved Issues and Problems

In formulating your conclusions, start by summarizing the effects that unresolved significant problems or issues have on the organization.

Failure to Meet Goals

Generally, a failure to meet goals can be identified easily, even without a formal diagnosis. An organization may have failed in achieving strategic goals such as diversifying through acquisition, fully developing a new product, or achieving market share.

Drop in Performance

A diagnosis generally will summarize existing data that indicate a drop in performance. Performance variances generally can be quantified, mainly because sufficient past performance criteria exist as a means of comparison. A drop in performance can be observed and often measured, from an individual all the way up to plant level and beyond.

Conflict

The diagnosis is an excellent vehicle for spotting conflict. When an organization experiences difficulty in dealing with a problem, and if a solution is difficult to achieve in a timely manner, often organizational conflict among individuals, leaders, and whole departments is observed. If such conflict continues, it will lead to severe dysfunctional behaviors such as turf protection, finger pointing, "back stabbing," manipulation, and other examples of political behavior notorious in American business today. Dealing with conflict must become a priority task; otherwise, working on the right problems becomes increasingly difficult, with employees concerned only about themselves, while the organization falls into disrepair.

Inaction

Even more troublesome than conflict is inaction. Inaction is indicative of people's feeling helpless and lacking direction. Thus, they fail to act because they feel that action would not help anyway, so why make the effort? At this stage, you are dealing with manifestations of despair and resignation, which can be extremely damaging and difficult to overcome without new and charismatic leadership.

Present Phase of Organizational Crisis

If, during the diagnosis, there are clear indications that a company is experiencing significant change and related problems, it is likely you are dealing with a crisis situation. In such a case it is helpful to determine the present phase of organizational crisis.

A particularly useful analytical tool for summarizing the present state of an organization is provided by Stephen Fink, Joel Beak, and Kenneth Taddeo,[1] who adapted the Kubler-Ross model (originally developed to help terminal patients deal with the eventuality of death). They devised an extremely useful matrix for examining the effects of the four phases that organizations go through when faced with major crises. These stages are shock, defensive retreat, acknowledgment, and adaptation leading to change (see Figure 9-1).

Figure 9-1. Phases of organizational crises.

Phase	Interpersonal Relations	Intergroup Relations	Communication	Leadership and Decision Making	Problem Handling	Planning and Goal Setting	Structure
Shock	fragmented	disconnected	random	paralyzed	none	dormant	chaotic
Defensive Retreat	protective, cohesive	alienated	ritualized	autocratic	mechanistic	expedient	traditional
Acknowledgment	confrontational	mutual	searching	participative	explorative	synthesizing	experimenting
Adaptation and Change	interdependent	coordinated	authentic, congruent	task-centered	flexible	exhaustive, integrative	organic

From Stephen J. Fink, Joel Beak, and Kenneth Taddeo, "Organizational Crisis and Change," *Journal of Applied Behavioral Science*, Vol. 7, No. 1 (1971), p. 18. Used by permission.

When a major crisis, such as a takeover or a radical environmental change occurs, the organization reacts in a fashion not unlike a person's state of physical shock. This state of shock can be observed in several key variables of organizational behavior. It often manifests itself in a high degree of fragmented interpersonal relations; disconnected intergroup relations, an example of which is strained relations among major departments; random communication; and paralyzed leadership and decision making. Other evidence of an organization in shock includes nonexistent problem handling, generally dormant planning and goal setting, and a chaotic structure.

The phase after shock is defensive retreat. Here you can observe a great amount of protective cohesion in interpersonal relations. Intergroup relations are likely to be alienated, with a tendency to blame other units for whatever problems are present. Communication is likely to be ritualized, heavily dependent on formal documentation and procedures, again a manifestation of defensive posture. Leadership and decision making, now recovering from paralysis, are likely to be autocratic. Problem handling is mechanistic and heavily procedure oriented. Planning and goal setting probably are expedient and short-term oriented. The leadership makes an attempt to get a handle on things by using autocratic means, thus restoring the organizational structure to a traditional, hierarchical framework.

The third phase toward recovery from a crisis develops when there is acknowledgment that a crisis has occurred. An organization in a state of acknowledgment exhibits a renewed confrontation in interpersonal relations, often evidenced by people debating and arguing points of view. This stage leads to a mutuality of interests in intergroup relations, an acknowledgment that the problems affect both units, thus making a joint solution imperative. The acknowledgement leads to a search for better means of communication. Leadership and decision making are likely to become more participative in order to allow for broad input from all levels; correspondingly, problem handling is explorative and no longer restricted to tried-and-true methods. Planning and goal setting now move toward synthesizing the input from and needs of various departments, and the structure undergoes a phase of experimentation in an effort to achieve more adequate means of organization.

The last phase leads the organization to adaptation and change. This stage occurs when interpersonal relations become interdependent and a feeling of mutuality is in evidence among the organizational units and individuals—a sense of common purpose. It means that intergroup relations will be coordinated, and communication is likely to be authentic (clear and unambiguous) and congruent (appropriate to the situation). Leadership and decision making are now task centered, problem handling is flexible and imaginative, planning and goal setting are exhaustive and integrative, and the structure is organic, as there is recognition of the need to organize according to the demands of the task at hand.

Such an analysis can be helpful because it leads management to recognize where the company is and what subsequent stages need to be addressed in order to continue along a positive developmental course.

Significant Organizational Strengths and Assets

Since by definition a diagnosis looks for organizational ills and ailments, it is possible to ignore the positive aspects, the unique strengths and assets that make an organization successful in spite of problems that may have been observed. Identification of "what is right" is an important element of a balanced diagnosis.

Organizations with inherent strengths can tolerate a significant number of problems that, in other organizations, could be fatal. A company that dominates through an overwhelming market share can afford to spend more on research and development and on the welfare of its employees. Providing personal computers when typewriters would suffice may seem a waste to more frugal organizations. On the other hand, if the money is there and if such expenditures constitute a minute fraction of a company's earnings, then such actions may be inconsequential.

Aspects of the Organization That Should Not Be Changed

A logical follow-up to the definition of an organization's strengths and assets is an examination of what should *not* be changed. A company survives because it has certain strengths, which enable it to remain alive, even prosper, in spite of problems and mistakes. These strengths should be traced to their source, which may lie in the company's culture, its unique prowess in areas such as technology or marketing, and possibly its status and image in the marketplace. If these have been consistent, it is likely they have held the company in good stead over the years.

Thomas J. Watson, who in 1914 came to manage IBM, built the company on three unwavering principles: (1) give the best possible service to the customer, (2) consistently strive for superior performance, and (3) respect the individual.[2] Some people think that the consistent application of these principles made IBM what it is today. Customers may pay more for IBM computers, which may not necessarily be the absolute best, but they know that they are dealing with a solid, reputable company that will provide service when needed.

A diagnosis strives to determine what needs to be changed in the organization to make it more effective and to be a better place to work. In the process, however, you must be careful not to change the very essence of what makes the company viable.

The good diagnosis is not unduly critical of the company and its leadership, because it recognizes the business climate within which the organization has been operating. The document does not criticize without also recognizing, in comparable measure, the significant contributions made by its managers to the well-being of the organization, its employees, and its constituency.

Diagnostic Recommendations

The last formal task before completion of the diagnostic report is the development of recommendations. This should be done by as many of the project team members as you can persuade to participate.

This particular task is quite demanding, because it inevitably results in much debate and discussion. It is remarkable how the same data and analyses can generate different solutions. Many of the issues are complex, and each member of the team brings his or her own philosophy, values, and orientation to this preliminary task. The team will have to work the differences through, and develop a set of general recommendations. I call this a preliminary task because the recommendations at this stage should be designed primarily to help management focus on the next steps, after it digests the diagnosis. It will be management that eventually develops the official action plans designed to address the appropriate issues or problems.

A study of this scope invariably leads to an extensive list of possible solutions. Often the approach is discouraging; it leads you to believe that the tasks of improvement and development are of such magnitude that results are out of reach. To prevent this reaction, the recommendations from the diagnostic team should be few and general in nature. First, addressing only a few critical areas in the long run eliminates many subsidiary problems. Second, this kind of diagnosis more than any other is designed to feed meaningful data back to the sponsor and ODC, so that they can do something about the stated conditions. The nature of a diagnosis, furthermore, is to help an organization understand its behavior and its present situation—what's going on, how it's going on—so that something can be done about it.

Appendix 1.9 provides a partial example of how diagnostic recommendations can be written. In order to be accessible to the average reader, they focus on general topics. Obviously, a comprehensive project also suggests interventions that involve finance and other technical disciplines.

Presenting the Diagnosis to Management

The Structure of the Diagnosis

The diagnostic report should include not only the main body of information, but also sufficient explanation about the process used for and the overall scope of data gathering. The following are general guidelines for structuring and writing the report.

The Introduction

The introduction to the diagnosis should set the stage for this important event by putting both the study and the organization it scrutinizes into perspective. As a minimum, it should cover the following.

Events leading to initiation of the study. Briefly describe how the diagnosis was initiated, and summarize the objectives as listed in the proposal originally submitted to the sponsor or council.

Duration of the diagnostic study. This information reinforces the fact that the undertaking was important. If a diagnosis has taken place over a significant period of time, often corrections to the organization's systems and procedures are made upon identification. This phenomenon should be acknowledged.

Process used to implement the study. Explain the process used to develop the diagnosis. Since it was commissioned, there may have been some changes in management, and these individuals, even though they might now be members of the ODC by virtue of their position, may not be completely familiar with the project. For this reason, and to give other members of the council an overview of the mechanical process that resulted in the report, provide a brief description of the methods used. Also, stress that the study is evidence of a powerful process of introspection by managers and employees at all levels, and that it reflects a collective perception of the organization's ability to cope with an increasingly complex environment. Indicate that the document reveals a high degree of candor and openness by all respondents. This candor should be regarded as reflecting confidence that there will be no recriminations. In effect, it should be seen as an acknowledgment that the organization has certain unresolved issues. Such acknowledgment is a prerequisite for organizational improvement.

Structure and content of the report. Offer some explanation of what the package in front of the executives is all about. Indicate that the study is presented in two volumes:

- *Volume 1* is a management summary that includes a description of the process used in the study, relevant background information, comments on major sections of the collected data, and general recommendations.
- *Volume 2* is a compilation of the data used in reaching the conclusions and recommendations in the management summary.

It is extremely important to point out that the second volume was developed primarily for use by the analysts. Indicate that its contents are deliberately compiled verbatim, in a logical structure. The undigested data were then used as the basis for the analytical work that led to the working hypotheses. The hypotheses were tested, necessary adjustments were made, and conclusions for the management summary were developed. The data-base volume is made available to management, to allow selective review of items that may be of particular interest.

Contributors. In a sense, all those who participated in the diagnosis are contributors. The contributions of line managers and staff people on the diagnostic team, key executives, and support employees deserve special mention. In particular, acknowledge the efforts of the line managers on the diagnostic team, who provided a substantial portion of the interview data, and were able to find time in their busy schedules to thoroughly review the material and substantially improve the quality of the finished product. Acknowledge the very important contribution also made by the executives and other employees who willingly allowed themselves to be interviewed, as well as the employees who spent considerable time filling out the questionnaires.

Participants. A list of all the people who participated in the study should then follow. This not only gives credit where credit is due, but also subtly reinforces the fact that the report has been assembled by a high-powered group. The sponsor or ODC will find it very difficult to ignore such a document.

The Body of the Report

The following are guidelines for writing and structuring the main section of the diagnosis.

Problems of the company as stated by its leadership. During the data-collection stage, you segregated the comments of company executives from those of line managers and the general employee population. This division sets the stage for the diagnosis, and lets you start with an overview of the company's problems and issues, as stated by its key executives.

A company's leadership is likely to be concerned about issues that have strategic implications, even though operational problems, if severe enough, will also be discussed. Quite often, you might hear concerns about the ineffectiveness of the company's planning process, the unequal distribution of technical capabilities within the organization, and the difficulties the company experiences in attracting and retaining qualified personnel.

Other common problems and related issues, often deal with:

- Competitive position and the need to increase sales:

  "Obviously right now business is of great concern. The tension is pretty well toward 'How can we best secure more work?'"

- Concerns about changing relationships with valued clients:

  "This company, for many, many years always worked at pretty high levels in the client organizations, and we really didn't get to know several managers at lower levels. We really weren't looking at tomorrow as we should have. Now all of the fellows are coming up in the organization, and are in position of power. Yet, we failed to cultivate them. Even worse, we haven't listened to what they were telling us back then."

- Similar concerns in regard to relationships with suppliers:

  "Most manufacturers would prefer to work with another firm, rather than put up with the difficulties of dealing with us. It's an attitude. Over the years we knew we were good. We thought we were the Cadillacs of the industry. We wouldn't listen to anyone else. I think this attitude still exists today, although for the first time, I think we are starting to question ourselves."

Some executives may be concerned that the company has not kept abreast of the marketplace:

"In the past, we knew the marketplace, we were attuned to it and we had some unique relationships which were working for us, but since 1973, that marketplace has completely turned around. If we continue in the same way as we have done before, we will be offering an Edsel. That doesn't mean we don't have the ability to come up with a Mustang or a Thunderbird, or whatever. It means that we have to reassess our objectives and the way we're going to reach them."

When writing this section, heavily use direct quotes to sustain the credibility and to give "color" to the data; quotes should also be used liberally throughout the remainder of the document as it is developed.

Major issue areas. The main body of the diagnosis, as we have already seen, is structured so that the data you collected, sorted, and categorized can be placed in a logical and coherent context. The balance of the diagnostic report, therefore, should cover your observations and conclusions regarding the organization—its history, background, and culture; mission, strategy, and structure; organizational resources; and organizational processes.

This portion of the diagnosis should be illustrated by representative data in the form of quotes related to each issue, integrated with the text in a way similar to the many examples in previous chapters and also as shown in Appendix 1.9. Certainly, the use of quotes in a narrative is difficult, because of the challenge it poses to integrate them in an elegant and fluid manner. It is worth trying, however, because the comments provided by the respondents are, to some extent, the purest form of feedback to management; generally they are colorful and express perceptions about various facets of the organization in the employees' own language. The number of examples you should use varies depending on the importance of the topic. In some major sections, additional interpretive comments are provided as necessary.

Topical background, guidance, and suggestions to facilitate analysis and interpretation of given issues should be incorporated throughout. A business issue that surfaces during an organic diagnosis still needs to be interpreted in relation to normative criteria of organizational effectiveness, exemplified by how successful organizations have handled similar situations. This guide should vary in depth depending on the topic area, and should not be all-inclusive; rather, it should be representative of the research you have done to place the issue in a proper context and to develop meaningful recommendations.

Prepare for the Presentation

Once the diagnostic report is completed, you need to prepare to present it to management. The best way is to schedule a meeting. In addition to the sponsor and the ODC, it is desirable to have several key members of the diagnostic team present, particularly line managers. How possible this is depends on whether the executives feel comfortable about having relatively junior people present. Should there be resistance, you can point out that having representatives of middle management at discussions that may have far-reaching effects could signal the beginning of enhanced teamwork among all levels of management.

Even though the content of the presentation will be extracted from the diagnostic document itself, topics covered and their sequence in your oral presentation need not necessarily be the same. The written document obviously is comprehensive and complete. The oral presentation covers highlights and is concerned more with providing the executives with guidance for their subsequent review of the document, both as individuals and as a group.

This presentation is crucial, and it demands a strategy of its own, particularly in respect to managing the potential defensiveness and denials that could lead to a rejection of the diagnosis itself. As shown in the discussion on transference in Appendix 2, even though the executives have sponsored and paid for the diagnosis, they are likely to subconsciously wish for its failure, in order to feel better about their inability to sort out the problems. At the same time, as the project manager, if you do not provide the new insights and meaningful recommendations the sponsor has paid for, you might be at risk. The manner in which the results of the diagnosis are presented thus becomes of crucial importance.

Deliver the Presentation

Introduction

Your first concern must be to establish the credibility of the data. A single controversial statement or half-truth will immediately lead to a challenge, and possibly an attack, by a member of the group.

The meeting should start with a brief review of the events that led to the commissioning of the diagnostic study, and a summary of the various steps that constitute its implementation, including time, resources, and cost. Most of this information will in all probability fail to register with the executives, who are likely to exhibit signs of impatience and anxiety in anticipation of the upcoming "revelations." In fact, a wise diagnostician goes out of the way to avoid surprises by keeping management informed as much as possible during the course of the diagnosis, so that during the formal presentation the context of the meeting can be more of a summary than a surprise. Nevertheless, the stage has to be set for immediate credibility with regard to methodology and validity of data.

A dramatic but highly effective way of presenting the content of the diagnosis is to briefly scan responses to the question coined by Harry Levinson, "Make believe the company is a person. . . . Describe that person to me." For some undetermined reason, which I will not attempt to fathom, when this question is asked of reasonably intelligent individuals, it elicits responses of extraordinary eloquence. When compiled, the results present a powerful and compelling picture of the very essence of an organization. This self-portrait can be communicated by projecting a few slides showing the respondents' statements. The following are representative:

> "The company is an old maid, a timid old maid."

> "The company is somewhat beyond middle age: conservative, slow to try new things, somewhat conceited, with such conceit based on conquests in the past. However, there is life in the old girl yet, but she needs a good goose."

> "The company today is a middle-class, middle-aged individual with conservative leanings, a modest desire for radical changes, marginal aggressiveness, great respect for tradition, and a tendency to adhere to 'preordained' philosophies and solutions to problems."

If the source of the comments is not immediately disclosed, it is inevitable that someone in the group will challenge them and their validity by expressing disbelief that they are representative of the general employee opinion. A somewhat risky but necessary response is to reveal that the comments come from the members of the group in attendance—the executives themselves. If the subsequent moment of silence can be tolerated without undue anxiety, the result is acknowledgment and ownership of those comments by at least one member of the group, followed shortly thereafter by confessions from the rest of the executives. This leads to a significantly heightened level of interest and alertness to what you have to say. A way of "breaking the ice," this method is powerful and creates credibility for both the method and the data of a long and involved presentation.

Summary Presentation and Discussion

The rest of the meeting should be a presentation of the diagnosis in summary, followed by a question-and-answer session.

Heavy emphasis on quotes from respondents during the summary presentation promotes immediacy, gives color and realism to the feedback, and further reinforces the credibility of the data. The summary presentation should cover a sequence similar to the following:

1. A summary of issues and problems as perceived by the respondents. (Generally, it is useful to identify the perceptions on the basis of organizational level: top management, middle management, and general employee population.)

2. Cause of the problems.
3. Internal issues.
4. Main strengths and weaknesses of the organization.
5. Perception of the leadership.
6. Quantity, quality, and adequacy of human resources.
7. External influences that need to be dealt with.
8. Appropriateness of mission and goals.

Additional coverage of specific items should follow the outline of the diagnosis itself.

Following the presentation, allow sufficient time for preliminary questions and answers. Don't expect to be able to provide answers to all the questions. Ask the group at this stage to focus on clarification, because the members will meet several times after they get an opportunity to review the report in detail.

Following the initial presentation, it is likely that the organizational development council or similar group of executives will ask for time to read the report thoroughly. Management has an obligation to the members of the diagnostic team, the employees, and the shareholders to consider the recommendations in a constructive manner. Prior to adjournment, discuss the response procedure to the diagnosis; they have four possible response options:

1. *Accepted.* Certain recommendations are accepted. Specify who is to implement the changes and by when. Request an action plan.
2. *Need more detail and information.* Specify who is to provide additional information and by when.
3. *Need more time to evaluate.* Indicate when the status will be reported.
4. *Rejected.* Specify the reason for rejection.

As they review the diagnosis on their own, the executives should also be asked to make notes, either on the document itself or on a separate piece of paper, regarding any areas that require clarification. They should then forward their comments to you, and as project manager, you will be responsible for preparing answers and clarification.

CHAPTER 10

Action Planning and Evaluation

Once the diagnosis is presented to management, the executives will need time for individual review. Top management will develop questions, which you should answer as thoroughly as possible. Then you and management should jointly commence working on an agreement about the issues or problems that should be addressed. Then the process of action planning details how and when the issues and changes will be addressed.

Review the Diagnosis With Management

A comprehensive diagnosis requires several months of study by the executives to ensure their understanding of the many issues and problems. During the course of this review, they will forward their written comments and questions to you.

Handle the Questions

The following are examples of how you can deal with such comments:

- *Comment:* "**The summary of the crises affecting the company was interesting. In regard to several of the crises having to do with control, scope of activities, and competition, it appears that these crises presently affect the entire industry, not just our company, as implied.**"

  — *Your response:* This observation is indeed true. It should be recognized, however, that the intent of this section was to examine how our company handles these crises, thus suggesting that a competitive advantage might be obtained by dealing with such problems before the competition does.

- *Comment:* "**Based on what I read about reactions to the bonus system, now is the time to rethink how we reward our performers. Up** to now, we determined such rewards based on annual profitability; at the end of the year, we split what's in the bonus pool. How would a change to this approach affect people who are used to year-end bonuses?"

— *Your response:* The feedback from our best people indicates that they would prefer a bonus system tied to reaching defined individual and group goals, both short term (annually) and long term (which could be two, three, or five years). The people are willing to do away with the guaranteed bonus, because it spreads the rewards too thin and does not adequately distinguish top performers from average employees. Making the bonus contingent on actual results is perceived as more fair, and is a better motivator.

- *Comment:* "There is a comment on page 41 that indicates there are present-day doubts about the long-term viability of our consulting services. Based on my own observations, I do not detect a widespread concern within this group."

— *Your response:* Your observation is correct. The members of this group are essentially focused on day-to-day operations. It appears that they may be somewhat sheltered from the marketing issues, which have a bearing on the future viability of the department. It is important to acknowledge, however, that such concern was voiced by several managers in other areas of the company, who are in a position to make such a judgment.

- *Comment:* "It seems that now is the time to start thinking about the development of a line of laser printers to supplement our regular product line. We have the funds available, and certainly the technology is no problem. However, don't we have an uphill fight, considering that the competition is already entrenched?"

— *Your response:* There is no question that many established competitors are marketing laser printers, and that many more are entering the field. However, the facts seem to work in our favor. First, the technology has been sorted out and the standards are now clear. The camp is divided between DPL and PostScript page-description languages. This means that we have only to decide which standard we will address. (It is even feasible to produce machines that can do both.) Second, the market is in its infancy. Sheer demand alone presents a significant opportunity for many suppliers. Another fact in our favor is our reputation. Our company's name is synonymous with reliability and well-thought-out design. The fact that we enter the market a little later should not pose any problems, because people know that when we introduce a product, it will work as advertised. Part of our strategy could be assurance to the customers that we don't experiment on them—we only sell field-tested products.

In some cases, an executive may make observations that require elaborate responses. Also, it is possible that inaccuracies in the diagnostic report will be pointed out. Regardless of the nature of the question, every effort should be made to respond promptly and thoroughly. Individual responses are appropriate, but it is best to issue consolidated questions and responses for all the concerned members of management to see.

Reach Consensus on Major Issues or Problem Areas

Following a thorough review of the diagnosis, and clarification of issues and problems as necessary, you should ascertain if the responsible executives feel they have thoroughly understood the nature and implications of the data they have examined. If the conclusion is positive, you are now ready to help management prepare an action plan that will, it is hoped, address the applicable problems, concerns, and issues. It is very likely that you and the diagnostic team will be asked to become an integral part of the solution, by helping management develop such action plans, milestones, and responsibilities. Certainly such participation, especially by the critical mass, was intended all along.

Generally, a diagnosis highlights both operational and strategic issues that affect the organization. The problem solving, decision making, and action planning that must ensue will probably occur simultaneously.

Action Planning

The best approach to action planning is to establish teams responsible for developing solutions and appropriate action plans, and to have such teams report to the council. Preferably, all of the managers of the critical mass should be involved. Members of the diagnostic team who are not line managers might remain involved in a facilitator role. It should be recognized, however, that at this stage the diagnostic project is essentially completed. Management has received feedback and recommendations. It is now up to management to take whatever action it feels necessary to address the identified problems and issues. The staff on the diagnostic team will become increasingly peripheral to the effort, as it should be.

Your diagnosis is likely to highlight a number of issues and problems that merit intervention. Clearly identified problems should be addressed and resolved as soon as possible, so that they do not linger and get in the way of more important goals. The remaining issues, which are likely to involve long-term development and strategic planning, can then be attacked systematically.

Operational, short-term issues can be dealt with by establishing task forces composed of the appropriate people to reach their resolutions. These temporary groups should be given a clear mandate and specific objectives, as well as the necessary time and resources to achieve meaningful and reasonably permanent "fixes" to the problems. The effort should involve the people most affected by the problem. It is preferable for top management not to get personally involved, except perhaps by appointing executive sponsors for the task forces.

Top management's responsibility is to deal with major issues, and with the demands of multiple and changing forces in the business environment. These executives will use the results of the diagnosis to develop priorities, goals, and strategic plans relevant to the future well-being of the organization.

Planning the Organizational Change and Development

A comprehensive diagnosis, to some extent, creates additional problems for management because it builds expectations for change on the part of the participants, and it presents many alternatives to reach certain goals. This means that executives must spend considerable time discussing which direction to take and choosing the people who should be assigned to given issues and problems. Such choices often depend on selecting the "best alternative," especially in regard to strategic directions. Executives will face complex dilemmas in determining priorities and solving problems, owing to the turbulence and uncertainty of today's business environment. Moreover, because of the critical issues that surround the alternatives, the best option is seldom one of continuing operations as usual. Rather, the choice is generally one that requires a significant change in organizational priorities and the way the company conducts its business and achieves its goals. All of these considerations demand a significant and sustained involvement by top management if the organization is to creatively cope with changing outside demands and increase the possibility for its survival and future success.

Reach Agreement on the Company's Core Mission

As previously discussed, the first choice management has to make is that of determining what constitutes the organization's core mission—its reason for being.[1] Once this choice has been made, management must engage in a series of activities to define the present state of the organization, develop a clear picture of the desired future state of the organization, map the route that will lead the organization from its present state to its future one, and manage that move.

Actual practice corroborates Beckhard's contention that is not unusual to find top corporate executives having differing views of their company's core mission, of the environmental forces that impinge on their organization, and of how the company should go about addressing those forces in the future. Resolution of these issues is one of the primary and most fundamental responsibilities of top management—a responsibility that requires much of their time, energy, and sustained involvement.

In making a decision about what constitutes a company's core mission, the following suggestions from Beckhard and Harris should be considered:

1. The operable decision about core mission is the one that the top management of the organization believes and uses to guide its priorities in goal-setting, resource allocations, and so on. It is always, in the final analysis, a personal judgment of one or a few key executives.
2. It is important—often crucial—that the key executive management of the organization have consensus about the mission. If they don't, their behavior can produce very confusing consequences, resulting in mixed commitment to organization goal priorities, which flow from mission definition.[2]

The diagnosis should assist management in identifying the different forces in the environment (government, competition, special-interest groups, labor, and so on) that make special demands of the company. These demands have to be sorted out in terms of the core mission and the goal priorities, and it should be determined whether they must be met or not.

Determine an Appropriate Response to the Identified Environmental Demands

Management must identify the specific response the organization is presently giving to each of its environmental demands. Attention must be paid to what is being said and what is actually being done. Again, as in the development of a core-mission statement, executives are not likely to be in accord on the level and quality of present organizational response. This means that they must work toward a consensus, a potentially positive process because it involves assessing the consequences of different responses.

Project Into the Future

The next step in this process is for management to make a projection of likely future demands if the organization were to do nothing significant in response to present demands—that is, if the company were to continue doing business as usual. This type of projection increases understanding of the current responses the organization makes to the different forces impacting on it.

Define the Desired Future State

The task here is to determine, on the basis of management's conclusions after reviewing the diagnosis, a desired end-state for the company, described in explicit terms. Many long-term plans state a goal of achieving a set bottom line or certain profitability criteria. However, a detailed description of what the company might look like in the future encompasses more than financial goals. We have already discussed how other elements in the picture might be the organizational structure, the company's size, its position in the marketplace, and so on. Whatever the elements, the key point is that management must produce a *detailed* picture of what it wants the company to be at a set point in the future. Being explicit about what the company will look like in the "new future state," and combining this picture with the assessment of the current state, generates the base for management to develop realistic action plans and timetables for managing the transition from present to future.

Organizational Interventions

The range of possible interventions is vast, and their planning, design, and execution may involve many people with skills and resources beyond what the diagnostic team can provide. At this point, addressing the many issues surfaced in the diagnosis will become the responsibility of management, which is likely to set both short- and long-term objectives to continue improving the organization.

Documentation of action plans, objectives, commitments, and milestones to measure accomplishment is absolutely necessary. These documents should have wide distribution and be subject to regular review. In most cases, the action plans will become part of a manager's performance plans and will be evaluated accordingly.

Evaluate the Effectiveness of the Diagnosis

A project with the scope of a diagnosis is expensive and time consuming. It can be justified because the results, or payoff, are expected to exceed the cost. For this reason, a formal evaluation of the results should be an integral part of the process. The basic questions which need to be answered are:

- What were the recommendations?
- What action plans were actually developed and implemented?
- What is the result of such interventions?
- In the balance, did the results matter? Did they justify the cost of the diagnosis?

As plans are implemented, a program of constant evaluation should be developed to assess whether the changes have indeed solved the problems. It is likely that in some cases additional actions have to be taken to address a particularly difficult issue. It is also important for management to recognize the problems that have been solved, by establishing regular feedback procedures with all concerned managers and employees.

The ultimate evaluation of a diagnosis's success is the resolution of the organization's main problems. It is unrealistic, however, to expect that the diagnosis itself will be credited for the positive changes likely to occur. Indeed, many managers have pointed out that changes that have occurred in their organization have taken place as data were being surfaced during the diagnosis process. Others indicated that change would have occurred with or without the diagnosis, primarily because the "pain" motivated such change. To a certain extent, these managers are correct. Sooner or later, organizations—as self-renewing mechanisms—change in order to react to their environment. It is also a fact, however, that a properly conducted diagnosis accelerates the process of positive change and development in an organization, primarily because it highlights the issues and problems in a systematic fashion, thus leading to proactive, rather than reactive, change.

The evaluation of the diagnosis can parallel the development of the project itself. It can be done through interviews or questionnaires.

It is important to recognize that such an evaluation is not necessarily for the purpose of appraising the performance of the diagnostic team. Rather, it is an assessment of whether the organization as a whole has been able to address the various problems and issues, how well it has addressed them, and to what extent. Even though key members of the diagnostic team may be involved in the development of action plans, implementation of such plans is generally in the hands of line managers. Of course, if some of the implementers are also members of the critical mass, which was part of the diagnostic team, the action plans have a better chance of succeeding.

Conduct an Evaluation Study

The most efficient way to approach the evaluation is to design questionnaires that are based on the recommendations and action plan themselves. Respondents should be asked to rate the progress made on each item in the questionnaire, using a scale of from 1 to 5, with 1 representing "not much progress" to 5 meaning "resolved."

Specific steps for evaluation can include the following items:

- Determine the current relevancy of the identified issues or problems.
- Analyze the extent of implementation of agreements and results achieved—i.e., issue has been:
  - Resolved
  - Unresolved, but action has taken place
  - Unresolved, no action taken
  - Expanded
  - No longer of concern
- Evaluate overall effectiveness of the action plans.
- Develop recommendations for future diagnostic projects.

In processing and organizing the data, it is useful to ascertain whether, on issues of global importance, there is any difference in perception among the various layers of management. As a minimum, the respondents should be categorized as:

- *Executive management*—President, executive and senior vice presidents
- *Upper management*—a significant sample of the managers who fit this category, all of them if possible
- *Middle management*—as large a sample of the population as possible, but not less than 10 percent

In some cases it may be desirable to include representation based on a diagonal slice of the employee population.

The questionnaire itself should be in two parts. The first section should list the recommendations in the diagnosis and whether they were accepted by management, with direction to develop appropriate action plans. The second section should list the action plans themselves. Appendix 1.11 provides an example.

Once the questionnaires are returned, you should first examine each major item to determine the amount of progress perceived by the majority of respondents, and note any significant differences in perceptions among the various categories of management. Next, study the verbatim comments made by the respondents, to give meaning to the resulting scores. The comments should be recorded and arranged in a way consistent with the original organizational grouping. All this material should be made available in the report as a data base to which readers may refer for elaboration. In writing the report, abstain from making personal judgments. You should, however, present the data in such a manner that the relevant issues come readily to the forefront. Refer again to Appendix 1.9, which illustrates the style and format of the main body of the evaluation document.

PART VI
Diagnosis as a Management Tool

Thus far, diagnosis has been treated as a large, complex, and comprehensive undertaking, whose scope encompasses the entire organization. In actual practice, diagnosis is also useful as a sophisticated tool to address specific issues. There is no reason why it cannot be applied to good advantage in any situation that requires meaningful background information in order to make informed decisions. This part discusses how such limited-scope diagnoses are conducted.

CHAPTER 11
Special Applications of Diagnostic Techniques

This chapter illustrates how diagnostic techniques can be applied in special situations, including mergers and acquisitions, strategy development, and team building. As an illustration of how different diagnosticians approach a project, each of the examples that follow is in a different style and format. It is up to you to choose an approach that best suits you, or even to develop your own approach, as long as the goals of an organizational diagnosis are met: The collection of meaningful data that, when analyzed, can be used by management to improve the organization.

Diagnosis in Mergers and Acquisitions

In the turbulent 1980s, an astonishing number of companies joined forces with or acquired other organizations that they believed would either complement their assets or add to them, in an effort to become more profitable or competitive in the marketplace. In theory, once the documents are signed the merger is accomplished; but in reality, the work has just begun. The complex task of integrating the cultures, histories, traditions, policies, and practices of the affected organizations determines whether such joining will come even close to meeting its original intent. There are many instances of failed mergers in the United States. According to *Business Week*, one-half to two-thirds of all mergers don't work; one in three is later undone. In 1985, for every seven acquisitions, there were three divestitures. Even if some mergers survive, studies estimate that 80 percent of them fail to live up to the expectations listed in their feasibility studies.[1] A postmortem reveals that the failures can be attributed in part to people's not thinking carefully about the companies' cultures and characteristic ways of thinking and acting. These characteristics cannot be meshed without a systematic effort to achieve such synergy.

The organizational diagnosis can be of significant help when a merger is contemplated, and can also be used to advantage shortly after the signatures have cemented the deal at the financial and legal levels. Owing to the secret nature of such transactions, preparing the affected people in the respective organizations is generally not possible, therefore the latter instance is more likely.

The following case illustrates how a diagnosis can help facilitate the creation of a new, combined organization by initiating a systematic program of communication and mutual support. It was conducted by a team of interviewers who talked to each group separately. They then prepared a diagnostic report that exposed the significantly different cultures and expectations of the two organizations.

*CASE: PHENIX S. A.**

Background

Phenix S. A., a manufacturer of high-performance European automobiles, was established as the result of a merger between two organizations: Axthel S. A., based in a suburb of a European city, and Mistral Racing Inc., located in a corner of a former army base in the English countryside. Axthel was a seventy-year-old manufacturer of economy automobiles and specialty off-road vehicles. Over the years, it had built a reputation as manufacturer of relatively small, no-frills autos all based on the same chassis. Differentiation among models was minimal, and generally consisted of either two or four doors and a limited choice of trim and options.

Manufacturing was very efficient because Axthel's production lines were highly standardized, and cost control was one of the best in European industry. The company managed to carve itself a niche in the market, which enabled it to sell around 100,000 vehicles a year. Customer appeal had been based on selling uncomplicated, reliable, if unexciting, vehicles at reasonable prices. Its customer base was primarily working-class, blue-collar people, with a smattering of young, college-educated couples who found the economical cars produced by Axthel ideal as a starter vehicle. Unfortunately, these people were rarely repeat customers, because they almost invariably upgraded as soon as they could afford to. As a general rule, few vehicles were sold to relatively affluent professionals, a group that made up an increasing percentage of the European suburban population in and around major cities. Another consideration was the lucrative U.S. market, where the relatively affluent yuppies seemed to prefer sporty, high-performance automobiles of European and Japanese origin.

Mistral Racing Inc. was founded twenty years earlier by Bill Desmond, a legendary auto racer who made his reputation by winning Grand Prix championships throughout the world. Mistral Racing specialized in the design and manufacture of racing cars for Formula 1 and 2. It was famous for the Mistere X engine, a twin-cam, four-valve per cylinder racing engine that was in much demand. It also converted luxury cars such as the Mercedes-Benz and BMW into superfast machines by modifying their engines and suspension systems to

---

*The names of all organizations discussed in this chapter have been changed.

optimum performance specifications. Most of the work was done by hand, one unit at a time, with the obvious result that its products were extremely expensive and the production level was low (less than five hundred units per year).

The merger of the two companies was a marriage of necessity. Axthel's management studied marketing reports indicating that the company's growth would be limited because the European public was buying an increasingly high percentage of domestic and foreign vehicles that, on average, were at least twice as expensive as Axthel's basic model. Moreover, new competition from other manufacturers, among them the Japanese and Koreans, provided vehicles priced below Axthel's, and had started to make inroads into Axthel's prime market area. If the company was to survive, it would have to make a new generation of attractive automobiles that could be sold at a significantly higher average price than its present product.

After examining many options, including the possibility of joint ventures with other European and Japanese firms, Axthel's management decided to merge with Mistral Racing. The reasons for this move reflected management's belief that the business should remain in domestic hands. Management also believed that Mistral Racing had the technology and credibility to design and produce a high-performance vehicle that could compete favorably with the likes of Audi, Volvo, and the larger Japanese models. The new product could compete at a significantly lower price, but would be much more profitable per unit than the vehicles presently being produced by Axthel. It was hoped that a new, outstanding car line—backed by Axthel's reputation for reliability of and spiced with the glamour and legendary engineering of Mistral Racing—would capture the emerging young-professional market and hold on to it by offering a choice of increasingly more sophisticated (and expensive) models when the customers were ready for an upgrade.

Bill Desmond and his people at Mistral Racing agreed to the merger out of necessity. The racing business was viable, but it ran hot and cold, depending on the fortunes of the racing business, and the result was that it was difficult to maintain a consistent backlog. Desmond was also concerned that legislation would impact on auto racing in general, with possible adverse consequences for his small company, which was entirely employee owned. By joining forces with Axthel, his people would get a crack at making reasonably exciting regular-production cars, not only to ensure steady income, but also to show the world that what they had learned in racing could be put to good use in making cars capable of world-class performance against all competitors.

The Diagnostic Interviews

The heads of both companies were concerned that significantly different cultures in the two companies would prevent the meshing necessary to make the deal work. They decided to address the problem by having a joint team of managers interview people on both sides, in order to identify the main differences in thinking and behavior. The following is a partial, composite transcript of typical responses from both sides. This transcript highlights how two groups with their own culture perceived the same issue quite differently.

Responses From Axthel. According to the data collected from interviews, shortly after the merger was announced a team of Axthel executives visited Mistral Racing, and were shocked. Mistral was located on an old army base, Quonset huts and all. It didn't even bother to put up a sign. Once inside, according to the respondents, there was no evidence of a disciplined production process. Instead of a steady, systematic sequence of production assembly, the Axthel executives observed groups of people working on several different cars at different levels of assembly in an apparently incomprehensible sequence. In addition, the workers somehow managed to modify Mercedes-Benz and BMW cars on the main manufacturing floor. The Axthel people felt that this kind of activity got in the way, particularly since the records showed that Mistral didn't make much money from it. The Axthel team also had difficulty finding a Mistral executive. You couldn't tell by looking at them, because they all wore overalls, and more often than not they were out there on the shop floor with their heads stuck in the engines.

In the view of Axthel executives, Mistral's president, Bill Desmond, spent more time allegedly testing the race cars on the track than doing what they thought he was supposed to do in the office. The financial controls at Mistral were perceived to be informal at best. Apparently, there was little budgetary control, and funds were used on a pay-as-you-go basis. There was no real cash management, and their collection record was inadequate. Marketing was judged by the review team to be nonexistent. The Axthel respondents felt that it would be necessary for them to take over operations, finance, and marketing.

In addition, the Axthel review team perceived that some of the employee-relations practices at Mistral were somewhat inappropriate. Every Friday afternoon they threw a beer party on the premises, at company expense. This kind of practice was not considered compatible with Axthel's conservative image, and most Axthel executives were ready to demand a stop to such activities because they felt they did not present a proper public image.

Desmond himself was perceived as highly competent, even more so if he could be persuaded to wear a suit and stay in his office. But the Axthel respondents felt that they would have problems with his immediate subordinates. All were very well qualified, with advanced engineering degrees, and most had racing experience, but they were considered light on management education and experience.

After talking to the Mistral people, the Axthel team felt that Mistral's expectations about the new venture were unrealistic. There is no question that the Phenix venture must come up with a new performance-luxury car. But it seemed that Mistral was setting its sights on going after Porsche, BMW, and the like, whereas the thinking at Axthel was to aim for something like Audi, Volvo, or Saab. The respondents felt that there was no way they could produce their kind of car in less than eighteen months, and it was even less likely that they could get away with charging the customer that kind of money for a newly designed automobile, no matter how good. What worried the Axthel people even more was that the Mistral people were reportedly talking about building cars with assembly teams instead of utilizing an efficient production line. Axthel executives believed that there was no way they would be able to produce the targeted 30,000 units for the first run, building up to 60,000 units by the second year. In any case, they felt that Mistral was going to have to give up its specialty car-upgrading work. The Axthel team also did not think the Phenix venture would have the resources to continue building racing cars. Mistral had its best people working on those, and they would be needed for the Phenix cars.

The Axthel people felt that they and Mistral were going to have to work together as a team, if they expected to be successful at a new venture of major importance to all of them. They also felt it would be necessary to get management all in one place, looking the part. They felt that they must create a new, lean corporate staff and an integrated product-development team. Then they believed they would have to get a good marketing campaign together. There was much work ahead. They felt an urge to move fast, because they didn't want people to get too nervous about the upcoming changes. Axthel executives felt that they couldn't afford to lose many of Mistral Racing's people, and obviously, they didn't want to hurt any of Axthel's own long-time, loyal employees.

Responses from Mistral. The Mistral people made no bones about their motivation for involvement with Axthel: **"They got the dough, we have the know."** According to Mistral executives, all that Axthel had to bring to the party was a checkbook to pay the bills, and Mistral would design **"iron which would blow the socks off BMW, and possibly even Porsche."** Their only problem was how they were going to make enough of the new autos, and this is where they hoped Axthel, with its "reasonably adequate" production technology, could help. The respondents figured that if Axthel could produce 100,000 of its uninspired vehicles, it could probably make at least 30,000 of the new cars.

Mistral people were somewhat concerned about Axthel's labor union, which in their eyes was a major obstacle to production and quality, but they understood that Axthel had done a better job than most at keeping things in harmony. Certainly, Mistral executives would prefer to hire more of their own kind of people, but they realized that these people would never get themselves tied to a production line. In any case, it would be impossible to get them to join the union. They frankly didn't know how they were going to solve that problem.

The Mistral people jokingly said that they didn't know how they would survive Axthel's well-deserved reputation for providing transportation mainly to working masses. They examined Axthel's four-wheel-drive vehicle, however, and admitted that with Mistral's engine and a little work, they could make an impressive off-road vehicle. They felt that perhaps it would be best to create a new company name, even though they hated giving up their own. In any case, they stated that Bill Desmond had indicated that a condition of the deal was that Mistral Racing remain an independent division involved in racing gear.

The Mistral people mentioned **"the predictable visit from a bunch of chaps in three-piece suits."** The racers seem to have enjoyed the reaction of

Axthel executives when they saw the rather spartan corporate headquarters.

The visit highlighted a major difference between the two companies: their operating methods. Mistral had no production line, no real warehouse, "**just a bunch of chaps working hard in the midst of divine confusion.**" They admitted it wasn't efficient but were quick to point out that "**it sure beats boredom.**" They explained that there was a genuine sense of camaraderie, with people working around each other, moving cars and components with overhead cranes and hand trucks and attending to several different cars at varying levels of assembly, in "**a delicious, harmonious mess.**" They reported that they also have five old Italian craftsmen, who still fit body panels by hand.

The Mistral executives said they like to be where the product is. "**I really love sticking my head under a hood, trying to squeeze the last bit of power out of a mill**" is a typical comment. Bill Desmond was said to spend more time "**burning rubber on the track**" than any of them, and was considered the company's best quality-control person.

The Mistral people admitted being a little sloppy with the finances. "**Some of the accounts are five months overdue; wealthy people are the slowest to pay up.**" Even so, the Mistral people claimed that they just didn't have the time or inclination to bother with cash management. They admitted that they could do better in this department, and suggested that Axthel handle this.

Traditionally, Mistral never worried about marketing; the customers just came to them. They recognized, however, that this would have to change if they were to sell 30,000 cars in eighteen months.

During the visit, the Mistral people invited the Axthel executives to join them in their customary end-of-the-week beer bust to see what team spirit was all about. The Mistral employees usually quit work at 4 P.M. on Fridays, roll in generous quantities of ale and stout, "**courtesy of Mother Company,**" set up a couple of large screens, and show racing movies. In the estimation of the Mistral group, the Axthel people came across a little stiff, but got a little better after "**we talked them out of their ties and into a few beers.**" In any case, they talked about how they would build the new Phenix cars. Mistral people made no bones about their preferences, which would be to build the vehicles utilizing teams around key component clusters. This way the workers would be responsible for quality, learn all the jobs, and avoid boredom by rotating.

The Mistral people were adamant: "**There is no way you are going to see our people here chasing a chassis on a conveyor. They like to work on something until it's right. I don't know how they are going to resolve this difference in philosophy.**" Disagreement also surfaced regarding the specialty car-upgrading work. The Mistral people admitted that their counterparts were right that Mistral didn't make much money from this activity. However, they said it was worthwhile because the employees got their hands on the new Mercedes, BMWs, and the like, and they learned a lot about new technology while trying to make the cars go even faster. Besides, a lot of these cars were brought to Mistral by the same people who commission the race cars. Also, once out on the street, everybody can tell a Mistral-customized car; it is a rolling advertisement for the company.

Looking at the Phenix venture, the Mistral people recognized the necessity "to get our act together soon. It is obvious that some things will have to change, and everybody knows it." They felt the decisions should be made soon, because they didn't want people to get too nervous about the upcoming changes. The sooner the details were worked out and announced to the people, the better chance to hold on to the "good guys."

Issues Explored After the Diagnosis

Part of the diagnostic process was an examination of the major issues facing the new venture. Accordingly, the diagnostic team presented management with a list of questions that needed to be addressed prior to any formal action to establish a new organization.

1. With the establishment of Phenix S. A., should the identities of Axthel and Mistral Racing be maintained?
2. Should existing products on both sides continue to be produced, in order not to lose the present customer base, or should they be phased out so that efforts and resources can be concentrated on producing the new Phenix line of high-performance automobiles within one year?
3. What should the Phenix identity be? What market segment should it address?
4. How will design of the new Phenix line be approached? Will former Mistral people develop the power train and former Axthel people the chassis and body? Should this be a joint effort? Should there be separate or joint project teams?
5. How will the Phenix line be manufactured? Should it be mass produced using Axthel's know-how and experience? Or should production methods be influenced by the way Mistral does things? Either way, is the product likely to meet the demands of the marketplace, in terms of quality and price?
6. Where should the Phenix line be built? It seems that the main manufacturing and assembly facilities will be at the Axthel facility on the Continent. Should Mistral people be relocated?
7. How will the labor union be handled? Is it likely to demand that Mistral people join? How will Mistral people react to the potential restrictions a union environment is likely to impose? How should these concerns be addressed?
8. The two corporate cultures—their similarities and differences—have been explored by the report. What bridges need to be built? How will the cultural differences be resolved?
9. A high-volume manufacturing process requires standardization and discipline. To the Axthel staff, such words mean order, predictability, no surprises. To the Mistral people, they mean boredom, routine, no imagination. How can these viewpoints be integrated?
10. It is inevitable that corporate staff groups be consolidated. These include finance, marketing, human resources, and research. How can this combining be accomplished with a minimum of trauma to the respective organizations?

Subsequent work involved the development of strategies for achieving a systematic and effective physical merger of the two companies. The executives worked to make the new entity a strong, integrated organization focused on a common goal and able to retain and effectively utilize the best talents available in both companies. A matter of vital importance was the retention of key employees, both managers and technicians, whose contributions would be vital to the future welfare of Phenix.

Management was particularly concerned about the negative reaction by employees on both sides at the announcement of the merger. Since the two companies were significantly different in their history, corporate culture, and product orientation, swift and decisive action was necessary to minimize speculation and fear.

Summaries of interviews conducted with key employees on both sides were used as a base for the planning. The diagnosis sensitized management to certain considerations regarding the change in organization:

1. A merger is a difficult, perilous task that carries with it significant uncertainty of success, because it attempts to introduce a new order.
2. Any planned or unplanned alteration of the status quo affects the structure, technology, and human resources of the total organization.
3. Failure to manage major change in an organization can result in its people feeling pain and frustration and exhibiting behaviors such as blaming others for a problem, forming subgroups, reacting contrary to data they possess, and acting differently outside the organization.
4. Radical change generally causes an organization to go through several stages, specifically shock, depression and denial, defensive retreat, acknowledgment, and finally adaptation. There is no way to avoid these stages, but the transition from shock to adaptation can be shortened dramatically if proper action is taken by management.

The Phenix management wanted to avoid dysfunctional behavior among the people of both organizations, which could have been caused by lack of awareness of what is really going on and fantasies about negative consequences they think the change will bring. They also became aware of homeostatic factors in organization, which have a significant impact on resistance to change. These factors are a reluctance to admit weakness; awkwardness; fear of failure; bad past experience with change; and fear of personal, professional, and financial loss.

Management was particularly concerned with minimizing behavior by employees that could make it very difficult to achieve the synergy so necessary to the success of the new company. It established a program of communication in an effort to find ways to reduce conformity to norms; loyalty to vested interests and sacred cows; rejection of outsiders; inappropriate use of power; adherence to a win-lose psychology; and choice of "safe" goals instead of reaching for excellence.

Phenix executives particularly wanted to use sound change-management strategies to lessen resistance to the new organization. They took the following actions:

- Involved employees in the change effort
- Provided accurate and complete information to minimize speculation
- Let employees air their objections
- Acknowledged each group's norms in an effort to find a way to accommodate their different perspectives
- Made only necessary changes
- Provided for adequate motivation by addressing meaningful rewards
- Encouraged the cementing of relationships, stressing the importance of every individual and team and each's involvement in decision making

Summary

A diagnosis employed *before* an organizational merger or acquisition has been officially consummated can help address the following issues:

1. *Diversification.* If the intent is on adding complementary capabilities or access to related markets, will the new business fit with the organization and will it be able to manage it?
2. *Changes in competitive strategy.* To what extent will the new strategy fit with the organization's assets and capabilities? Will the acquired organization indeed enable the execution of the new strategy? How soon and by what means?
3. *Rapid growth.* How can management keep what is good and valuable about the organization? What should be changed, especially if management is going to combine forces with another company that has its own culture and way of doing things?
4. *Potential for serious conflict between major groups in the merged company.* What aspects of the respective cultures or subcultures could lead to conflicts? How would a broader corporate culture help resolve these differences?
5. *Retrenchment.* What parts of the planned organization are likely to no longer be viable? How can they be downsized humanely? How can the company preserve its assets while retrenching?

A diagnosis employed *after* consummation of a merger or acquisition can help address the following issues:

Feelings of the employees. Employees on both sides are likely to resent being sold as a commodity. To a certain extent, such an event violates their past expectations, because they may feel that they chose to work for a specific organization that no longer exists. They may create negative fantasies about their lack of knowledge of the other organization, and they are likely to be very much aware of the possibility of consolidation and downsizing. Left untreated, there is the potential for conflict and hostility. A diagnosis soon after merger can bring all these concerns to the surface, and suggest immediate action and communication to maintain morale and retain the best employees.

Acceptance of the merger. People need to understand the reasons for the merger, and recognize that they may gain from such a union. Why did the merger take place? Will this result in the creation of one new, single organization, or will they be able to retain their identity and a certain measure of autonomy? What is the plan for the future? A diagnosis, especially if done through interviews, will reveal the most troublesome questions in the minds of the employees, and help prepare a communication campaign to address such concerns.

History of the respective organizations. A study of company history, which is also effective if conducted prior to a merger, can help explore serious questions such as, Can the respective cultures indeed be meshed? What are the strengths and weaknesses of these cultures? What makes each individual and unique? To what extent are they likely to resist combination with each other?

Respective autonomy. If indeed changes are to be made in administration, personnel practices, benefits, and compensation systems to include converting retirement plans, a diagnosis can help determine as soon as possible how such changes can be carried out with as little trauma as possible.

Performance evaluation. Invariably, each merged organization will have its own method of appraising performance. A single system needs to be developed immediately, but it cannot be done arbitrarily because of the resentment that could cause. A diagnosis can help management study the relevant criteria for performance in the new organization, and recommend a synergistic system appropriate to the new situation.

Career considerations. In a merger, people fear for their jobs, but the best of them have options and they are likely to jump first and ask questions later. A diagnosis can help evaluate who these valuable people are and determine what career opportunities will be created in the new structure. This can enable retention of high-potential people by helping them see what opportunities lie ahead.

Knowledge transfer. Who can teach what to whom? How will this knowledge help both parties? Since a merger implies the desirability of a technology exchange, how can such an exchange take place as soon as possible and in the most constructive and synergistic manner feasible? A diagnosis can help identify who can teach whom, thus leveraging technology around key skilled individuals who are then able to develop their teams.

Adherence to broad corporate policy. Even if the intent is to have the merged units operate as independently as possible, it will be necessary that they comply with broad corporate policies. A diagnosis can help define exactly what policies should be developed, for what purpose, and how they need to be administered.

Marketing. What will the new products be when the capabilities of the merged companies are put to the test? Will marketing be combined or separated? Will the above factors help or inhibit the market's perception and willingness to buy? A diagnosis can help test assumptions about the probable acceptability of the new company's products.

Crisis Intervention

A merger is a threat to people in the system, no matter what the corporate propaganda says. Employees know that this change is no longer business as usual, and that sooner or later they will be affected. A lot of time will be spent worrying about what might happen, with resultant negative effects on productivity. A diagnosis can be a vehicle for preventing such problems by analyzing at the beginning what is likely to happen and thus providing management with the opportunity to develop programs, procedures, and communications that significantly improve the chances of a successful merger.

Diagnosis to Analyze Problems in Diversification Strategy

Development of an organization's grand strategy requires the concerted efforts of many people who are able to view the present capabilities of the company with an eye to development for the future. When it comes to implementing strategy, it is not unusual for the process to break down. Perfectly sensible plans don't seem to work in practice, or they may be misapplied.

Whenever strategic initiatives fail, the consequences can be disastrous, and management may not always be able to tell exactly what caused the failure.

The following case illustrates how a diagnosis that focuses on strategy development can help in examining what has happened and why. The study was conducted at the request of the chief executive officer by a team of managers from various units of the corporation. The team spent approximately one month gathering data, primarily by interviewing a representative sample of employees at all levels in most operating units. They also interviewed several outsiders, primarily bankers and members of brokerage firms. The team then spent a month analyzing the results. The following is a summary of the report that was prepared for management.

CASE: POWER ENGINEERING COMPANY

Background

In reviewing the situation presently facing the company, we recognized the importance of our heritage as an organization, not only with respect to the culture it has spawned, but also the effect that historical actions continue to have on present management practices. We would like to briefly review a chronology of events from the founding of the company to the present, because it helps explain our condition today.

Power Engineering Company (PEC) is an eighty-year-old enterprise that has specialized in manufacturing boilers, reactors, control instruments, and simulators for power plants. In the 1970s, its operations had spread to providing equipment to utilities in many areas of the world, including breakthrough contracts to supply boiling water reactors (BWR) to Taiwan, Korea, and the Philippines. However, the bulk of its income came from the domestic market, where PEC was regarded as a highly competent and responsive vendor by its client utilities.

PEC was also known as an exceptionally good employer whose policies included very competitive salaries and benefits, promotion from within, and maintenance of full employment by carefully scheduling its work to minimize swings in personnel demand. In the occasional slow periods, employees who were temporarily off the direct production process were assigned to overhead "development groups," task forces charged with review and improvement of specifications and procedures. The respondents feel, and so do we, that over the years such efforts were responsible for the high degree of technical expertise in the company and the resultant high quality of its boilers, reactors, and related product line. Moreover, the company, being one of the largest employers in the town, is a bulwark of community support; it not only donates significant sums to improve the quality of life in the community, but also encourages its employees to become active in civic matters. PEC employees are very supportive of their employer, and exhibit a high degree of pride at being part of a first-class organization.

In the late 1970s, PEC found itself with significant cash reserves, owing to consistently high earning for the past few years. Management took this opportunity to acquire several companies, some in related businesses such as specialized tool manufacturers, others in industries such as oil and gas exploration, marine mechanical services, and even a logging mill. The bulk of its holdings, however, focused on servicing the needs of electric utilities, particularly on the nuclear side.

Having been consistently successful appears to have promoted a feeling of complacency, so that management neglected to take into account the impact of serious changes in the business environment caused by:

- The Three Mile Island incident, the lack of understanding by the public, the frenzied fanning of public fears by the press, the jumping on the bandwagon by local and national politicians, and the hardening of NRC policies.
- The increasing strength of environmental groups, relatively few in numbers but highly vocal and politically active, which were hostile not only to nuclear power but also to perceived pollution by fossil power and the oil exploration industry.
- The oil crises brought on by OPEC since 1974, and the consequent significant jump in oil prices, not to mention the prospect of long-term price and supply instability resulting from strife and lack of cohesion in Middle Eastern countries and the OPEC cartel.
- The weak, uncoordinated, underfunded, and predictably ineffective public-relations efforts of the energy industry in general, which mistakenly hoped that its problems with public perception would eventually blow away.
- The inroads in international markets made by German, French, and Canadian manufacturers of boilers and nuclear reactors, not to mention Japanese turbine and heavy-equipment manufacturers. These companies were also fully supported by their national government, whereas the U.S. government burdened the domestic industry with

regulations, restrictions, and tax policies that made it more difficult to deal with an increasingly tough and cynical international market.

We all know that PEC's problems started to surface in 1985, when most of senior management retired without having provided for adequate succession. A pioneer in the industry, PEC historically did not have to sell very hard, and as a consequence, developed its managers to be strong in the technical areas. It is also fair to say that PEC's management did not encourage much of a marketing orientation, and was particularly neglectful of bringing up a new generation of managers attuned to the realities of a tougher environment. According to records and discussions with respondents, the board felt that there were no candidates for the job of president who met these qualifications, and brought in an experienced executive, Mr. Peter Gold, to head the company. Mr. Gold came from a large, international CPA and consulting firm, and was chosen primarily because of his financial expertise, which the board felt would benefit a company in transition.

As the new president, Mr. Gold made some immediate changes. He established a strategic planning group reporting directly to him. He brought in a personal friend and associate, with whom he had worked well for years, as his deputy with the title of executive vice president. Over a period of one year, Mr. Gold gradually replaced over half the major departmental heads with outside executives. He then proceeded to put into place an ambitious program of divestiture and acquisition in an attempt to achieve a better portfolio of businesses that would help the company weather the business cycles of various industries.

The acquisition program proceeded much faster than the plans for divestiture of unwanted businesses. Over a period of two years, PEC acquired several companies unrelated to the power business, ranging from computer software developers to department stores. To ensure proper corporate control, Mr. Gold replaced key executives in each acquired company with hand-picked, financially oriented managers.

On the other hand, the planned program of divestiture for some of the unwanted businesses, most of them in the oil and gas and petrochemical-service industry, was a complete failure. There just weren't any buyers in a market full of competent firms and not enough work to go around. The business environment for the energy-service industry had collapsed. No new power plants and refineries were being built in the United States, and foreign competition was cornering what was left of the international market. Since the U.S. nuclear industry was unable to build new facilities, it started to rapidly fall behind in technology, as compared to the foreign firms. Owing to these factors, most mainline businesses of PEC started to lose money in 1985.

The situation was made worse when new acquisitions meant to produce cash to replace the declining business units in general did not work out. The managers PEC imposed on its new subsidiaries, according to many respondents, **"used a bean-counter mentality on businesses they didn't understand, with the disastrous effect of causing the departure of these companies' most talented people who went to the competition and clobbered**

us." This acquisition program was generally regarded as such a disaster that its architect, the executive vice president, was dismissed under fire. Many respondents suggested that he was a scapegoat, because he was only responsible for arranging the acquisitions and not for running them in the manner prescribed by Mr. Gold himself.

Responses From Management

The old-line employees of PEC were upset with what happened to the company, and exhibited signs of significant frustration at their inability to control what appeared to be a runaway situation. They particularly resented a fundamental change in the way employees were treated. They recall that in previous years there was a sense of family, of being in touch with a management that spent a lot of time talking to the employees and, even more important, listening to them. The new management was perceived to be more interested in strategic issues and grandiose expansion programs, and was accused by the employees of treating them like minor cogs on a big wheel.

Most of these employees blamed the existing management for the company's problems, and were highly critical of the acquisition program, which they perceived as contributing to the company's ruin. **"We should have stuck to our knitting,"** they said. **"Dealing with things we don't know drains us of the energy we need to fight the problems facing our mainline business."** They felt that the "losers" that were acquired only squandered the company's money; they not only failed to contribute but actually drained whatever resources were left. This attitude of PEC managers and employees had never been a secret, since they took every opportunity to express their views and suggest in the strongest terms that the new companies be dumped so that no more good money was thrown after bad to salvage a poor investment.

For their side, people at the recently acquired companies were just as vocal. Their alternative suggestion was that the old-line, moribund, and no longer viable energy-service businesses be the ones to be cut, because there was no prospect of keeping those people gainfully employed until new refineries, chemical plants, and power plants started to be built, and that was not going to happen until the year 2000. They felt their own businesses being wrecked by managers imposed on them by the parent company, and these new managers did not understand their corporate cultures and knew nothing about their industries. They believed that PEC bled them to death in order to keep the price of the stock up, by meeting the quarterly dividends out of operating funds instead of nonexisting profits and retained earnings. This, they perceived, was done to avert a takeover and save the cushy jobs at headquarters. In addition, they resented PEC's reluctance to invest in capital projects, which could have made the difference between their companies' survival or oblivion. The favorite slogan directed against PEC management by the subsidiaries was, **"They know the price of everything and the value of nothing."**

The suspicion and defensiveness appeared to be so acute that managers of the various units started to view with extreme skepticism any legitimate venture that involved more than one PEC unit, fully expecting that the other department or company would attempt to take the lion's share of the profits.

There was a general feeling that, if left alone, each unit could take care of itself. As a result, resistance to virtually any new directions from corporate management intensified, even when the corporate marketing group communicated legitimate business opportunities for some of the subsidiaries. Just the fact that the leads came from corporate headquarters was reason enough to suspect that **"they were up to something."** Several of the companies openly criticized the marketing group's failure to produce much new business; some of the most powerful top managers took matters into their own hands and dispatched their own executives to see potential clients in order to solicit business. This created new problems, because without central coordination, the clients were visited by several PEC units competing with each other for business.

The clients started to be irritated about having their time wasted by redundant calls by PEC people, and became even more incensed when they found out how difficult it was to complain, because things were allegedly so fragmented that it was rare for any executive to have authority over more than a few diverse units.

Even though some top PEC executives felt under siege, many of the older executives were somewhat optimistic, feeling that the situation was bound to change, because sooner or later the government, if no one else, would have to deal with the upcoming energy crisis. This group believed that it still had a good company, and that the job at hand was to **"batten down the hatches, lower the sails, and wait for the storm to pass."** Thus it directed the reinstatement of an austerity program and issued new procedures that controlled budget expenditures all the way to the top.

Some younger executives felt that all this was only a denial—that the company was not just going through a difficult period, but was facing fundamental changes in its business environment that would force it to do things significantly different in order to survive.

For the first time in PEC's history, people stated that the unthinkable had to be faced. Severe downsizing actions might be necessary, including layoffs, curtailment in operations, and in some cases, closing down businesses outright.

Recommendations

1. Review the report with all key executives in the various companies.
2. Ask each of the above to provide his or her own succinct diagnosis of what the problems are.
3. Jointly decide on specific actions that have to be taken to ensure the survival of the company.
4. Prepare a specific plan for communicating changes to the employees, along with a plan for obtaining employee cooperation and commitment to making the changes happen.

This diagnostic report was designed to provide management with an unbiased survey of people's feelings and perceptions regarding the effects of the strategic initiatives. Subsequent to the report, management made significant decisions that led to downsizing and restructuring, including writing down significant assets that could not be utilized or sold. It is presently working on establishing a closer and mutually supportive relationship among the remaining units by restoring much of their former independence.

Diagnosis in Team Building

A significant part of the work done in organizations is performed by small work groups and teams that have been established to control and direct activities, solve problems, or develop products. In theory, work groups and teams are able to:

1. Plan and carry out their work in a way that is appropriate to the task.
2. Distribute work among the members in a way that is equitable and draws optimally on their individual capabilities.
3. Notice and take care of both individual and group needs.
4. Cope with crisis and conflict in a way that promotes the mission of the group while maintaining morale.

Organizational development consultants who study work groups have found that such groups evolve through specific sequential phases, creating social structures within the formal structure that allow them to meet their needs and work effectively. In this evolution, certain leadership roles emerge in the group to carry out crucial aspects of developmental process. Working systematically with these groups and task forces to improve their interaction and achieve synergy is called "team building," particularly when a facilitator is used.

Team-building techniques are further categorized, depending on the composition of the team. They include:

- *Family-group teams*—composed of a supervisor and his or her direct subordinates.
- *Functional teams*—composed of people with the same job or function but from different departments or divisions, who come together to plan or solve problems of common concern.
- *Project teams*—composed of key technical personnel assigned to a project on a relatively temporary basis, generally under a matrix structure. This kind of group generally is led by a project manager.
- *Intergroups*—two or more discrete teams that get together to address issues or concerns that affect them both.

All of these interventions are dependent on an initial diagnosis, which helps determine the nature of the facilitating process required to deal effectively with the situation confronting the team. The balance of this chapter covers how diagnostic techniques are used to help such teams deal effectively with the issues and problems normally encountered in these settings. Since the process is similar, regardless of the team's composition, we will cover only family group and project teams.

Family-Group Team Building

Family-group teams, as noted earlier, generally involve a manager and his or her immediate subordinates. When a diagnosis is done, a preliminary step to team building takes place, and issues raised and subsequent work usually occur in the following areas:

- Mission of the department
- Individual roles and responsibilities
- Timing and control of work
- Communications
- Conflict
- Morale

The best way to understand how such a project is conducted is to review an actual case in the financial industry. The following is an example of a diagnostic project with the objective of helping a vice president create a better level of teamwork among his managers. Following a week of interviewing, a diagnosis was written and was subsequently used as the data base for the team-building session that followed.

CASE: FINANCIAL BANK—WHOLESALE COMPUTER-SYSTEMS DEPARTMENT

Background

This project was initiated at the request of the vice president of a computer-systems group responsible for supporting wholesale banking operations. The decision to use internal human resources people with facilitating skills was made by the vice president after a lunch at which all parties got acquainted and discussed how the project would be executed.

The purpose of the project was to determine the organizational effectiveness of the bank's Wholesale Systems and Planning Department, particularly in relation to its plans to establish a matrix organization.

The personnel involved in this project were the vice president himself, his direct reports, and several staff members reporting to his office.

On the scheduled day, two external consultants and the internal OD person conducted individual, unstructured interviews with each of the participants. The interviews each lasted less than an hour and focused on the individuals' perception of issues likely to influence the department's effectiveness and implementation of a planned matrix organization for the group.

During the interviews, comments were recorded as accurately as possible.

The comments formed the data base from which the analysis and recommendations of the report were developed. Typical quotes were as follows:

> "We are going through the pains of change. The department is getting larger and more interdependent, and communication is more critical than ever."

> "The corporate computer network is being defined in isolation."

> "A significant staffing problem in the overall systems and planning groups has to do with management depth. Because of fast growth, many good people moved up, and not enough qualified people were available to replace them."

> "The current ratio of consultants (programmers) should be reduced to enable the permanent staff to gain better systems familiarity and to improve morale."

> "Wholesale Systems and Planning made a mistake in considering the International Department as just a wholesale banking business instead of treating its computing needs on a separate, dedicated basis. This should have been done, because International consumes 50 percent of our data processing capacity."

The following is a partial reproduction of the report that was submitted to the vice president and his staff.

The Challenge of Change

Change was seen by the respondents as a key element having an impact on the entire bank. Comments focused on two issues: the increasing sophistication of the systems and applications, and the continuing decentralization of the data-processing function itself. The participants were very much aware of the "growing pains of change." They observed that the department was getting larger and more interdependent, necessitating more effective communication at all levels. This was perceived as particularly important, because in the past **"there used to be little interface among groups."** Even though the decentralization of data-processing centers was perceived as a potential operational improvement, concerns were expressed that all the benefits claimed might not necessarily be realized.

Computer Resource Constraints

In this area, respondents perceived five basic issues. First, inadequate funds limit acquisition of equipment to do the job. Second, there are interface problems owing to some equipment kept in the wholesale fund-transfer system area. (These complaints revolve around the cumbersome process of budget approval when additional hardware is needed by the cash-management systems, thus delaying acquisition of needed equipment.) Third, the recently resolved episode regarding past arguments and negotiations with the hardware manufacturer is blamed for the bank's inability to update the operating system for one and a half years. The need to incorporate at least 1,000 software changes into the system to make it work is viewed as a further complication. This episode is also responsible for its present inability to use the powerful new operating system recently installed for anything other than test runs, owing to a lack of updated software. Fourth, there is a lack of direction in the wholesale computer facility technical-support area. Fifth, the corporate network is being defined in isolation.

Inadequacy of Human Resources

Significant inadequacies in the quality of human resources in the data-processing groups have been stressed by the respondents. These inadequacies are allegedly manifested in a scarcity of people fully qualified to deal with applications presently being implemented and a need for additional training of new employees before they become productive, owing to high turnover.

Scarcity of data-processing personnel within the organization is quoted as "the biggest problem." This results in "**not having enough help to complete the work on time and within budget.**" The problem is further intensified by the relatively high turnover in the organization, attributed in part to the national scarcity of data-processing people in general. The inability of the organization to acquire as many data-processing people as it would like is further attributed to two factors. First, there is a perceived inadequacy in the current salary structure, even with the acknowledgement that salary ranges have been adjusted upward along with raises for the existing staff: "**This has helped somewhat in recruiting, but we still are dealing with a competitive environment.**" Second, it was felt that personnel familiar with the bank's computer equipment were difficult to find. The planned switch to IBM equipment was perceived as a potentially favorable move.

There are also concerns regarding management depth in the overall Wholesale Systems and Planning Group, generally attributed to fast growth, which enables many good people to move up but does not allow for the timely development of new people to replace them. This general weakness in terms of skills and experience is observed at the project-manager and group-manager level. Further concerns exist regarding a clear trend for technical people wanting to become project managers, even though they may not be at all suited to that position. If allowed to continue, this trend may further weaken the technical capability of the group. A significant shortcoming that needs to be addressed is the perception that a lack of training exists in the area of managing people. Staff upgrading is perceived to be constrained by the existence of "dead wood," which reportedly is virtually impossible to clean out under current personnel policies and practices.

Use of Consultants

Concerns were expressed regarding the utilization and handling of both domestic consultants and foreign nationals under contract. Issues common to both categories of personnel indicate a "demoralizing" of the permanent staff and a weakening of system familiarity because of frequently changing consultants. Difficulties arising in the use of foreign workers point to a need for additional training to make them effective, and to resolving the very cumbersome and complex administration, which the human resources department is apparently unable to deal with satisfactorily.

Additional Topics

The remainder of the diagnosis covered the following areas:

- Administrative support
- User relationships
- The Wholesale Systems and Planning Group itself:
  — General perceptions of the people themselves
  — Concerns with accountability
  — Key staff relationships
  — Reward systems and growth within the organization
  — The planning process
  — Project management
- Perceptions of the matrix organization
- Communications
- Diagnostic observations
- Recommendations

The interviewers, in a thorough report, noted that a great degree of anxiety originated from people's perceptions of the restraints and ambiguity a matrix organization would impose. As a result, in its diagnostic observations section, the report treated in detail the pros and cons of such a structure.

Recommendations

The recommendations were as follows:

1. Distribute the report to all respondents and other key people at an equivalent level, and announce management's intention to follow up on the consultants' recommendations.
2. Hold a two-day feedback session with the area managers. At this session, one half-day will be spent reviewing the report in detail and discussing key issues of concern to the group. The rest of the day will be utilized to train the participants in the details of operating in a matrix organization. The second day will be spent entirely on finalizing development of the project coordinator/project manager role, along with specifying roles and relationships, interfaces, and problem-solving mechanisms.
3. Hold a training session with key staff including project managers and project coordinators to review the substance of the report, as well as matrix theory, roles, relationships, interfaces, and problem-solving

mechanisms developed by the area managers at the previous session. Feedback from the participants should also be solicited.
4. Hold a meeting with area managers, project coordinators, project managers, and other key staff as appropriate, to develop a strategy and procedures for dealing with constraints and concerns external to the wholesale group.

Following a review of the recommendations, all were implemented. Internal facilitators continued to provide the necessary support.

Project Team Building

The following case study illustrates how a project manager, with the assistance of trained human resources professionals, can develop and enhance a project team by addressing the stages of team formation from undeveloped through mature. Activities include establishing an environment necessary for group formation, clarifying the goals and roles, dealing with mutual expectations and concerns, and addressing difficulties of matrix organizations.

CASE: WESTERN POWER COMPANY FAR HILLS UNIT 3 PROJECT

Background

The Far Hills Unit 3 Project is a nuclear power plant into its ninth year of design and construction. It is located in a relatively remote area sixty-five miles from the utility's headquarters. Most of the engineering and design work was done by an integrated team involving the utility's own engineering staff, supplemented by a group provided by the engineer-constructor as a principal contractor. The company also maintained a relatively small site-engineering group responsible for supporting the construction effort and for coordinating with quality-assurance people at the plant site.

As often happens, a project of this magnitude is extremely difficult to manage. The theoretical feasibility of effectively integrating proper design, engineering, construction, and startup with a comprehensive schedule based on predetermined budgets is invariably countered with the reality, perhaps the inevitability, of work falling short of objectives and missing milestones when equipment fails to arrive on site when scheduled, or the inevitable labor and public relations problems develop. Not surprisingly, the project demanded the customary sacrificial lambs, in the form of mass replacement of project-management staff and key-discipline engineering and construction personnel—once in the middle of the project and, more recently, about two months before the consultants were asked to help. A year before, the company installed a new resource-constrained, comprehensive planning, scheduling, and cost control system. Implementing the system at this advantageous stage of the project had been difficult, but management felt that it was essential to finally track what was going on and what needed to be done.

Goals and Objectives

The overall goal of the project team was to plan, organize, and manage the project such that cost, schedule, and quality performance clearly exceeded the industry norm. Major areas of project management have emphasized:

1. Establish and motivate the project team at the site and at the home office. Promote and ensure clear and timely communications between the construction group at the site and the support departments at the home office. Encourage team building.
2. Establish a mutually supportive relationship with the contractors.
3. Establish, integrate, and follow up on the most aggressive credible work schedules for all areas of the project.
4. Obtain necessary licenses and permits.
5. Control unplanned work on the project and resolve claims with the contractors, such that the cost efficiency of the project consistently increases.

The Project Manager

R. K. (Bob) Jones, the new project manager, had previously operated out of the home office as an assistant project manager. This was in order to be involved with the engineering and design aspects. Now that the construction stage of the project had advanced, Bob, as newly appointed manager, relocated to the construction site; as a consequence, he became actively involved with construction management, including organization, staffing, and discretionary participation in problem or high-potential-payoff areas.

Essentially all project-management goals and activities were accomplished through people. A project of the magnitude, duration, and changing conditions of Far Hills Unit 3 required capable, experienced, and highly motivated individuals in key leadership positions on the project team, and cohesiveness in project operations. With few exceptions, such individuals are by nature aggressive and ambitious, with substantial needs for recognition and self-fulfillment. Establishing and integrating a leadership team of such individuals, and maintaining growth and continuity of such personnel on the project, was directly influenced by the style of project management.

Bob subscribed to the approach of influencing (and learning) through interpersonal communication, rather than by directing the performance of key leaders on the team. In reality, the magnitude and pace of the project made it challenging for any individual to do more than establish broad goals, maintain relevant knowledge, and selectively influence those areas of the project where an investment of time had a cost-effective payoff in project performance. This meant that day-to-day operation of the project had to be organized and staffed to proceed without mandatory operational involvement on the part of the project manager. To effectively achieve this goal, the key members of the project team must feel fully responsible, authorized, respected, and expected to manage their areas of the project.

In spite of sincere attempts to operate as described above, the project still faced significant problems not atypical of the latter stages of design and construction. To deal with the various issues and problems in an efficient fashion, Bob Jones asked key members of the project team to participate in a team-building session.

On December 15, 1986, the new project manager issued a memorandum to key members of the project team, announcing the scheduling of a team-building session "to explore ways in which we can make our work as a team even more effective.... As an outgrowth of this meeting," the memo stated, "attendees will be expected to follow up with team-building sessions of their own with their respective teams at the site or at the home office."

The Diagnosis Process

Prior to the team-building meeting, internal human resources professionals interviewed each participating member of the team. The interviews focused on two basic questions:

1. What are your expectations for this meeting?
2. What specific issues affecting your work and the work of the team would you like to see discussed at this meeting?

The data obtained from the interviews were then grouped into major preliminary categories, indicating the general source of the comments. A data base was prepared that presented a compilation of the interview data arranged into source categories, some of which were further broken down to allow for more detailed differentiation. The interview data clearly reflected the pressures, concerns, and problems encountered by the project team, which was trying to meet a very tight project schedule. Some respondents characterized the schedule as "impossible" and "totally unreasonable." Quotations from project-team members were transcribed as closely as possible to the way in which they were related. No attempt was made to identify the respondents, other than to categorize the source by the departments to which the people were assigned. The comments that made up the data base took up twenty-four pages.

Using the direct quotes obtained in the interviews, the facilitators prepared a short summary intended for use during the upcoming team-building meeting. Whereas the data base itself was arranged merely to indicate the general sources of the information, this summary provided a narrative based on major issues. To reinforce the immediacy of the issues, as expressed by the respondents, the facilitators made liberal use of quotes from the data base. The following are excerpts from the diagnosis:

Summary of Issues and Perceptions

The interview data reflected problems and difficulties created as the focus of the project moved toward startup activities and Central Engineering phase-out. Communication remains problematic, with the emerging role of Site Engineering as a point of contention with most individuals surveyed. The following issues have been mentioned as key to the present functioning of the project team:

Central Engineering phase-out. The rapid completion of major engineering tasks at the home office seems to have created some communication problems—in particular, concern over split responsibilities of key personnel. Most engineering drawings have been transferred to the site. However, **"Site Engineering cannot answer a lot of questions, and we are still dependent on key personnel at the home office, who are not always available."** Stated more succinctly: **"Nothing's wrong with the interface, but nobody is left at the home office."**

Those individuals who need home-office input feel that information flow from the site to the home office is **"still a gray area."** They feel that the **"flow of information should be more standardized."** For example, many state that the previously agreed upon procedure for implementing three-way telephone conversations is not taking place: **"Construction Engineering still asks Field and Central Engineering the same thing at the same time, then waits to see who does it first."**

There is a feeling that project management has **"encouraged using Central Engineering as a scapegoat."** The overriding concern is that **"now that Central will not be available, we'll start pointing fingers at each other."** The situation as expressed by the project team suggests that the emerging relationships between Field Engineering and the construction group should be a priority concern.

Startup activities. The project as a whole seems to have experienced difficulty in making a transition from active construction to startup activities that may reflect new priorities. As indicated by one project member, **"The startup operation pushes hard on its priorities. Sometimes, it conflicts with the requirements and priorities of the major construction effort."**

Many individuals seem to be giving little credence to startup at all: "Up to now, startup has been primarily finger-pointing." "The schedule date [for startup] is extremely optimistic. We have been given a date because of politics."

As stated by another project member, **"an overriding task facing the project is to re-orient people to think of startup dates as a reality, rather than engage in 'fire-fighting,' which has been going on for so long."**

The remainder of the diagnostic report was written in a similar fashion, addressing the following problem areas:

- Communication
- Project-team management
- Field Engineering, particularly its relationship and interaction with Construction Engineering, the construction group itself, as well as its own internal dynamics
- Planning and scheduling
- Maintenance of the project schedule
- Morale

The diagnosis was then discussed with the project manager and a few key project personnel. The team-building session was then scheduled.

The Team-Building Session

Once the key members of the project team were assembled, they were given an opportunity to examine how they work together and to find ways to maximize their effectiveness as a team.

Following a brief introduction to the concept and purpose of team building, the group was given a problem-solving exercise. The purpose of this exercise was to highlight the differences between facts and perceptions, and to point out actions required of the group to overcome those differences when engaged in a problem-solving mode.

The data previously compiled by the facilitators was then distributed to the participants in a data-feedback session. This was done in order to:

1. Present a summary of problems or issues that seem to influence the effectiveness of the project team
2. Gain a common understanding of these problems and issues
3. Arrange the issues in order of priority and importance to the team members
4. Determine, as a team, who will address the issues and problems, and when

Questions resulting in further clarification and understanding of the issues were encouraged and considered. The project team was divided into three groups and asked to: (1) indicate their feeling about this team-building activity, (2) identify any other issues that had not been addressed by the data base, and (3) rank the issues in order of priority.

The team then proceeded with the discussion and developed a ranking of issues in order of priority, as follows:

- Communications
- Interfaces among groups
- Last-minute design changes
- Project personnel turnover
- Paperwork
- Insufficient resources

It was acknowledged that the interface relationships among various groups in the project team were central to the team's ability to function effectively. If those relationships were to be improved, many other issues would be of less concern, because the team would be able to deal with the issues more effectively. Following receipt of the report of this meeting prepared by the facilitators, the project team agreed to:

1. Have representatives of the various disciplines participate in an intergroup team-building session.

2. Establish action committees to work toward resolution of each prioritized issue.
3. Establish special committees to investigate how to balance the project schedule with high quality standards.

Following the initial meeting, several sessions took place during which the team hammered out solutions to the various issues. Resulting agreements and commitments were put into writing.

One of the most useful aspects of this type of intervention is the documentation and follow-up that ensue. With today's technology, it is easy to keep track of commitments by preparing status sheets on a word processor.

This case illustrates how a properly conducted diagnosis, which essentially feeds data back to the principals themselves, enables a work group to acknowledge the existence of problems and issues. Since the data are provided by the principals themselves, they have inherent credibility. And since the facts are made public, they demand resolution. The rest of the work is essentially aimed at guiding the people to work on their problems in collaboration. It can be argued that the job would have been accomplished in any case, but it must be recognized that a properly conducted diagnosis can greatly enhance the problem-solving ability of a project team.

CHAPTER 12

Conclusion: Issues and Problems of Organizational Diagnosis

An organizational diagnosis is a powerful process that carries significant implications about how a company develops, how it has been managed in the past and is managed in the present, and what its likely prospects are for the future. The process itself requires time, resources, and perseverance. Its successful application must take into account the possibility of hitting several obstacles, which need to be recognized at the outset.

Predictable Problems in Diagnostic Projects

Management Resistance

Contemplating the possible benefits of an organizational diagnosis is one thing. Actually being allowed to begin one and successfully executing it are entirely different matters. Several difficulties stand in the way. In particular, getting management to agree to a diagnosis is difficult for the following reasons:

1. *Lack of understanding.* Since a diagnosis is a relatively new technique, it is likely that top management may not be aware of what it is and the potential benefits it could generate.
2. *Apprehension and defensiveness.* Even the most powerful executives become apprehensive when faced with serious scrutiny of their operation, especially if they have been associated with it for a long time. They also become defensive whenever something wrong is found, and are likely to rationalize and even defend past actions to the extent of denying that the problem exists at all.
3. *Perception of postponing action.* A manager who favors a "bias for action" may be skeptical of any process that takes time and does not

promise immediate results. Often, he or she is after a quick solution to the problems and is likely to resist a long-term commitment, especially if the process requires time and resources.

System Resistance

Even if a diagnosis is authorized, several problems remain. For example, people may not be as available as they should be, sometimes because of time pressures, other times because they would rather not be associated with someone who asks a lot of questions.

The biggest problem is the phenomenon of unconscious hostility toward the project leader. When someone is hired to do a job he or she assumes that the employer wants the employee or contractor to be successful. This is not necessarily so in a diagnosis. It is not unusual for the manager who commissions a diagnosis to become an obstacle in the way of its successful conclusion. This is manifested in resistance to accepting facts and rationalization and justifications of past actions. We have seen how this leads to a feeling of dependence, which Harry Levinson calls "transference." Further feelings of inadequacy and guilt stem from the fact that had the manager managed "correctly" in the first place, it would not have been necessary to conduct a diagnosis.

Conditions for Success

The following is a summary of considerations that must be taken into account when conducting a comprehensive diagnosis.

1. As discussed in Chapter 2, for a remedial diagnosis, there must be sufficient "pain" in the system to generate enough incentive to engage in a comprehensive self-examination, which may lead to significant change. In most cases, without such pain it is highly unlikely that a diagnosis will be authorized in the first place.
2. In a developmental diagnosis, there must be at least one individual or group with sufficient insight, ambition, perseverance, or forbearance to see the significant benefits a diagnosis can provide, particularly if the company is contemplating growth, diversification, or acquisition. To initiate a diagnosis, such individuals must have sufficient power and authority to persuade others in the organization to go along with the project.
3. Top management must be intimately involved in a project of this magnitude. The establishment of a council, to whom the diagnosticians are responsible, is virtually a necessity. Management must establish parameters and objectives for the diagnosis—in essence, expectations that define what kind of organization it wants the company to be.
4. The process of change must be data derived (through a diagnosis), with feedback to all members of the organization. Furthermore, the

diagnostic model must be based on the organization, not just outside research. This is why the organic approach, which collects data and perceptions from the organization's own members, is inherently and directly relevant to the company and its environment.

5. A diagnosis conducted by members of an organization has a better chance of producing valid data and of generating commitment to change. Furthermore, a diagnosis is a line-management responsibility. Consultants and staff people can help line managers do the job, but they cannot do it for them. The data, and the diagnosis that follows, are much more powerful if developed by an organization's own people. A side benefit is that diagnostic processes become part of how managers do their job.
6. By its very nature, a diagnosis promotes open communication, with confrontation of facts. Problems solving can be effective only if based on data. Furthermore, problems cannot be ignored, in the hope that they will go away.
7. A comprehensive organizational diagnosis must be a multigroup effort. It cannot be restricted to a department or unit within the organization if lasting effects are to be expected.
8. The diagnosis must have a systems orientation. It must be based on a sound approach, and it must take into account systems other than the human system.
9. A viable diagnostic effort requires commitment of time and resources.
10. Commitment to the diagnosis and the changes it generates must be developed. It is important to identify who should do the job. A critical mass has to be defined. This should be significant people with the power to hinder or facilitate the change process. Once these managers have been identified, a plan must be developed to obtain their commitment. Ideally, these managers should be involved in the diagnostic process, preferably as part of the diagnostic team itself. They must be people with the necessary clout to mobilize resources and keep the momentum going, people who have the respect of the present leadership as well as that of the change advocates, people with effective interpersonal skills. Involvement of these managers virtually ensures that the resulting recommendations will be seriously considered by management. Ignoring the advice of the critical mass is significantly more difficult than ignoring the advice of external consultants. Once these people have been identified and charged with the responsibility, they must be supported by management.

Conclusion

Organizations need to better understand how properly designed and conducted diagnostic efforts can be of significant value when problems must be identified and addressed. Moreover, the value of such techniques for organizational development is such that they might significantly improve the strategic planning process itself. It is hoped that this book has clearly explained how such diagnoses are designed and implemented. The use of a relatively simple, yet sophisticated method such as the organic diagnosis should be encouraged and eventually added to the standard repertory of management skills. These techniques can help managers develop data relevant to the issue in a timely and systematic manner, enabling them to think things through before committing to inappropriate action—or, worse, to no action at all.

Organizational diagnosis is a powerful technique that, when used in the proper context, generates new data and insights, often presenting management with options it may have not thought about before. A comprehensive diagnosis is also a galvanizing experience for everyone involved, since it forces people to talk and work with each other, to look for solutions jointly, and—just as important—to reaffirm what they have been doing right, thus confirming the most desirable aspects of an organization's culture while assuring that it remains open to new ideas.

PART VII
Appendixes

The three appendixes that follow offer some additional guidance in both practical and theoretical aspects of diagnosis. Appendix 1 consists of numerous forms, checklists, and sample reports that you and the other employees in your organization can use in developing your own diagnostic tools. Appendix 2 covers three different categories of methodologies that organizations have found useful in diagnosing problems. This appendix also describes the theories of various pioneers who have contributed to our understanding of diagnostic and intervention models. Appendix 3 provides an account of how I developed, conducted, and followed through on an organizational diagnosis at a specific company.

APPENDIX 1
Examples, Forms, and Checklists

Appendix 1 offers examples of actual components of diagnostic projects. In addition, several checklists and forms provide templates, which can be modified for your own use.

It is important to consider this appendix as a guide only. Review the various checklists, forms, and other instruments to gain a sense of how they are developed, but do not follow them slavishly. For example, a proposal for management should be developed with your own organization in mind. Use your data and incorporate your own writing style. The same holds true of the forms and checklists. A successful diagnosis depends on proper preparation. It is best to have these resources fully developed and available before you start interviewing.

Since organizational change and improvement, and the commitment that is necessary to make things happen, are dependent on communication with the employees and participation of all the key players in the organization, you are urged to involve as many people as you can in the development of these tools. This might slow you down, but ultimately the project will become much more meaningful, because the people who will be responsible for organizational improvement will have participated in the development of the diagnostic aids and tools. Such participation will not only reinforce the validity and credibility of the diagnosis, and the plans that will result from it, but will also minimize the perception that such changes are being imposed on the line managers and employees. Involvement means that members of the staff will have had a say in the proceedings *throughout* the diagnosis; thus, they will feel that they "own" it, and will be more committed to the implementation of necessary plans or changes.

1.1
Sample Proposal Structure

Objectives

Conduct a systematic (comprehensive or restricted) organizational diagnosis to achieve the following:

- Collect relevant data expressing:
  - *Perceptions* of a defined respondent population that may (will) include executives, managers, employees, former employees, and consultants
  - *Relatively neutral* facts from researchers and outside data sources such as newspapers, publications, and commercial data bases
- Identify and define the issues, problems, and challenges facing the organization today and in the proximate future
- Assess the present level of organizational effectiveness in relation to the identified issues, problems, and challenges
- Develop specific recommendations to:
  - Capitalize on the organization's strengths and unique capabilities
  - Improve relevant aspects of the organization in order to increase its effectiveness

Scope of the Project

The range of diagnostic coverage should be defined. The study could be comprehensive or restricted, based on a specific model or conducted along organic principles. If the scope of the diagnosis is restricted, the areas of inquiry should be defined at the outset. These may include any or all of the following:

- Historical data relevant to present circumstances
- Corporate culture
- Structural data, including organization, policies, procedures, and communication
- Functional and operational data
- Attitudes, internal and external

In a restricted diagnosis, management may wish to specify additional areas of particular interest, such as evaluations of the competition, product-development evaluations, strategic-portfolio analysis, financial review, and so on.

Data-Collection Methods

These methods should be specified. They may include one or a combination of the following:

1. *Structured interviews*—following a prescribed series of questions developed by the interviewing team along with management, or questions provided by a diagnostic model
2. *Unstructured interviews*—nonleading questions aimed at generating the respondents' own definition of relevant problems and issues
3. *Questionnaires*—paper-and-pencil instruments developed by the diagnostic team in conjunction with management, or commercial products
4. *Survey-research methods*—involving data collection by consultants and subsequent feedback of the data to management

Respondent Population

To obtain a representative sampling, indicate that it is desirable to collect data from at least 10 percent of the employees. The respondents should include:

- All officers
- All department heads
- Selected managers representative of all major functional areas
- Selected professional personnel from all relevant areas
- Selected clerical personnel from all relevant areas

Interview or Data-Collection Schedule

The people selected to participate in data collection should receive orientation and appropriate training over one month. The actual interviews should be scheduled for the subsequent two months, more or less, depending on the number of respondents. Data review, analysis, and interpretation should take about three months. Preparation of the diagnostic report itself should take about one month.

Resources Required

Human and financial resources are necessary for effective implementation of the diagnostic project. These may include:

- *A sponsor or an organizational development council* (ODC), who should budget enough time to function in advisory, evaluative, and monitoring roles during the conduct of the study and during subsequent development and implementation of action plans
- *A project manager,* preferably a respected member of middle management, who will probably work on the diagnosis full time
- *A diagnostic team,* composed of two groups:

  — Qualified and fully trained OD professionals, preferably members of the human resources staff, who will form the core team responsible for the overall conduct of the diagnosis.
  — Selected line managers, members of the critical mass, who will participate in data collection and to a certain extent in analysis and interpretation. All of them will also be reviewers of the diagnostic drafts, and act as resources to the project manager when necessary, particularly when detailed data about the organization are sought. To anticipate potential objections to the utilization of busy managers for such an undertaking, you should acknowledge the burden they will be asked to bear. Point out that you are fully aware that the individuals are key managers who already face great demands on their time. It is important for the sponsor and the council to realize, however, that those individuals are the people who "make things happen" in the organization. Employing their talents, credibility, and clout at the initial stages of the diagnosis not only will facilitate the conduct of the project but will also give them a long-sought opportunity to lead the company toward meaningful change and development.

  Attach a list of the proposed diagnostic team to the proposal. Part of the time commitment sought will be for training of all concerned in the diagnostic methodology.

- *Financial resources,* in the form of an adequate budget, should be requested. Sufficient detail should be provided, along with a cost estimate for the following items:

  — Salaries of the project manager, team, managers of the critical mass, and equivalent of one hour's time for each respondent at average rates. (Remember, schedule two hours for interviews.)
  — Research, particularly if extensive library searches are conducted; this may include paying graduate students
  — Consultants, if utilized
  — Equipment such as word processors, computers, dictating machines, typewriters, and duplicating machines used during the course of the project
  — Data transcription, preparation of drafts, and final typing
  — Reproduction of the report, including artwork, duplication, binding, and similar expenses

Diagnostic Report

Upon completion of the report, you should plan for the presentation to the sponsor or ODC. Advise the sponsor or ODC that the presentation will be made in the afternoon, and that the report should be reviewed overnight. The council should also plan to meet the next morning to discuss the report in detail.

The sponsor or ODC should be advised that, after the report has been discussed and the necessary points clarified, the people involved will need to budget time to work on the next steps:

1. Develop objectives for organizational change and development
2. Identify the more promising variables, whose alteration is likely to produce the desired results with the least possible effort or disruption to operations
3. Develop an action plan with specific objectives, budgets, milestones, and progress-measurement criteria

If a formal model will be used, the outline and list of questions should be attached.

1.2

Master Project Checklist

Task	Dates		Responsible Task Leader
	Start	Complete	

Plan and Organize the Diagnostic Project

Preliminary Assessment and Start-up

1. Define your role as a diagnostician _____ _____ _____
2. Understand the reasons for the diagnostic project _____ _____ _____

   a. Determine the focus of the diagnosis _____ _____ _____

      (1) Diagnosis for remedial purposes
      (2) Diagnosis for developmental purposes

   b. Determine the scope of the diagnosis _____ _____ _____

      (1) Limited (issue and problem specific)
      (2) Comprehensive

3. Analyze the political environment _____ _____ _____

   a. To what extent is the sponsor or company management invested in, or responsible for, the way things are?
   b. Is the sponsor in a position of sufficient authority to legitimize the project with other key managers?
   c. Who are the significant players making up the critical mass? Is it necessary to get them involved as part of the diagnostic team?
   d. Does the situation demand the establishment of an organizational development council?

4. Present a detailed proposal _____ _____ _____

Task	Dates		Responsible Task Leader
	Start	Complete	

    a. Objective
    b. Scope
    c. Kinds of data
    d. Data-collection methods
    e. Respondent population
    f. Interview or data collection schedule
    g. Resource requirements
    h. Product to be delivered

5. Obtain final approval to proceed   _____ _____ _____
6. Organize the project

    a. Establish a political support system   _____ _____ _____

        (1) Establish a council
        (2) Enlist a critical mass

    b. Establish an administrative system   _____ _____ _____
    c. Assemble the diagnostic team   _____ _____ _____
    d. Train the diagnostic team   _____ _____ _____

        (1) Interview the critical mass   _____ _____ _____
        (2) Conduct a workshop   _____ _____ _____

Collect and Process Diagnostic Data

Data Gathering

1. Organize the logistics of interviewing

    a. Confirm the availability of interviewers   _____ _____ _____
    b. Notify the respondents   _____ _____ _____
    c. Match interviewer with respondent   _____ _____ _____
    d. Schedule the interviews   _____ _____ _____

	Dates		Responsible Task Leader
Task	Start	Complete	

2. Develop a reference data base

    a. Perform background research

    b. Interview key management personnel

        (1) Part 1: Strategic issues interview

        (2) Part 2: Regular interview

3. Develop the main data base

    a. The process of diagnostic interviewing

    b. The interview procedure

        (1) Prepare the interviewer

        (2) Prepare the respondent

4. Review the interviewing process

Process Collected Data

1. Establish administrative tools
2. Transcribe notes
3. Control paper flow
4. Review volume and progress
5. Organize collected data

    a. Review the transcripts

    b. Code the data cards

6. Select the team for the balance of the project
7. Prepare for the analysis and interpretation

    a. Develop issue categories

Master Project Checklist

Task	Dates		Responsible Task Leader
	Start	Complete	

Analysis and Interpretation

Corporate History and Culture

    1. Write corporate culture module
    2. Write historical development module
    3. Write corporate indoctrination module

Planning, Strategy, and Structure

    1. General planning practices in the organization
    2. Strategic planning
        a. Core mission
        b. Environmental scanning
        c. Scenarios and strategies
        d. Strategy implementation
        e. The prospects of strategic planning
    3. Operational planning
    4. Organizational structure
    5. Evaluation of strategic advantage

Organizational Resources

    1. Financial resources
        a. Goals of financial management
        b. Financial-statement analysis
        c. Analysis of financial goals

	Dates		Responsible Task Leader
Task	Start	Complete	
2. Technological resources	_____	_____	_____
3. Physical resources	_____	_____	_____
4. Human resources	_____	_____	_____
a. Employee-turnover patterns	_____	_____	_____
b. Turnover trend analysis	_____	_____	_____
c. Performance appraisal	_____	_____	_____
d. Management development	_____	_____	_____

Organizational Processes

1. Leadership and power characteristics

   a. Assess the types of leaders in the organization   _____ _____ _____

      (1) Proactive leaders
      (2) Homeostatic leaders
      (3) Mediative leaders

2. Authority and power
   a. Assess predominant bases of power   _____ _____ _____

      (1) Coercion
      (2) Influence
      (3) Expertise
      (4) Information
      (5) Position
      (6) Interpersonal skill
      (7) Resources

   b. Assess major indications of power, influence, and politics   _____ _____ _____

      (1) Forcing
      (2) Smoothing
      (3) Avoiding
      (4) Bargaining
      (5) Confronting

Task	Dates		Responsible Task Leader
	Start	Complete	

    3. Assess problem-solving practices _____ _____ _____
    4. Assess decision-making practices _____ _____ _____
    5. Assess reward systems _____ _____ _____
    6. Assess work and productivity _____ _____ _____

        a. Assess levels of performance deficiency _____ _____ _____

Feedback, Action Planning, and Evaluation

Complete and Deliver the Diagnosis

    1. Develop diagnostic conclusions _____ _____ _____

        a. Summary of significant issues and problems
        b. Indicators of unresolved issues and problems

    2. Assess present phase of organizational crisis _____ _____ _____
    3. Assess significant organizational strengths and assets _____ _____ _____

        a. Aspects of the organization that should not be changed

    4. Develop diagnostic recommendations _____ _____ _____
    5. Present the diagnosis to management

        a. Write and structure the diagnosis _____ _____ _____
        b. Prepare for the presentation _____ _____ _____
        c. Deliver the presentation _____ _____ _____

Action Planning and Evaluation

    1. Review the diagnosis with management _____ _____ _____

Task	Dates		Responsible Task Leader
	Start	Complete	

    a. Handle the questions
    b. Reach consensus on major issues or problem areas

2. Action planning
   a. Resolve operational problems   _____   _____   _____
   b. Resolve major issues and problems   _____   _____   _____

3. Plan the organizational change and development

   a. Reach agreement on the company's core mission   _____   _____   _____
   b. Determine an appropriate response to the identified environmental demands   _____   _____   _____
   c. Project into the future   _____   _____   _____
   d. Define the desired future state   _____   _____   _____

4. Plan and execute organizational interventions   _____   _____   _____

5. Evaluate the effectiveness of the diagnosis

   a. Conduct an evaluation study   _____   _____   _____

1.3

Master Interviewing Schedule

	Mon. 14	Tues. 15	Wed. 16	Thurs. 17	Fri. 18
Interviewer Respondent Time	A. Jones T. Brower 9:00 A.M.	G. Hern H. Jackson 9:00 A.M.	A. Jones J. Hall 9:00 A.M.	A. Jones P. Saunders 9:00 A.M.	R. Deals F. Scala 9:00 A.M.
Interviewer Respondent Time	S. Gower A. Quentin 11:00 A.M.	B. Horn W. Gens 11:00 A.M.	J. Calzi O. Levant 11:00 A.M.	A. Confort I. Kipnis 11:00 A.M.	D. Ness W. Weitz 11:00 A.M.
Interviewer Respondent Time					
Interviewer Respondent Time					
Interviewer Respondent Time					

1.4

Interview Data-Recording Guide

Memorandum

To the Interviewers:

To help compile the data generated during the interviews, please follow this guide as closely as possible. On the transcript, indicate the following:

1. Code designation of the respondent
2. Date of the interview
3. Your name
3. Name of the questionnaire used

The body of the transcript should reflect the responses as accurately as possible. Exact quotes should be indicated as such.

Provide a brief summary of your impressions about the interview, when they occurred, and why you feel they are valid.

Indicate if any of the questions were a "flop," and why.

Please send your transcripts and the tape (if you use a recorder) to me as soon as possible.

Jack Smith
Project Manager

1.5

Core Mission and Strategic Planning Issues Analysis

> Memorandum
>
> To: Mr. Howard Greeley, Vice President, Finance
>
> The importance of clearly defining the core mission of a company can best be brought to light by the following real-life example:
>
>> The top executives of the O. M. Scott Company, a manufacturer of fertilizers, spent one year deliberating whether the core mission of Scott was "to manufacture fertilizers" or "to keep lawns green." It was ultimately concluded that the company's core mission was "to keep lawns green." The implications of such a decision were of critical importance for the planning of this company's future direction. With the core mission being "to keep lawns green," Scott geared itself to manufacture not only fertilizers but also all other paraphernalia needed to keep lawns green.
>
> The following questions have been formulated around key factors external and internal to our own company, and deal with issues related to helping the company define its core mission and develop responsive strategic plans for the future.

Note: This instrument was adapted from a model originally developed by Noel Tichy and Ian MacMillan for a diagnosis conducted at Ebasco Services in 1987. The core mission concept is based on the work of Richard Beckhard.

Step 1

In order to develop or enhance strategic plans, the company must be able to clearly state its core mission—that is, what the company is in existence for. Using whatever words, phrases, etc., are most comfortable, relevant, and meaningful to you, write your own view of the company's core mission.

As I see it, the company's reasons for being are as follows:

_____

_____

_____

_____

_____

Step 2

Focus on key internal factors that either help or hinder the company's ability to accomplish its core mission <u>as you have stated it in Step 1</u>. Identify what you consider to be the key external factors in the environment (markets, government, customers, economy, etc.) currently affecting the company's ability to carry out its mission. These factors can be either positive or negative. List as many factors as you think are necessary to map the key external factors (no more than ten).

The key internal factors affecting the company's capacity to achieve its core mission as I have stated it are:

_____

_____

_____

_____

_____

Step 3

For each of the key external factors you've just listed, specify what you perceive is the demand or pressure it exerts on the company. Attempt to write the demand or pressure in very specific terms. For example:

Key Factors	Demand or Pressure (Positive or Negative)
Government regulatory agencies	They demand immediate compliance.
The current administration	It seems to de-emphasize government participation in energy projects.

List each of the key factors you mentioned in Step 2, explain the related demand or pressure:

Step 4

For each of the demands and pressures listed in Step 3, indicate the response that the company currently makes to these demands. (Responses might include the company's ignoring the pressure and doing nothing.)

Key Factors	Current Organizational Response
_____	_____
_____	_____
_____	_____
_____	_____
_____	_____
_____	_____
_____	_____
_____	_____
_____	_____
_____	_____
_____	_____
_____	_____
_____	_____
_____	_____
_____	_____
_____	_____
_____	_____
_____	_____

Step 5

Keeping in mind your statement of the company's core mission and projecting five years into the future, what do you feel will be the relevant key factors at that time? Specify the demands and pressures of each key factor.

Key Factors Five Years Hence	Likely Demands and Pressures in Five Years

Step 6

What response mechanisms do you think must be developed to effectively cope with the stated future demands and pressures? That is, in order for the company to carry out its core mission (as you have stated it) five years from now, what response mechanisms are needed to deal with the key external factors you have predicted for that year? (Responses might include doing things between now and then to alter the predicted demands—for example, lobbying for certain legislative changes or developing new markets.)

1.6
Equipment Control Log

Dictaphones

No. 1	No. 2	No. 3.	No. 4.
Serial No. 099219	Serial No. PG448768	Serial No. EL735190	Serial No. 4835903
Date Name	Date Name	Date Name	Date Name

1.7

Transcription Control Log

Interviewer Name and Respondent Code ( )	Date Tape Submitted	Date Transcript Received	Date Transcript Sent to Be Proofed	Date Transcript Returned	Date Tape Erased
_____	_____	_____	_____	_____	_____
_____	_____	_____	_____	_____	_____
_____	_____	_____	_____	_____	_____
_____	_____	_____	_____	_____	_____
_____	_____	_____	_____	_____	_____
_____	_____	_____	_____	_____	_____
_____	_____	_____	_____	_____	_____
_____	_____	_____	_____	_____	_____
_____	_____	_____	_____	_____	_____
_____	_____	_____	_____	_____	_____
_____	_____	_____	_____	_____	_____
_____	_____	_____	_____	_____	_____
_____	_____	_____	_____	_____	_____
_____	_____	_____	_____	_____	_____

1.8

Document-Review Control Cover

CONFIDENTIAL

Operational Improvement Study

Section: Organizational Procedures

Title: B. Administrative

Draft review copy for: George S. White

This material is for the addressee's eyes only.
Copies of any kind should not be made at this time.

Please return to June Aaronson upon review

1.9

Sample Diagnostic Report

[*The following is an example of the <u>main body</u> of a diagnostic report.*]

Problems of the Company as Stated by Its Leadership

The company's most critical problems, as seen by its officers, revolve around issues of the organization's ability to meet the challenges of the competition and to acquire more work when there is less to go around. Part of this concern is attributed to the company's recent performance record, which indicates difficulty in completing work effectively and efficiently. Corollary problems cited by the executives included:

- The ineffectiveness of the company's planning process
- The unequal distribution of technical capabilities within the company
- The difficulties that the company experiences in attracting and retaining qualified personnel

The problems, and their corresponding issues, are summarized.

Competitive Stance and the Ability to Acquire More Work

As one executive views the problem: "Obviously right now business is of great concern. The tension is pretty well toward 'How can we best secure more work?'" Several executives see the problem as originating in past associations with the clients:

—1—

> "This company for many, many years always worked at pretty high levels in the client organizations, and we really didn't get to know several managers at lower levels. We really weren't looking at tomorrow as we should have. Now all of the fellows are coming up in the organization and are in position of power. Yet we failed to cultivate them. Even worse, we haven't listened to what they were telling us back then."

Other executives indicate problems with different elements of the business equation, in this case, the manufacturers and suppliers:

> "Most manufacturers would prefer to work with another firm, rather than put up with the difficulties of dealing with us. It's an attitude. Over the years, we knew we were good. We thought we were the Cadillacs of the industry. We wouldn't listen to anyone else. I think this attitude still exists today, although for the first time, I think we are starting to question ourselves."

Some members of management are concerned that the company has not kept abreast of the marketplace. One executive compares the company to an automobile:

> "In the past, we knew the marketplace; we were attuned to it and we had some unique relationships that were working for us, but since 1973, that marketplace has completely turned around. If we continue in the same way as we have done before, we will be offering an Edsel. That doesn't mean we don't have the ability to come up with a Mustang or a Thunderbird or whatever. It means that we have to reassess our objectives and the way we're going to reach them.

[*The following is a partial example of a* topical analysis.]

Policies and Procedures

Theory Base

This section is concerned with the company's operational rules: its efforts to maintain a common mode of operation. Policies and procedures are the methods by which the organization accomplishes its work economically and according to certain standards. We will explore how the individual is expected to go about getting work done. The more formalized these efforts are, the more bureaucratic the organization. However, some bureaucratic measures may have positive value for the organization—for instance, maintaining the quality of the product or service, or protecting the employee or company from injury or legal action.[1]

Introduction

Policies and procedures may evolve in two different ways. One way is for policies to be laid down by upper management, and these policies are then codified into written procedures. A second way is for procedures to be written down as a description of how things are done; once these descriptive procedures are approved, they then become policy. In the company, overall procedures can generally be described by the first pattern, while departmental procedures have typically been developed by the second model.

There are several reasons why an organization may document its procedures. One is to codify the existing systems, to set them down as reference points to which questions of procedure can later be addressed. A second reason is to control operations, to establish a standard mode to which all operations are required to adhere. A third reason is educational, to help new employees learn how to carry out operations in a manner that is consistent with company practices. A fourth reason is a response to pressure from clients and regulatory agencies to standardize the way operations are carried out as a means of ensuring quality or safety.

In addition to more formal procedures, certain company policies may exist only in unwritten form. Some of these may be norms, or descriptions of "the way things are usually done around here." Or they may be expectations that the organization has of its employees.

Written Procedures

The company's written procedures seem to have developed as a result of both internal and external forces. Internally, written procedures were needed in order to have a record of "our way" of doing a job. Department heads and other knowledgeable personnel were retir-

—3—

ing at a time when the company was expanding, and it became necessary to document how jobs and tasks were getting accomplished so that those methods could be retained. Externally, the federal government began demanding that we institute quality assurance and safety measures. This led to the development of company or interdepartmental procedures and to documentation of various standards and guidelines, such as criteria, specifications, and design guides.

The thinking among most managers is that corporate procedures should be followed as written. The degree to which these policies and procedures are followed, as well as the way they are interpreted and carried out, varies greatly from individual to individual and from department to department.

One project manager agrees that everyone has to follow corporate procedures, although he allows that there might be occasional exceptions. A manager in Engineering says it is necessary to keep in line with general company regulations, both technical and administrative. An Atlanta manager lists as belonging to this category "**codified manuals such as design guides, company and project manuals, projects procedures manuals, etc.**" For example, personnel are expected to abide by the rules of the Project Management System when working on a project, according to a project manager. He adds that, in a similar manner, people have to abide by all requirements of the Quality Assurance Program on a nuclear project. A Chicago manager says that his department follows the basic "rules" that are covered in the Personnel Practice and Procedures guides and the Office Practice and Procedures guides. The latter guidelines are also referred to as E-Procedures (*E* for engineering); there are now around eighty of these guidelines. Two procedures are referred to specifically by the managers as rules that have to be followed: Corporate Procedure 5, which relates to manpower planning and control; and Procedure 34, which deals with feedback from customers and external relations.

Company procedures are used as guidelines, according to a manager of projects. They can be deviated from if they hold up the accomplishment of objectives, but this must be done sensibly and with supervisory approval.

Procedural Effectiveness

Just as managers are undecided regarding the proper interpretation and execution of policies and procedures, so are they undecided about the effectiveness of the procedures themselves. Some managers think the written procedures are effective; others feel they are not so effective.

An Atlanta manager thinks that the company has good corporate and engineering guides. A senior officer comments that engineering and project procedures work effectively and are followed.

An Engineering manager says that these various rules work fairly well; he thinks the written procedures are good. A manager in Purchasing concludes that corporate policies are **"all right"** and are generally being followed. Most "rules" are effective and can be carried out, according to a manager in Construction. He adds that there is current updating of procedures to eliminate problems.

Rules concerned with criteria, specifications, and contracts work well, according to a project superintendent. He thinks this is the case because these rules are better defined than some others.

A project manager says that the rules **"work pretty well, generally,"** and that corporate procedures are followed. However, he feels that sometimes too many things are demanded of individuals, particularly lead engineers, from a procedural standpoint.

Procedural Ineffectiveness

A large number of managers contend that the rules do not work as well as they should. A project superintendent thinks this is because there is no attempt by management to follow the basic policies and directives of the company. Instead, he says: **"There seem to be direct attempts to get around them."**

An Engineering manager feels the procedures do not work well because the company **"doesn't have a balance between what its people have to do according to the procedures, and their being able to use their initiative to do it."**

A Chicago manager contends that **"project managers still don't adhere to the intent of the procedures."** He thinks this causes problems for all concerned. Similar problems are discerned by a manager of projects, who comments that **"company procedures and departmental procedures are sometimes in conflict."** A department head in Engineering comments that: **"The matrix system has a built-in conflict: the overall goals of the Engineering Department are concerned with engineering excellence, and this is sometimes at odds with a scheduling-oriented Project Management Team."**

A project superintendent also thinks people often have problems with the policies of the company. He feels that people just complain instead of confronting these problems. Some managers theorize that the trouble lies in the procedures themselves. Another group of managers feel that there are too many procedures, or that they are too voluminous. Other managers feel that the trouble lies in the way the procedures are implemented. And a number of managers refer to specific instances of problems with policies.

The Procedures Themselves

A manager in Engineering refers to procedures as "**one of our sore spots, one of our weakest points.**" He thinks the procedures are poorly written: "**They are conflicting, they are redundant, and they generate inefficiency. The company needs good writers to go through all the procedures.**" A project manager says that these procedures are written by technical people who cannot communicate. An Engineering manager considers it "**a poor commentary that the company procedures manual needs to be reworked.**" One manager thinks that "**the rules don't work well because of lack of consistency and perhaps because of poor procedures.**" A similar perception is held by a project superintendent. In his view, "**the company lacks a great deal of uniformity in the format of corporate procedures.**" He feels this makes them unusable to supervisors and managers for quick reference. A consulting engineer says that engineering procedures are extremely difficult to understand and to follow.

A department head in Engineering feels "**there are no standards established by the procedures. The only real measurement is schedule and budgets.**" As he points to all the manuals on his shelf, he says: "**We have books around here that are full of procedures. These procedures work poorly. No one understands how they work. Procedures don't help, they hinder.**" He adds: "**The procedures are used after the fact to point to individuals to justify some deficiency. Procedures are not used as standards before the fact to help the individual avoid the deficiency.**"

A department head in Planning cites procedures as another instance of the conflict between Engineering's work execution and Project Management's emphasis on schedule and budget. It is the contention of a manager in Business Development that "**the company is practicing certain procedures that the industry has thrown out, that the industry isn't using any more. We are not keeping current.**" An Atlanta manager expresses a similar concern: "**Many of our standards, specifications, and guides are outdated, antiquated, and based upon information that is no longer valid.**"

A branch-office manager calls the specifications "**bureaucratic documents." They are "burdensome and ludicrous. They get longer instead of shorter; they get added to instead of subtracted from." In response to vendor complaints, he was able to cut a specification from 140 pages to 40; he felt it was just as meaningful as before.

A Seattle manager feels that the design guides are not geared for rapid performance, but to assure that designers don't make technical errors. A department head in Engineering includes engineers as well as designers in that comment, and thinks that is an appropriate objective for the design guides.

Number and Volume of Procedures

"There are too many guidelines," says a consulting engineer. He thinks they are not followed because of their volume. The rest of the organization, except for Construction and Quality Assurance, has too many procedures, according to a senior officer. A department head in Engineering agrees; he thinks procedures need to be segregated for individual use.

An Engineering manager comments that there are too many directives geared at middle-management people, making it impossible for them to function as managers rather than as administrators. **"There are too many rules, and there is too much bureaucracy,"** says another Engineering manager. He indicates that to keep up with all the changes, he would have to spend one day a week to read what comes out of Licensing, Projects, and other departments. He says, **"It doesn't help just to read the title; it's necessary to read all about the subject."** A project manager says that one problem with the procedures is that his staff just can't keep up with the changes. A senior officer adds:

> "The regulations that you have to go by are just ridiculous, absolutely ridiculous. You've got a guy trying to get something done, and the Quality Control guy is watching what he does, and the Quality Compliance guy is watching what the Quality Control guy does, and the Quality Assurance guy is watching the Quality Compliance guy, who is watching the Quality Control guy. It's a tough way to do things . . . you write all kinds of paper. . . ."

According to another senior officer, "Directives have recently been issued by upper management to reduce the volume of certain procedural manuals."

Sample Diagnostic Report 227

> The remaining analysis elaborates in the following areas:
>
> - Implementation of procedures
> - Poor dissemination of procedures
> - Other causes of procedural ineffectiveness
> - Unwritten policies
>
> —8—

You may find that this approach is too cumbersome or time consuming for your own project. Also, it may not be necessary to fully document your findings when presenting your conclusions to management. Appendix 1.10 is a summary of the same issues, which is a format that may suffice in most situations. In any case, the scope and thoroughness of the report should be defined and negotiated with the sponsor or council beforehand.

1.10
Sample Topical Analysis Summary

Policies and Procedures

Source: pp 12.1–12.18

Comments

Although managers contend that written and unwritten corporate procedures are an important basis for the company's operation and production, the degree to which those policies and procedures are actually followed, as well as the way they are interpreted and implemented, varies considerably from individual to individual and from department to department. Factors contributing to discrepancies in the application of policies and procedures are:

- Departmental and company procedures with conflicting requirements
- Procedures used to identify delinquencies rather than to establish correct methods
- Abundance of procedures that constrain productivity rather than support it
- Inadequate and nonsystematic dissemination of and orientation to procedures
- Cumbersome or noncomprehensible procedures, which thus often are ignored

The underlying contradiction between belief in and use of procedures may imply managers' general ambivalence and resistance to changing technology and organizational processes. For example, managers accept the need for policies, set up rules and guidelines, and even revise or add rules, but they do not enforce them. Moreover,

—1—

managers often retain copies of procedures but do not systematically inform employees. Resulting gaps in knowledge of policies and procedures exacerbate communication difficulties and increases feelings of manipulation and deficiency among employees, while also potentially affecting the quality of their work and the implementation of new methods.

Much of the inconsistency is a reactive adaptation to change brought about by a growing and possibly turbulent internal and external business environment. Managers need written procedures that reflect a flexible and change-responsive structure and climate. Moreover, they need controls that emphasize evaluation of results more than they need detailed inspection of work methods and procedures.

The unwritten policies or norms define implicitly what the employee owes the company. Of significance is the absence of any mention of a psychological contract or a set of unwritten expectations between employees and company. Instead, unwritten policies focus on performance practices and relationships with the clients. Rules illustrating this are cited by managers as **"everything by the book," "zero errors,"** and **"if it interferes with the client, you are off base."**

While nonadherence to procedures is perceived as a major cause of not getting things done, an argument can be made that policies and procedures will not work unless they are sound and are properly enforced. The flexibility favored by managers, on the other hand, could be viewed as an important element in making the Project Management System work. (See Project Management, pp. 6.6–10, 7.1–12.)

1.11
Diagnostic Recommendations

[*The following is an example of the recommendations from a diagnostic report.*]

Strengthen the Project-Management System

Referring back to the basic components of an organization (structure, process systems, reward systems, and people), we have identified certain areas where action should be taken.

Establish a Clear Balance of Power

The matrix is basically a balance of power between the goals of the technical disciplines and those of a specific project. This means that the two-boss concept must be legitimized. The roles, responsibilities, and authority of key personnel should be clearly defined. Adherence to a single point listed in the "Green Book" would go a long way toward reaching this goal:

- The project manager specifies <u>what</u> is to be done.
- The functional department is responsible for defining <u>how</u> it is to be done.

Implement a Viable Planning and Scheduling System

Coordination problems with the various disciplines suggest that additional effort needs to be made to develop mechanisms for gathering, processing, and disseminating information in congruence with the adopted structure. The present lack of an acceptable schedule for major projects prevents both the disciplines and project management

—1—

from addressing issues of productivity, performance measurement, and on-time completion of work.

Establish a Dual Performance-Appraisal System

Behavior is a function of the individual and the role you put him or her in. Appropriate reward and evaluation systems channel behavior in a desired direction. The reward system needs to be thoroughly revised so that:

1. Personnel assigned to a project are appraised jointly and with equal emphasis from both the discipline and the project management.
2. There is a change from the present practice of the project manager's filling out an evaluation form on the project engineer, which can be used by the chief engineer as input to the formal evaluation if he or she chooses.
3. Both the chief engineer and the project manager sit in on evaluation feedback with project engineers and lead engineers, and advise the employees of salary changes together so that rewards are not construed as having been secured from only one side of the matrix.

Institute a Formal Program of Development for Project Managers

As has been discussed, project managers cannot rely on authority to achieve coordination. They must have excellent interpersonal skills and extensive personal networks of people they can work with.

- Interdepartmental rotation and experience help the potential project managers build larger networks of people they know, while at the same time enabling them to gain an understanding of the various disciplines.
- A viable performance-appraisal system must be used to identify potential project managers. Selection criteria must identify people who know how to affect others' behavior in a positive manner. Potential project managers must be:
    — Interpersonally competent
    — Leaders with an attitude of: "What can I do to help people do their jobs?"

— System engineers, rather than single-discipline people

Develop High-Level Career Opportunities in the Technical Areas

The company is clearly in the business of selling technical services, not project management per se; the latter is only a means of control. Yet people in the organization perceive project management as one of the few avenues of promotion. Project managers need to be developed, of course, but the company can ill afford to lose top technical talent to project management. In the long term, the company's unique competency in the technical areas must be preserved. In order to do so, outstanding technical talent must remain in the various disciplines. This means finding appropriate avenues of promotion and upgrading within the technical areas.

Provide Training Relevant to the Project Management System

One of the conspicuous educational needs too often forgotten is an understanding of the nature of the matrix. Differences in the capacity of individuals to deal with ambiguity exist, but all individuals new to matrix management lack some of the knowledge and skills necessary to navigate through the ambiguity and conflicts of a matrix.

People literally have to be socialized into a matrix. In the company's case, two areas must be addressed:

- Develop an understanding of what the Project Management System really is, not what it is perceived to be. The positive aspects of the system should be pointed out as well as the shortcomings that need interdepartmental cooperative behavior as compensation for them.
- Develop skills to enhance the interpersonal competence of key personnel throughout the organization: listening, communicating, conflict resolution.

Examine the Necessity for Personnel Adjustments

Some people, although competent under normal circumstances, are not able to function in a matrix organization, even if help is provided. Such people should be reassigned to positions that do not require such interaction.

A process of self-selection is also important. To avoid surprises, prospective employees should be told about the Project Management System prior to joining the company.

Summary

In reviewing the general characteristics of an effective matrix, we have emphasized the quality of flexibility. By looking in some detail at the key roles unique to the matrix, we have concluded that flexibility comes from individuals who are challenged by the matrix to respond to each new situation in a fresh manner. This approach is admittedly at odds with the present tendency of the company to rely more and more on written procedures to make things work. The fact is that a matrix organization was never meant to rely heavily on procedures; it should depend on the flexibility of the personnel within it. This should be the focus of development.

APPENDIX 2
Diagnostic Models and Intervention Methods

We have seen that diagnostic studies are part of a broad range of organizational intervention methods; in fact, they are a necessary first step for most of them. Such studies range from very simple interviews and surveys to complex and time-consuming large-systems diagnoses.

The following is a description of some of the better-known diagnostic and intervention models. The intent is to familiarize you with what's available, and to give due credit to the various pioneers in the field. These are the diagnostic approaches that have been most influential over the past several decades, and they divide into three different categories: (1) behavioral-science models, (2) special-purpose models, and (3) comprehensive models.

The purpose of these categories is to help identify the provenance and overall perspectives of the various types of models—where different analysts "are coming from"—and not to "label forever" the theoretical work of individual analysts or all applications of any particular approach. In applying these models, for example, practitioners in organizational diagnosis have been known to stray far from the original views of the model's creators, and some practical applications represent a polyglot of theoretical approaches.

Still, it is useful for discussion purposes to consider the bulk of organizational development and diagnostic models under the general heading of behavioral-science models, certain others as special-purpose models, and an "advanced class" of theory and practice as comprehensive models.

Behavioral-science models are primarily psychological in their orientation, and attentive to the personal and interpersonal characteristics of people in the organization; they assume that behavioral change in people will create change in the organization of which they are a part. These models include a broad range of diagnostic and intervention methodologies, but are typically "micro" oriented, or limited to the confines of the organization or department under analysis. And for the most part, behavioral models are limited to strictly "people" issues, largely ignoring financial, technological, and economic matters.

Special-purpose models, as the name suggests, are usually concerned with a specific problem and its solution. In performance analysis, for example, such models might focus on whether an individual's performance problem is related to deficiencies in training or to constraints in the system that prevent the person from performing as desired.

<u>Comprehensive models</u> are ambitious, complex, time consuming, and expensive, and attempt to examine virtually all aspects of an organization in an attempt to clearly define problems and seek solutions. Their focus is not only on the organization itself but also on its interaction with the business environment, particularly its ability to deal effectively with change and the threats and opportunities such change implies.

Behavioral-Science Models

During the past twenty years, a number of methodologies based on the concepts of behavioral science have been developed and placed into practical use by organizations. The main focus of such interventions has been the encouragement of change to new modes of behavior by individuals and groups in order to help the organization develop. This general field of behavioral science has been called organizational development (OD).

OD theory generally assumes that in organizational functioning there are overt, readily identifiable behavioral components, as well as covert, less apparent, and certainly more subtle elements that in some cases may be more significant. Much like an iceberg, what's below the waterline can be ignored only at the observer's peril. A manager intent on changing an organization cannot act only on the basis of formal organizational components, such as organizational structure, job descriptions, strategic objectives, and personnel policy practices. He or she must also understand what's below the surface in order to construct a complete picture of an organization and how it functions. The manager will then be concerned with covert components such as emerging power and influence patterns, value systems, and informal power and influence networks (see Figure A-1).

Most OD interventions confine themselves to dealing with the behavior of people in organizations, and they generally either ignore or don't consider important structural and overt components.

Most OD interventions stimulate and foster the behavioral and emotional development of individuals, with the objective of enhancing their ability to respond creatively to problems or opportunities. An extension of this concept assumes that behavioral change in individuals also applies to the organizations they form.

Attitude Surveys

Theory and Concepts

The employee attitude study—and its modern refinements including diagnostic studies that survey perceptions, processes, and work relationships as well as "attitudes"—is a historical tool of organizational diagnosis. Typically, such studies take the form of questionnaires filled out or marked by active

Figure A-1. The organizational iceberg.

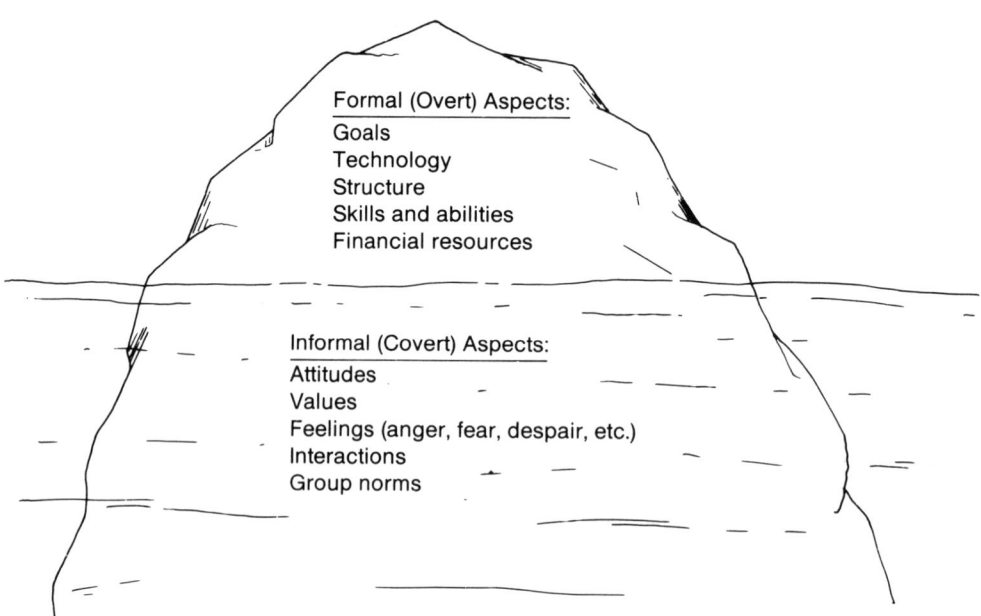

From Wendell L. French and Cecil H. Bell, *Organization Development: Behavioral Science Interventions for Organization Improvement,* 3rd ed., © 1984, p. 19. Reprinted by permission of Prentice Hall, Inc., Englewood Cliffs, New Jersey.

members of the organization. As Camman and others[1] have noted, such members are "uniquely qualified to report their own personal beliefs, opinions, expectations, and affective responses," as well as "the work, work environments, and organizational activities in their respective areas of the organization."

The theoretical justification for the use of questionnaires usually includes the following:

- It is a cost-effective means of reaching large numbers.
- Many different people may have information or attitudes that are relevant to organizational diagnosis; even if the majority of respondents provide data through interviews, it may be necessary for practical and economic reasons to use questionnaires to canvass a larger sample of the population, or at least to supplement the data provided by the primary target population.
- Confidentiality promotes honesty (a basic guideline of attitude survey design is to ensure anonymity to respondents). It should be noted, however, that the need for anonymity is not necessarily universal; it generally is a function of organizational climate.
- Results may be aggregated or analyzed in a variety of ways: by management level, job function, tenure, demographic characteristics, or other variables.

Today's questionnaire-based diagnostic studies, as Walter Mahler[2] points out, go "far beyond the familiar attitude surveys of the past." For Mahler, survey design includes such features as individualized questionnaires (instead of companywide instruments), confidentiality of results within departments, mechanisms to improve the involvement of participants, a "balance sheet" approach that reports strengths as well as weaknesses, various types of reports, and repeat studies.

Others have noted continuing shortcomings in the questionnaire approach, however. "They do not create the kind of personal involvement and dialogue that is so valuable in changing hearts and minds," say Jack Fordyce and Raymond Weil. "The information garnered by questionnaires tends to be canned, ambiguous, and detached—i.e., cool data rather than hot. The replies may be interesting, but they lack punch."[3]

But because such criticism applies mainly to ill-conceived or poorly administered attitude surveys, these shortcomings are minimized and tolerated because of the efficiency of questionnaires, which are much less costly and time consuming than interviews. The effectiveness of these surveys can be enhanced by including managers and other employees in the formulation of questions and survey items. Advance research can shape items that respond to specific investigative needs, such as ways to test adherence to certain agreed-upon management styles. Also, as a statistical approach, the accumulation of codable survey data suitable for computerization permits the implementation of quality-control procedures and validity assessment.

Ultimately, the issues surrounding the theoretical validity of questionnaire-type attitude surveys become moot; most OD diagnosticians see questionnaires as a useful tool in combination with interviews, observations, and other data-gathering methods that may be more suitable for some organizations or OD objectives than others.[4]

Process

The application of questionnaire-type attitude studies in organizational diagnosis begins with the determination of topics and coverage. What organizational characteristics will be assessed? Whose attitudes and perceptions are being sought in this form of data gathering? Other developmental issues, such as the establishment of scales, validity measures, language to be used, and interpretive meaningfulness, are important but remain relatively technical issues compared to the "what" and "who" of questionnaire design.

Typically, the more specific the content of the questionnaire, the more likely its development will require a modular approach, with different sets of items or questions for different functions or levels in the organization. General attitude studies, seeking opinions on broad subjects such as satisfaction with pay or the corporate climate, can be developed as a single instrument to cover diverse employee populations. But when the meaning of terms and concepts is different in different parts of the organization, or when functionally specific information is sought, modular construction or entirely separate questionnaires are required.

In general, two paths are open to the study developer. Based on the objectives sought, the specific problem or issue to be addressed, and the survey population, the analyst can devise a survey instrument and methodology appropriate to the task at hand. Mahler, for one, asserts that "the first step is to define outcomes. What are the results that are to be expected if a study is to be conducted?"[5] Among the range of different basic studies from which to choose—to get specific attitudes in different situations—are climate studies, organizational studies, coaching-practices surveys, authority-analysis studies, power-conflict studies, decision-flow analyses, performance studies, and time analyses.

A second approach is represented by the Michigan Organizational Assessment Questionnaire (MOAQ) and similar survey instruments that are developed in modules, some of which are administered to all employees and others which are tailored to specific segments of the employee population. Some of the "packaged" survey instruments have the added advantage of providing ways to measure certain questionnaire responses against responses from employees in general, in the U.S. work force or in an industry. The MOAQ, for example, consists of seven separate modules.[6]

Module 0: Demographics. This module, in which respondents indicate age, race, sex, education, family status, and other personal information, permits analysis of responses according to differentials that arise because of different personal perspectives. Data from this module can provide additional meaning to results or help explain anomalies. For example, fringe benefits are more likely to concern employees with many dependents, pension characteristics escalate in importance with age, and so on.

Module 1: General attitudes. This part of the Michigan survey uses scales to assess "outcomes," such as overall job satisfaction and intention to stay with the company, and "psychological states," including levels of satisfaction with work, pay, and such quality-of-worklife factors as job involvement.

Module 2: Job facets. The objective in this module is to more specifically link employee attitudes to aspects of the job and job rewards, to determine where and to what extent parts of the job are contingent on good performance. For example, respondents are asked whether they believe that if they perform a job especially well, they will (1) have a chance to further develop their skills and abilities, (2) be promoted, (3) feel better personally, (4) gain the respect of colleagues, and so on.

Module 3: Task, job, and role characteristics. The focus in this module is on the work itself, rather than its surrounding conditions. Task characteristics in this module, for example, ask about employees' perceptions of freedom in their work, variety, and feedback. Job items view the employees' jobs within the organization. And role characteristics focus on psychological states presumed to arise in connection with work, such as perceptions of challenge, meaning, responsibility, and knowledge of work results.

Module 4: Work group functioning. This module assumes particular importance in surveys of employees who typically work in teams or groups, sharing a common workplace, job goals, supervisors, or similar tasks. In the Michigan study, items cover five aspects of work groups: homogeneity, goal clarity, cohesiveness, openness, and fragmentation. The administration of this module requires an advance definition of what constitutes the "group," a definition that must be clearly communicated to the respondents.

Module 5: Supervision. In quality-of-worklife studies such as the MOAQ, supervisory relationships and perceptions of leadership styles are critical elements. Items in this module assess supervisors' control of work, their ability to solve problems, any bias, special considerations, and overall competence.

Module 6: Pay. Psychological aspects of pay administration are evaluated in this module, with items that address such issues as perceptions of equity with others in the organization, the relationship of pay to performance, pay importance to the respondent, and overall satisfaction with pay.

The MOAQ is called a "living instrument" by its proponents,[7] adaptable to different circumstances. The modular approach used in this process provides a means of tailoring attitude surveys to the particular organization, focusing attention on tasks, relationships, work flows, or other characteristics pivotal to diagnostic objectives.

Finally, most proponents of attitude studies urge users to repeat the surveys, using identical item language and scales. Over a period of years, annual studies can identify trends in the organization, as well as trends by job function, level, location, or other variables that may correspond with the issues that should be addressed in an organizational change effort. For example, a one-time study that shows mediocre attitudes about supervision in one department may have many reasons, but if ratings on this subject plunge significantly in one year of an annual survey, the reason may be identifiable.

Action Research

Theory and Concepts

Action-research models for diagnosing problems and generating data about an organization are claimed to be a departure from "packaged" OD diagnostic methods, which action researchers see as (1) piecemeal or nonsystematic, such as Blake and Mouton's GRID organization development training programs, which run for a week or so and cover only top executives;[8] (2) overly concerned with "content," such as a new organizational chart, to the exclusion of "process," such as the new relationships among people on the chart; and (3) lacking in adaptive flexibility, because they approach the organization as a static, rather than a dynamic, entity.[9]

Central to the idea of action research are three basic concepts. First, the research is shaped by actual conditions rather than by preconceived models.

Second, action-research models are based on collaboration between the behavioral scientist and the affected members of the organization; the participation of the latter is intended to assure accurate identification of problems and agreement on plans for their solution. In a diagnostic phase, the members of the system and the OD practitioner jointly use the data to define and explore organizational problems and strengths. The significant feature about such a process is that the joint collaboration of the consultant and the client is an integral part of it—the process does *not* consist of a prescribed relationship where the expert alone does the work, reaches conclusions, and decides on the remedy.

Third, organizational problems represent moving targets and require continuing flexibility in their analysis and evaluation.

The place of diagnosis in action research is as part of a continuum, an inseparable stage in a process that is being carried out by researchers and clients who are effectively "the same people." Marvin Weisbord[10] puts diagnosis after data collection (and before the related steps of action and evaluation), and defines it as the identification of "gaps between 'what is' and 'what ought to be' as supported by the data."

Other action researchers have constructed more elaborate steps of activity that include diagnosis as one phase, stressing the iterative nature of the process (see below) and the uniquely collaborative nature of the diagnostic stage in action research. Figure A-2 provides a diagram of the action-research process as it relates to organizational development.

Though the repetitions of the cycle described in the "Process" section below, the researcher-client team in action research is expected to accomplish solutions to real problems, and at the same time to develop new knowledge that can be applied by the behavioral scientist.

Finally, it is worth noting that action research is a term of long standing; it originated in social research focusing on ethnic minorities[11] and was the subject of review papers as early as 1950.[12] Whether viewed as a basic OD characteristic,[13] or as a distinctly different approach, the term "action research" has been around for many years and has been applied to a countless array of OD efforts, not all of which have recognizable similarities. In other words, the term has been notoriously misapplied by self-described "action researchers."

Process

Action research is a cyclical process of research, change, evaluation, integration of learning leading to further research, change, and evaluation in cyclical fashion. The results of research produce ideas for changes; the changes are introduced into the same system and their effects are noted through further research. The number of cycles may be infinite.[14] Action-research methodology focuses on the creation of specific changes that develop people for individual change and ability to adapt. This includes a didactic element, which involves the generation of new knowledge of the process of change, of specific change methods and techniques, and of specific changes of a technical, structural, or process nature. The training element includes sharing research methods needed for collecting data, understanding a problem, and evaluating previous attempts at change. In this scenario, the consultant also fulfills the roles of trainer and researcher.[15]

Action research is a cyclical, an iterative, and—its practitioners hope—an educational cumulative process. The cycle proceeds through phases or steps

Diagnostic Models and Intervention Methods 241

Figure A-2. An action-research model for organizational development.

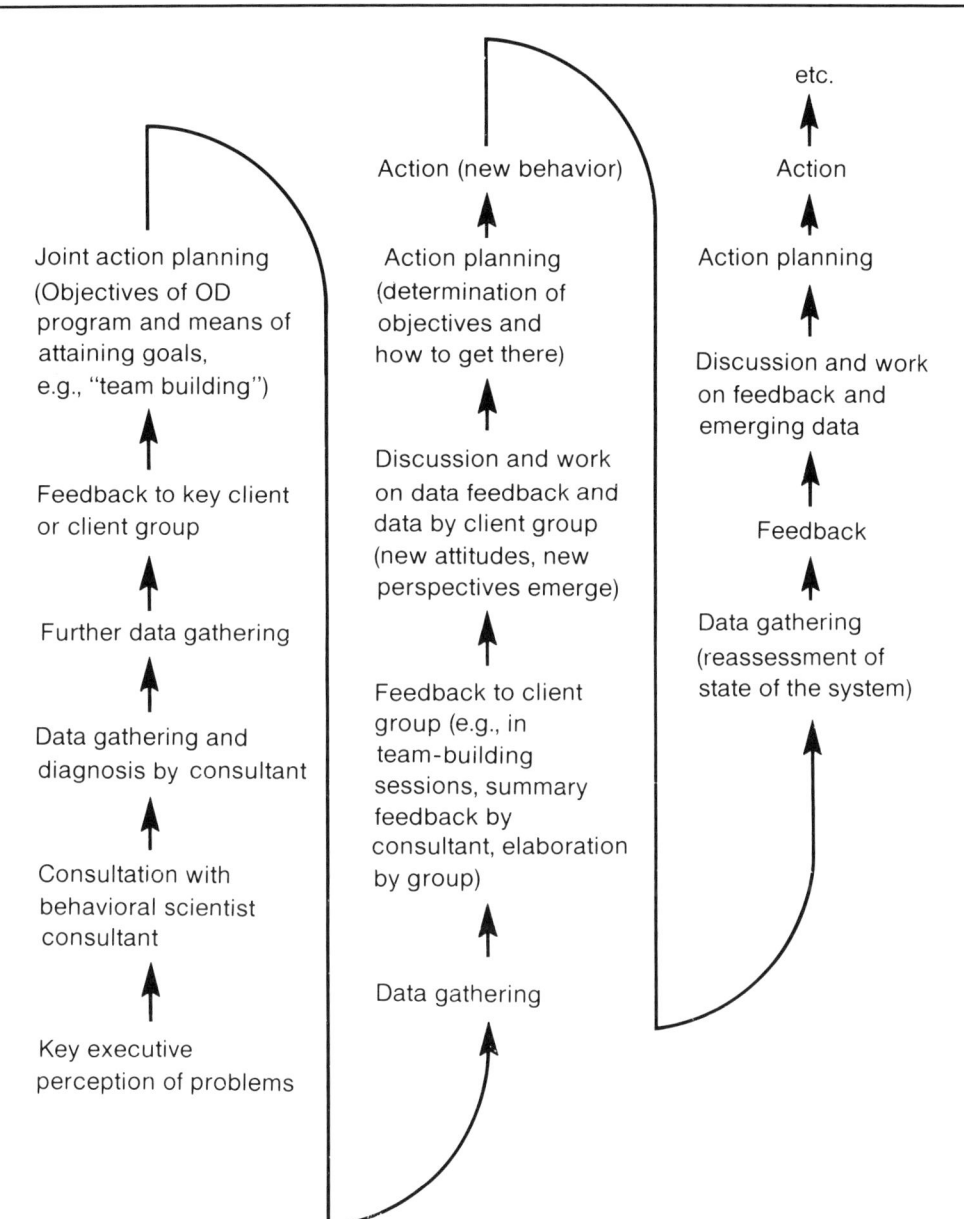

© 1969 by the Regents of the University of California. Reprinted/condensed from the *California Management Review*, Vol. 12, No. 2. By permission of The Regents.

that include research, diagnosis, action, and evaluation, and then begins again with research based on the results learned from the preceding cycle. Theoretically, the process may be infinite, and the new knowledge and skills gained in each cycle apply both to the organization and to the action researchers—a client-consultant team working together—who are expected to apply improved understanding and new insights to each repetition of the cycle.

In Weisbord's simplified action research model,[16] the steps are (1) data collection, (2) diagnosis, (3) action, and (4) evaluation. Others[17] propose a more elaborate range of phrases that are "similar to other models" (e.g., Lippitt, Watson, and Westley)[18] and that include:

1. *Scouting.* This is the research-oriented opening phase of disclosure between client and consultant. The client provides basic information about products or services, technology, demographics, structure, external relationships, and other significant data, and the analyst provides an initial application of the methodology that will be used to understand these data—what Kolb and Frohman call the consultant's "descriptive-analytic theory,"[19] revealing consultant biases or theoretical approach. This preliminary research should result in a decision whether to proceed to a formal arrangement for OD.
2. *Entry.* The process of establishing a collaborative client-analyst relationship. Action-research models, more than most other OD models, put great emphasis on the importance of open, interactive communications between clients and consultants, and stress the early and continuing support from upper-management people for the process.
3. *Data collection.* The research in which the client organization assumes a more active role, and which involves interviews, questionnaires, observations, or a combination of these methods. Data are usually classified by organizational level or according to major areas of concern, and methods of obtaining data are worked out.
4. *Data feedback.* A phase that includes the development of mechanisms for returning collected data to the client system for discussion of organizational strengths and weaknesses, often through team meetings. This phase is closely related to diagnosis, which follows.
5. *Diagnosis.* A phase of action research in which the emphasis returns to research, and during which client-analyst teams work together to define and explore organizational issues or strengths and weaknesses. In action research, diagnostic conclusions are the products of collaborative client-consultant analysis at this stage. Further, diagnosis of data may reveal an insufficiency of data or ambiguities that require further data collection. In this instance, the process is recycled to the data-collection phase, with newly specific subjects for inquiry.
6. *Action planning.* The development of specific action plans to address the issues diagnosed in the preceding phase. This planning includes the determination of who will implement plans and how the results will be evaluated.
7. *Action implementation.* The phase in which an intervention is actually

introduced, monitored, and made to produce new data for evaluation. The actions may range from weekly problem-solving meetings to a new corporate structure, but in any case the action is ideally perceived—in action research—as a joint client-consultant product and the source of new data, which will be evaluated in the next phase and used to begin the next iteration of the overall process.

8. *Evaluation.* The final phase in the cycle, based on procedures established in the preceding phase. It is possible, of course, that evaluation will reveal either that the problem has been solved or that the OD approach is inappropriate.

In summary, action research focuses on the creation of specific changes that have both organizational and individual impacts. The organization's problems are addressed, as are the capabilities of people in the organization to see and effect the needed change. The training element includes an unusual degree of openness on the part of the consultants, a sharing of research methods and initial "biases," and a dual role for the consultant, who is both trainer and researcher.

At the focal point of diagnosis—the critical phase of this or any other model of organizational development—the action-research methodology stresses the vital importance of collaborative effort, an analysis that emerges (or perhaps *seems* to emerge, which is almost as helpful) from the joint minds of the analyst-client team. Moreover, the iterative nature of the process—with each new diagnosis supposedly improved by new information, new skills, greater collaboration, and the like—fits well with the reality that organizational change efforts usually take time and rarely proceed to a "fixed point" that will be optimal ever after. More often, organizational change aims at developing an adaptive organization, one capable of further change as conditions require.

Hertzberg and Maslow

Theory and Concepts

Both Frederick Hertzberg and Abraham Maslow focused on motivation of the individual. Their theories are well known, but no less relevant if the focus of a diagnosis is on the factors around the employee himself. Hertzberg[20] postulated that people are not necessarily motivated by pay and working conditions; inadequacy in these areas are demotivators, however. Restoring these variables returns people's perceptions to a state of neutrality, which takes such "maintenance" factors for granted and are not necessarily motivators. In order to be motivated, employees need interesting and varied jobs. Hertzberg coined the phrase "job enrichment" to describe the redesigning of jobs. This redesigning motivates employees by removing them from monotonous tasks and adding responsibility and variety to their jobs, in contrast to keeping them in assembly-line positions where they are only required to attach the same part to many automobiles.

Abraham Maslow[21] described a hierarchy of needs present in all individuals. He also postulated that in order for an individual to engage in higher-order needs and seek what Maslow called "self-actualization," the basic survival and social needs had to be met.

Process

In diagnosis, the consultant particularly wants to know to what extent the needs and potentials of the people constituting the organization are not being fulfilled or capitalized on, for the benefit of the individuals and the organization. A consultant stresses the need for meaningful work for employees by helping the client become more aware of this need and designing procedures that provide for more responsibility, authority, and frequently greater complexity. The consultant concentrates mostly on the removal of blocks to individual motivation. He or she especially urges management to develop processes whereby the employees can realize more of their potential. A central part of the diagnosis is to understand the level of employee complaints—that is, whether the complaints are largely about working conditions or about not receiving appropriate recognition for outstanding performance.

B. F. Skinner and the Behaviorist Approach

Theory and Concepts

B. F. Skinner was a key figure in the development of behaviorism, a school of psychology that tells us we can change behavior, and consequently performance, in one of two ways: by modifying the behavior repertory itself, or by modifying the environment. Behaviorists would say that, in any case, we are modifying behavior. As an extension, Skinner postulated a reinforcement theory—that is, arranging feedback and consequences so that desired behavior is encouraged and rewarded. A behaviorist consultant urges management to ignore subperformance on the part of its employees and to stress instead the positive reinforcement of competent performance. He then helps the client devise ways of providing praise and appropriate rewards for people who perform well.

Process

The behaviorist engaged in a diagnosis particularly looks for aspects of the organization that manifest punitive controls. He or she is an advocate of incentive systems, especially those which provide consistent rewards but not necessarily in a predictable pattern. In a diagnosis, the behaviorist searches for the positive and negative reinforcers of behavior—that is, what factors reward and punish the employees.

Kurt Lewin

Theory and Concepts

Kurt Lewin is credited with having introduced the concept of action research.[22] He founded the Research Center for Group Dynamics in 1945 at M.I.T., was a central figure in the origins of the National Training Laboratories, and "had a profound influence on both organizations and the people associated with them—and his influence continues today."[23]

As discussed in the section on action research, Lewin's approach to diagnosis of systems was based on a collaborative, interactive method of empirical fact-finding and action planning. The process is iterative, so that the findings from one diagnosis become part of the data gathered for the subsequent cycle.

Lewin stressed that the design and implementation of the diagnostic effort be a team effort, strongly involving members of systems that will be changed. This participation helps to motivate changed behavior and attitudes. He noted: "This result occurs because the facts become really their facts (as against other people's facts). An individual will believe facts he himself has discovered in the same way that he believes in himself."[24]

Apart from his original work on action research, and the applied behavioral-science thrust he gave to both laboratory training and survey research,[25] Lewin is seen as a founding father of the human relations movement, along with Mayo, McGregor, Roethlisberger, and others.[26] Certainly, the implications of the action-research methodology, which includes participation at all key levels of the client organization and a heavy emphasis on self-determination and mutual trust, put him at the leading edge of that movement.

Process

In a Lewinian diagnosis, the consultant's approach to understanding such organizational behavior as morale, productivity, and motivation is to distinguish between induced forces—for example, decisions that are imposed—and own forces—for example, employee participation in decisions that directly affect them and their work. The approach to intervention is to change certain norms to which people conform, rather than to change individual patterns of behavior or personality structure. The consultant pays attention to power dynamics particularly in terms of who attributes power to whom, rather than who has authority for what. In a diagnosis, the consultant believes that the most important dynamics to understand is the organization's unique pattern of norms—that is, those rules and standards of conduct to which employees conform. A Lewinian consultant prefers to intervene in terms of reducing restraints on people rather than on creating conditions that will provide inducements for change.

Rensis Likert

Theory and Concepts

In his 1961 book *New Patterns of Management*,[27] Rensis Likert presented his comprehensive theoretical statement of participative management. He saw organizational management as placed in a continuum ranging from System 1 (exploitative-authoritarian) and System 2 (benevolent-authoritative) to System 3 (consultative) and System 4 (participative). In his view, System 1 was infrequently used in the United States. System 2, he believed, was characteristic of the decades immediately preceding the 1960s; System 3 was perceived as a way station to System 4, which appeared at that time to be an emerging and desirable standard. Likert also believed that System 3 management was inherently unstable, leading to a move to either System 2 or 4. In later writings,[28] he added the notion of a System 0, an essentially laissez-faire or undeveloped management system. The essential management concepts articulated by Likert focused on leaders being supportive, close to their people, and egalitarian. He saw the manager as the linking pin by which the organization is held together and its efforts become coherent.

Process

Operationally, a consultant using the Likert technique, when working with a group, would rather deal in a fairly structured manner with what people's perceptions are of the group and the organization, rather than underlying, unconscious issues of the group and the larger organization. When the consultant finds that group decision making in an organization is other than by consensus, he or she advocates a change to consensus. The consultant feels most comfortable when using research-based forms to collect data, thereby achieving a sound basis for analysis. In diagnosis, the consultant especially considers organizational structure, particularly in terms of provisions made for effective vertical linkage. He or she believes that certain organizational structures, especially those based on group problem solving and decision making, are better than others, irrespective of organizational objectives or worker characteristics.

Chris Argyris

Theory and Concepts

Chris Argyris has been a pioneer in the development and testing of T-group methods, also known as sensitivity training.[29] Sensitivity-training laboratories provide the means for one to learn about the interaction among individuals in a group, about deeply felt experiences and feelings as opposed to intellectual content. Small groups, usually numbering about twelve, together with one or two facilitators, work intensively over a period of three to five days and evenings with each other. Argyris's approach is oriented exclusively toward changes in people and behavior, and is relatively unconcerned about technological or structural change. Particularly, no attempt is made to go outside the system (work groups or organizations for resources or help) with the exception of the process consultant himself. All of the collected data are generated within the client system, consistent with a philosophy that the aim is to create effective, adaptive internal changes in behavior. The most common vehicles for organizational development are the family group (a manager and his or her immediate subordinates) and task groups. The methodology has three primary objectives: (1) to generate valid information by establishing a climate that allows open expression of opinions and feelings, (2) to enable the participants to make clear and informed choices on the basis of the valid data that has been generated, and (3) to encourage continuing commitment to change by learning and improving through interpersonal processes. These are done over time, with a facilitator trained in such matters working with the group. The central strategy is to work with the members of the group so that they acknowledge and accept responsibility for their own thoughts and feelings, become open and accepting of the thoughts and feelings of others, continue to experiment with new thoughts and feelings, and help others to do the same. The focus is primarily on developing an extraordinarily open relationship among the working group, with organizational effectiveness only as a secondary goal.

Process

Operationally, a consultant using Argyris's concepts believes in being authoritative with the client about behavioral theory, research, and practice. This consultant values the client's attacks and mistrust as serving an important client need and as useful points of departure. Consistent with the group concept of development, in diagnosing organizational behavior, the consultant pays particular attention to whether people openly and publicly state their ideas, opinions, and feelings. In an organizational development sense, he or she believes the system will not change unless the behavior of the top management group changes. The consultant also believes that the data collected become the basis for a conceptual map that sets the course for action steps that will lead to organizational change.

Warren Bennis

Theory and Concepts

Warren Bennis helped introduce a historical perspective to organizational development in his 1969 book,[30] and was among the first to stress the importance of identifying and changing culture, the "system of beliefs and values ... within which people work and live," in order to change organizations. Writing at the end of the turbulent 1960s, Bennis also stressed the need for a new "social consciousness" among individuals and collectively in the organization—an awareness "essential in the kind of world we are living in."

The historical perspective, no less valid in the late 1980s, presents a Hegelian premise that successful organizations develop "an organizational form most appropriate to the genius of that age." The "determinant conditions" of the age, as Bennis saw the latter third of the twentieth century, include an environment that fosters interdependence among organizations (rather than independence), turbulence and uncertainty, large-scale organizations, and the growth of complex, multinational enterprises.

Another key determinant of the age to which organizations must adapt, Bennis observed, is education. Educational attainment levels of workers and the population as a whole are escalating, and the pace of technological change increasingly requires refresher training and various forms of advanced education. Among the implications of higher educational levels is the need for greater involvement and autonomy on the job.

Bennis was among the first organizational analysts to promote the idea of organizational structures made up of "adaptive, rapidly changing temporary systems," consisting of task forces of professionals and specialists "arranged on an organic rather than a mechanical model." He foresaw a time when organizational charts "will consist of project groups rather than stratified functional groups."[31] These new-style organizations he called *"adaptive"* structures.[32] Seventeen years later, the Conference Board held a two-day meeting entitled "Creating the Adaptive Organization: Organizing for a New Era."[33]

Bennis believed that consultants *should* work in an environment of trust, collaboration, and valid data, and be able to "discount power based on and channeled by fear, irrationality, and coercion"—power that "leads to augmented resistance to change, unstable changes, and dehumanized and irrational conflicts." Still and all, Bennis warns, "one had better understand these irrational and powerful forces."[34]

Process

The purpose of organizational diagnosis, from Warren Bennis's perspective, is to develop evolving, adaptive organizational forms that are more in tune with their times, more democratic and humane. Systems that foster satisfaction with the work itself—the Hertzberg goal—are the ultimate model. Nonetheless, Bennis stressed that a wide range of diagnostic techniques may be useful in organizational development to meet this goal, from data-feedback sessions to confrontational meetings, and that the most important consideration is that "data are generated from the client system itself."

The goals or subjects examined in organizational diagnosis, Bennis makes clear in a 1965 article,[35] are at the heart of the difference between organizational development (OD) and operations research (OR), another optimization technique to emerge in postwar management. The variables that classify OR problems—inventory, allocation, routing, sequencing, and such—are usually economic and engineering variables, factors that are highly quantifiable. In contrast, the variables that define OD problems are, to Bennis, essentially human and less quantifiable; they include factors such as mission, values, collaboration and conflict, leadership, and communication.

Sociotechnical Systems Theory

Theory and Concepts

The view of the organization as a sociotechnical system, a term first developed by Eric Trist and his associates (Rice, Emery, Davis, et al.) at the Tavistock Institute in England, stresses the interrelated impacts of technology, organizational inputs, and social interactions on worker productivity and morale.

This approach has been defined as "the organizational concept emphasizing that both human and non-human factors—including technology, structure, and process—interact to determine individual and organizational functioning"[36] Moreover, A. K. Rice and his Tavistock colleagues have focused on the importance of differentiation within organizations when it comes to solving problems of worker collaboration and other dysfunctional patterns.[37]

The diagnostic concept employed begins with an effort to bring "comprehensibility" to the "complex interdependence of forces which culminate in organizational behavior, most particularly that behavior whose results can be measured by more or less objective levels of productivity, subjective senses of satisfaction, and the sometimes ineffable signs of human, group, and organizational development."[38]

Process

The sociotechnical consultant typically works more with workers than with management. He or she typically advocates a composite system of organizational structure—i.e., combining a simple formal organizational structure with complex work roles rather than a complex structure with simple work roles. The consultant believes that it is a necessity for top management to sanction a change effort, but their involvement otherwise is not required. In an organizational change effort, the sociotechnical theorist typically arranges for an experimental group to try the new approach—e.g., structural change in the organizational chart—before intervening with the change to other parts of the organization. The consultant usually explains to management clients the belief that a manager's primary job is that of relating the system to the environment; in other words, the manager's involvement with internal organizational problems should be oriented primarily to the organization's external relationships.

Special-Purpose Models

Performance Analysis

Theory and Concepts

Performance analysis is a process of problem solving based in part on behaviorist approaches and initially developed by Robert F. Mager[39] to help instructional designers to assess a performance problem. It is used particularly to detect, early on, whether an individual's performance deficiency is indeed due to lack of training. The concept was then expanded by Thomas H. Gilbert and the Praxis Consulting Organization.[40] This technique is rather narrow in scope, because it is primarily a front-end analysis prior to designing training programs. It has, however, been used to train supervisors and in situations where identification of a performance problem with people needs systematic evaluation.

The performance-analysis methodology takes the user through several distinct and logical steps and uses a flowchart that moves through a disciplined series of decisions and subsequent suggestions for appropriate action.

The main steps involve (1) problem identification, to assess whether the problem is there and whether it is worth solving; (2) problem analysis, primarily to compare actual behavior with desired or model behavior; and, most important, (3) problem classification, to assess whether the problem is due to a lack of skill or a problem in execution, or to generally external factors beyond the control of the individual.

Process

The analyst approaches the problem by asking a disciplined series of questions. He or she starts with problem identification, to assess if the problem is worth solving. If so, the analyst tries to find a role model to which actual performance can be compared. This will enable assessment of a discrepancy and computation of the value of bringing everyone up to the level of the best performer. The most important stage of this analysis is an examination of whether the problem is due to skill or knowledge deficiency—in which case training may be appropriate—or to execution deficiency; restraints owing to lack of feedback or consequences for not performing as desired; or task interference, preventing a person from performing as desired.

Kepner-Tregoe Analysis

Theory and Concepts

Charles H. Kepner and Benjamin B. Tregoe wrote a book[41] and established a firm that successfully promoted what became known as the KTA method of problem solving and decision making. This is essentially a way to solve operational problems, but it is sufficiently popular to merit review as a variation on diagnostic practice.

The KTA method is a disciplined, sequential approach designed to better define the nature of a problem, followed by a series of steps that lead to decision making and prevent the reoccurrence of the problem in the future.

Process

The person trained in KTA technique starts by looking at a problem as a deviation from what *should* be happening, specifying it as what *is* happening and what *is not* happening: where, when, and to what extent. This step is called problem analysis. Once the cause of the problem is found, objectives for resolution are developed and alternative actions are developed. The objectives are classified as aspects of the solution that either must be there or that the manager wants to be there. *Musts* must be there, or the solution will not be acceptable; *wants* are a relative fit. The next step is a potential-problem analysis, in which an assessment is made of adverse consequences of a potential solution, and actions are planned to minimize the threat. This technique is still very popular in applications where a specific outcome (such as production from a manufacturing department) can be measured.

Comprehensive Models

Marvin Weisbord's Six-Box Model

Theory and Concepts

Weisbord[42] believes that there are many equally valid theories, techniques, methods, and instruments—too many, in fact, to make an exact science of organizational diagnosis. Given this uncertainty it is important to resist the temptation to gather data for a diagnosis from every conceivable direction. As a framework for such a study, a model must be employed that provides a cognitive map. The six-box model that Weisbord developed fills such a need (see Figure A-3).

The strength of Weisbord's model is in its ability to encompass interpersonal and group issues as well as complex management systems, processes, and structures.

Process

Weisbord does not subscribe to any given method of data gathering. Rather, he suggests methods of grouping collected data into the general categories shown in the boxes in Figure A-3. Whatever lies outside these boxes constitutes the environment, and the constraints and demands that it imposes.

The power of such a model lies in its relative simplicity. For this reason, it is popular among practitioners who prefer to avoid the rigors of more complex diagnostic approaches.

Lawrence and Lorsch Model

Theory and Concepts

Lawrence and Lorsch believe that (1) there is no one "best" way to organize, (2) there is no one "best" way to manage, and (3) to be effective, an organization must fit the environment.

To deal with increasing complexity and a changing environment, organi-

Figure A-3. The six-box model for organizational diagnosis.

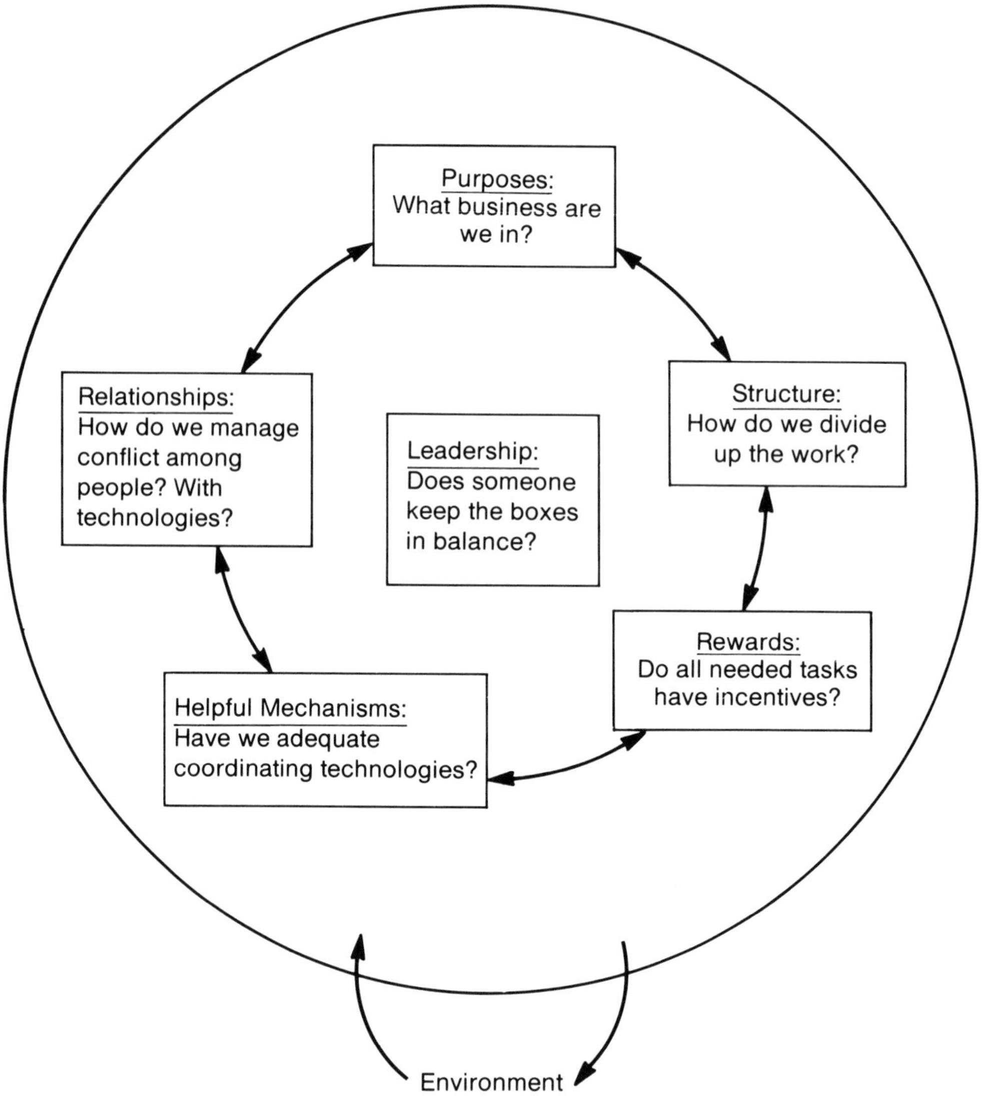

From Marvin Weisbord, *Organizational Diagnosis*, © 1978, Addison-Wesley Publishing Co., Inc., Reading, Massachusetts. Reprinted with permission.

zations engage in differentiation. This is breaking an organization into clearly defined departments that are specialized, sometimes to an extreme degree. For example, one unit performs only value-design application work, while another concerns itself exclusively with metal stress-analysis calculations. This differentiation is more than organizational; it extends to the attitudes and time horizons of the people involved.

Differentiation, as justified and necessary as it may be, requires a certain degree of integration, and this integration toward a common goal must be achieved while allowing the various differentiated units to maintain their distinctive competence and identity. The situation necessitates carefully designed integrative mechanisms. These may be explicit lines of authority, such as the management hierarchy, which get three or four units tied together to a single boss; manuals and procedures; committees and project teams with individual integrative roles (such as project managers and team managers); and rewards and measurements, such as profit centers. Integrative mechanisms can be temporary (task forces) or permanent (a project management system).[43]

The positive aspects of differentiation are that it enables each organizational unit to cope with the environment by virtue of its specialization, and that it allows each individual within that unit to obtain a sense of competence. There are, of course, several considerations and issues on differentiation/integration that are problematic: the greater the differentiation, the greater the need for interpersonal orientation to bring about effective integration. Another dimension is time orientation: the greater the differentiation, the longer the time needed to receive feedback on organizational action.

Various interfaces exist, and a diagnostician will attempt to examine how effectively the planned transactions among several dimensions take place: (1) the organization-environment interface; (2) the group-to-group interface; (3) the individual-organization interface, and (4) the individual-individual interface.

Process

The consultant with this approach feels very comfortable working with any number of different means as long as they are based on quantitative data and primarily address the organization in systems terms—e.g., the organizational structure, information flow from one unit to another, and so on. In diagnosis, the consultant analyzes the task demands placed upon the organization by its environment, and also examines the needs of individual contributors, in order to make a normative prescription of what organizational characteristics best fit those task requirements and individual needs. He or she pays particular attention to the behavior patterns used to manage intergroup conflicts, and looks for possible problems with the organization's structure, especially in terms of which organizational units need to work more interdependently. The consultant pays particular attention to how the organization is structured, and whether there is an effective match of structure (organizational chart) with environment (e.g., market demands). As a consultant, he or she is not necessarily an advocate of participative management, since managerial style should be contingent on the situation.[44]

Harry Levinson

Theory and Concepts

In his definitive work *Organizational Diagnosis*,[45] Levinson provides an awesomely comprehensive framework for analysis, and emphasizes that description of any organization must be viewed in its historical context. The diagnostician must know (1) how historical forces evolved, (2) which historical forces continue to influence its activity, and (3) how the organization is functioning at the present time and why. Levinson uses the analogy that a person:

> has uniqueness, personality, and the capacity to act on his environment in a host of spontaneous ways. He is, of course, a product of his history as well as his capacities. So it is with organizations. They achieve uniqueness in their way of performing their functions despite the similarities of their organizational structures, marketplaces, personnel, techniques.[46]

Levinson applies the psychoanalytic approach to organizations by suggesting that a company has a developmental course that begins at its founding. An analysis of an organization's practices and values often reveals that the underlying assumptions of the founders have continuity. A lot of what is going on today, both positive and negative, can be attributed to past practices that in some cases still go unquestioned, even though the company may be operating in a different environment and with another set of variables. The portion of the diagnosis that examines historical development asks questions such as: What led the company to be the way it is today? How did the company adapt? What crises molded the company into what it is today? The study of past crises often provides valuable insight, because it generates explanations of how an organization's characteristic adaptive patterns have led to present problem-solving behavior.

Levinson considers three issues in consultation: (1) case-oriented consultation, intended to deal with a problem or a given set of problems; (2) task-oriented consultation, to help the individual do a job better or help a group of people deal with a task, and (3) organizational consultation, to help the whole system. To help the whole system, the consultant needs a perspective on the organization as a whole, he must stand outside the system in order to maintain detachment, and he must have an active relationship with key members of the organization, although he cannot expect to be able to work with everyone. This view leads to certain key assumptions.

First, no intervention can be made without affecting the whole system. For this reason, according to Levinson, effective consultants often have a systems orientation.

Second, consultants are elite persons in respect to their training and knowledge. They do indeed know something that other people in the client organization either do not know or are not allowed to use. Consultants bring a frame of reference that may not exist in the organization. In essence, they must be authoritative in the expert sense, in order to gain credibility and be effective. The client is, in this context, dependent on the consultant, and this dependency is a fact.

Third, consultants must deal with the psychological phenomenon of transference on the part of the client—that is, the bringing to the present attitudes from the past relating to other power figures. This transference necessitates dealing with the four major feelings that every human being experiences: love, hate, feelings about dependency, and feelings about one's self-image. The feelings people have about dependency are what affect the extent of transference in relation to the consultant. No human being can survive without being dependent on someone else.

For some executives, to be a little dependent is the same as being totally dependent. This unconscious factor and the resultant negative feelings about dependency stem from the helplessness of infancy; in some cases, these archaic feelings are brought to the fore in adult behavior. This means that a consultant must be aware of transference throughout the consulting relationship, because he or she might be seen as an enemy by some people, who are likely to test the consultant repeatedly. It is, therefore, important for a consultant to expect and accept the hostility of the system when change is introduced.

In order to manage this transference, consultants must understand why clients are coming to them, and why they are coming now, rather than at some other time. This knowledge may help consultants manage people's dependency by enabling them to preserve their self-esteem, which, for example, could be destroyed by premature feedback.

The acceptance of client transference and the subsequent hostility from clients are crucial and natural parts of the process. It is also possible that, at some point during the intervention, a consultant might get angry at the client, thus leading to counter-transference, because the consultant has his own dependency needs. When this happens, the consultant should stop and examine the reasons for his feelings. One way to cope with counter-transference is to have a co-facilitator. The latter may be a much-needed support system in a difficult situation. Another way for consultants to cope is to be aware of their own limitations and to get outside help when needed. Knowing one's own limitations is also important from the point of moral and ethical responsibilities. Consultants should know under what conditions certain techniques must be used, since no one technique is applicable to all situations. Unless consultants identify their own boundaries of competence, they reach a point of vulnerability and are likely to get in trouble. During diagnoses, consultants are likely to face some crucial problems. Thus they must pay particular attention to their behavior and how it affects the system. They must also be aware, as was pointed out before, of how the organization affects them. It is, therefore, important to realize that consultants are their own antennas—the most important and fundamental.

Process

An important part of the Levinson approach to diagnosis is the differentiation the consultant makes about the key elements or variables in the situation. He is aware of the interrelation and complications arising from three sources: the consultant himself, the leadership of the organization, and the organization itself.

The consultant. While performing a diagnosis, the consultant should periodically ask himself two questions: "What am I here for?" "What is this doing for me?" The consultant must be particularly watchful of his or her feelings of guilt about interfering in a system, feelings akin to being a voyeur: "What right do I have to look into a system?" This guilt stems from ancient and archaic sources in childhood, and it appears to be a universal experience of new consultants. If these feelings aren't managed, they may cause the consultant to back away, and prevent him from digging out the appropriate information and asking the painful questions. This could develop into a serious problem if the consultant becomes frightened by a seeming inadequacy of people in the system, without realizing that this inadequacy is due to a temporary focus on deficiencies during the early stages of a diagnosis.

The opposite attitude could also be a problem for the consultant. Levinson quotes two terms coined by Karl Menninger, *furor therapeuticus* and *furor inandes*. *Furor therapeuticus* occurs when a consultant has a need to intervene. He or she thus gets into a system whether or not the intervention is needed. This, according to Levinson, is "the great OD sin" and the most likely to do damage. In *furor inandes,* the consultant exploits the client, out of his or her own need to cure or to get a good result. The client is thereby an instrument for the consultant's gratification. There is no way to do a good job in consultation by trying to satisfy one's one gain.

According to Levinson, it is important to realize that the fundamental issue is the consultant-client relationship, and not the technique. This is facilitated if it is recognized that some problems cannot be resolved. Coping with this fact means that a consultant must set his or her own limits and limits of the system. It is also important to anticipate what will happen when the relationship with the organization is terminated. This is a particularly real issue for internal consultants, who are not able to escape the long-term consequences of an intervention.

The leaders. Levinson's psychoanalytic approach stresses the importance of examining leaders as people with their own needs and wants. Being in a position of power, they generally exercise their needs by influencing the workings of the organization. A close examination of top leadership reveals that these people have usually adopted certain postures to meet their own needs. These postures may be difficult or painful to sustain; nevertheless, they serve to maintain their equilibrium. The net effect may be resistance to accepting painful facts. This resistance is usually a manifestation of the following equation:

$$\text{Self-esteem} = \text{ego ideal} - \text{self-image}$$

If the self-image does not measure up to the ego ideal (and often it does not), a person may get to the point that he dislikes himself, resulting in anger, an uncomfortable feeling of inadequacy, and consequently guilt. The greater the gap between ego ideal and self-image, the more unhappy and depressed a person becomes. In extreme cases, this condition may result in anger and self-destructive behavior.

Levinson points out that the ego ideal is not necessarily one we want; nevertheless it drives us. A leader who offers resistance to a diagnostician, in spite of the fact that he may have hired the latter precisely to help a situation, might be doing so unconsciously. His resistance might also be a testing behavior that has to be dealt with. This is why a consultant must accept the hostility of the system when change is introduced. As a matter of fact, according to Levinson, hostility in the initial stages of consultation should be expected, and the actual occurrence should be considered normal. It also reinforces the need to cope with leader resistance, by finding out what the nature of the person's ego ideal is, and by getting a grip on how he handles aggression and dependency. (It is important to realize that we are dealing with equilibrium-maintaining systems.)

The organization. In Chapter 1, we introduced Levinson's assertion that the process of consultation starts by identifying where the pain is, what it is like, how long it has been going on, and what has been done about it. It's important to know whether pain exists. If there is no pain, there is no motivation to change. This means that if there isn't sufficient pain, the consultant should not intervene. The pain must be conceptualized and identified. The consultant should describe in words why he has reached certain conclusions about the organization. He should then organize information as he goes along. As the information is conceptualized, he should keep in mind how it relates to the pain.

The formal part of the Levinson diagnosis is normally performed in four stages. The first is the development of historical data about the organization, intended to gain an understanding of the company's history. The way the company approached its past crises reveals a characteristic adaptive pattern leading to present-day organizational behavior. The second stage involves a description and analysis of the current organization as a whole. This yields structural and process data. The third stage deals with interpretative data, focusing on current organizational functioning as well as attitudes and relationships. The fourth and final stage comprises the analysis and conclusions. This section addresses the effect of the environment on the organization, its assets and impairments, and closes with a summary and recommendations.

The Levinson model is comprehensive and complex, and for this reason, it demands a high degree of professionalism. Being comprehensive, the model provides a framework for most categories of data. It does not attempt to simplify something that in fact is not simple. It reflects the true scope of such an undertaking.

APPENDIX 3

Organizational Diagnosis: An Experience

To help illustrate the process of organizational diagnosis in large systems, the following describes a developmental diagnostic effort that I planned and directed in 1977–78, with continuing follow-up and evaluation to mid-1986.

Background of the Organization

This large, precedent-setting effort was conducted in 1977 at ENCON,* a 5,000-employee, seventy-year-old engineering, construction, and consulting company that throughout most of its history had enjoyed a well-deserved reputation as a pioneer in the electric industry. ENCON provided a wide range of engineering, construction, and technical consulting services primarily to electric utilities in the United States.

The design and construction of large projects, particularly nuclear power plants (which constituted approximately 80 percent of ENCON's work at the time), required the application of fairly complex technology, involving many technical disciplines over a project life that often reached twelve years and cost upward of two billion dollars. The highly differentiated structure of technical disciplines that ENCON employed was typical of organizations in this field.

Because of the great need for coordination, ENCON had nine years prior established a matrix management system, called Project Management. This system was intended to provide a business focus by way of a single head for each project, who would decide what and when various activities were to take place, and professionals in the technical disciplines, who provided people to the project, along with technical direction.

In 1977, ENCON was starting to feel the effects of the OPEC embargo, which caused utilities to significantly reduce orders for new power plants. Moreover, intense competition had eroded the company's market share from its peak years in the 1940s. The matrix organization needed improvement, particularly because of bitter conflicts between the project organization and

---

*The name of the organization has been changed.

the technical disciplines. Moreover, the company was trying to cope with its third takeover in ten years. Following an industry trend, turnover among young, talented professionals was high.

Despite these problems, the company had remained profitable. The intent was to stay that way by taking some sort of action to deal with a slowly deteriorating business environment in the field of power engineering and construction.

The Diagnosis Is Commissioned

Early in 1977 the chief executive announced his decision to retire by the end of the year. For all practical purposes, the company was to be run by a triumvirate of top executives, one of whom had been charged with establishing a centralized manpower planning and development department. I was appointed to lead the group on the basis of a proposal that I submitted, justifying the consolidation of such activities at the corporate level. More important, I accepted the job on the condition that the organization conduct a comprehensive organizational diagnosis. The management triumvirate agreed to do so, primarily because such a study was perceived as timely, given the environmental realities the firm was facing.

An Organizational Development Council Is Established

Recognizing that the support and understanding of top management were essential, I asked for the establishment of an organizational development council, composed of the top ten officers of the company. The intent was to build legitimacy and a strong, supportive political organization from the top down. The council would also ensure the direct involvement of management in the anticipated change effort, and would be a direct channel of communication to a yet-to-be-named new CEO.

The council sat through two day-long sessions, designed primarily to establish a base of common understanding about the scope and implications of the proposed diagnosis. Part of the deliberations involved examining various diagnostic models, which included survey research, paper-and-pencil instruments, and other relevant models. The council was concerned with the possibility of attempting a "quick fix," which would not have had lasting effects on the organization. It was the council who selected the organizational diagnosis model originally developed by Harry Levinson, and explained in his book *Organizational Diagnosis*.[1] I had presented the model, never expecting that it would be adopted because of its apparent complexity. At the time, I was unaware that the model had never been used in its entirety, certainly not in an organization the size of ENCON. The council nevertheless decided to go with this model, mainly because it did not appear to oversimplify what it takes to understand large organizations and their problems, issues, and challenges.

The Power Diagnosis

Recognizing the magnitude of the upcoming project, I became concerned about potential opposition from powerful members of middle management. I called this second level of managers in the power network the "critical mass," a term I heard during a workshop with Richard Beckhard,[2] and particularly appropriate to people with a background in nuclear power. These were the people who could make or break any change effort—the people who, whatever their titles, held the real power. I identified who they were by first asking department heads, managers, and the rank-and-file who had the power, and then asking those named if they thought they indeed had power and influence in the organization. A correlation of responses indicated that twenty-four managers were indeed "powerful." I then asked the council to let me have these managers participate in the diagnosis as a supplementary team. The intent was not so much to get help with the upcoming mass of interviews, but to have the critical mass involved at the outset, so as to obtain their commitment to the project and their cooperation in implementing any changes it would generate.

I received permission to ask for the participation of the critical-mass managers, and I persuaded this group to become part of the diagnostic team, at least for the interviewing phase. Later, they also participated in portions of the analysis and interpretation, and all of them reviewed and commented on the diagnostic document itself, prior to finalizing it.

The Study

Several problems arose during the study. Some of the critical-mass team members resisted at each step along the way. Some were afraid of reprisals if they spoke out against management. Others were cynical about the possibility of change. Still others couldn't acknowledge their negative feelings, but dragged their feet in getting work for the study completed. The OD and supplementary teams had to work in an atmosphere of anxious rumors. Lower-level employees who weren't told much about the study became pessimistic about the company's future. Some people worried about what the study would find. Word went around that the company was in financial trouble, that a management shake-up was imminent, that another takeover was in the works. As those in the study learned of these unfounded rumors, they dissipated them by presenting the facts and explaining the real purpose of the study. They worked hard to keep people as informed as possible, and coped with vast amounts of paperwork—sending memos explaining the study, thanking people for their participation, and informing people about what they had learned so far. When the interviews were completed, the diagnostic team found itself overwhelmed by the data. The team had more information than it knew what to do with, and its members nearly panicked. They didn't know how to sort it, pare it down, or use it to support the general conclusions they'd come to. After trying several methods that failed, they finally cut each piece of relevant information from the transcripts and pasted it on separate cards—20,000 of them. They separated the cards by topic headings taken from organizational diagnosis and divided the topics among volunteers, who would analyze and write them up. Given the fact that computers were not used, this turned out to be the only way to handle all this data and maintain an objective view of what was going on.

A basic premise during the study was that a diagnosis conducted by members of an organization has a better chance of generating data valid to the participants and leading to a commitment to change. Valid data can be generated by consultants and other professionals. The only problem is, you don't know if the data generated are going to be valid to the people in the organization. And that's what really counts.

Historical Methodology Applied to Organizational Diagnosis

Part of the diagnosis included a thorough study of the company's development since its inception. Much of management's approach, both positive and negative, could be traced back to past practices that were successful in their day, but in some cases still went unquestioned even though the company was facing a different environment and a different set of variables.[3]

We have seen how organizations have stages of potential growth in their life cycles, and that each organization experiences crises and situations demanding certain indispensable management and organizational responses, if the organization is to achieve its next stage of growth.[4]

By tracing the continuum of the organization's life through three developmental stages—birth, youth, and maturity—we could gain a better understanding of where the company was, and to what extent flexibility existed to plan and implement the changes a diagnosis would almost certainly identify as necessary.

Having evolved as the service arm of a holding company that at one time owned over 11 percent of all the electric utilities in the United States, ENCON had built sizable cash assets from divestiture of most property, as directed by the government as part of an antitrust action. The high liquidity made the organization attractive as a takeover candidate; in fact, it was acquired by a conglomerate in 1968. Shortly thereafter, the latter siphoned off all the liquid assets of its newly assimilated subsidiary, and after a stormy five years, divested it to a holding company that, among its various assets, had a company in the same business as ENCON. This second marriage did not last long, for it was promptly challenged by the government on antitrust grounds. The action culminated with a further divestiture of the company. At the time the diagnosis was conducted, the owner was an energy conglomerate based in Dallas, Texas.

The diagnosis included a thorough examination of the company's seventy-year history, as a means of explaining its present characteristic behavior. One reason for incorporating a historical study in the diagnosis was the desire to find an explanation as to why the organization was not effective in dealing with tough problems facing it at the time. Management did not want to be restricted to the traditional management-consulting method of problem identification and action planning, because it felt that traditional methods would not address the fundamental problem. Management wanted to know *why* the company's behavior and perceptions appeared to be out of touch with the demands of the marketplace.

The first portion of the study identified and examined three major evolutionary phases of the organization. The first phase—the period between 1905 and 1935—was termed the firm's "rise to glory." The second phase was the "holding action"—a period when the organization fought a government order to divest itself of most of its subsidiaries. The third phase covered the period from the 1950s to the present, and was called the "search for new beginnings." This particular approach was consistent with Levinson's view that "a key developmental phase is an experience which significantly changes the direction, size, effectiveness, or strength of the organization."[5] In the analysis, an attempt is made to distinguish between conscious choice of strategy and one that arrives by itself. In the course of the study, emphasis was placed on identifying whether such phases would eventually be positive or negative in the long run. Levinson defines these phases as follows:

> A positive key developmental phase is one which reflects growth, greater sophistication, greater maturity, greater stability through diversification or financing, or greater access to personnel or financial resources. A negative developmental phase is a type of organizational aging or failure. One evidence of such a phase might be a decline in profitability because products become obsolete, declining membership, or lower quality of job applicants by virtue of uncontrollable external events. Positive or negative phases depend heavily on the organization's ability to perceive its environment objectively."[6]

Since this issue was very much a concern at the time, it was hoped that the diagnosis would enable a better understanding of this aspect of the inquiry.

The diagnosis traced the major events through the organization's history and analyzed them within the Levinson model, supplemented by a developmental framework patterned on a concept by Lippitt and Schmidt (Creation, Survival, Stability, Pride, Reputation, Contribution, Uniqueness, Adaptability, and Maturity).[7]

Phase 1: The Rise to Glory

Creation

In 1905, a major manufacturer of electric-generating equipment created an electrical holding company (EHC) for the purpose of managing a large portfolio of securities received in partial payment for capital equipment supplied to newly established electrical utility companies.

Survival

Under the leadership of a very capable chief executive, EHC expanded by creating a vast structure that helped meet the demand for electrification in the nation. He did this by (1) forming subsidiary holding companies to hold common stock of the geographically dispersed operating companies, (2) setting up workable financial structures, and (3) establishing a central service organization to provide technical help to these newly established utility companies.

Stability

The service concept of EHC became successful through the establishment of an effective operating pattern that developed efficiency and strength with sufficient flexibility to meet the needs of the time.

Pride, Reputation, and Contribution

By the early 1920s, EHC had successfully stabilized the earnings of the small, geographically dispersed operating companies, and increased their visibility to investors while simultaneously providing lower-cost electricity to customers. This was a remarkable achievement by any standard and exemplified great insight and leadership. By 1925, EHC generated almost 12 percent of the nation's energy, thus making it the largest supplier in the country.

Uniqueness and Adaptability

This early period of EHC's history set the pattern for the firm's continuing operating style, and for the technical services that it provided to operating utilities. Characteristic of this period was the fact that none of EHC's services required active marketing, because its clients were its own operating utility companies.

Since EHC entered the business early in the period of rapid technological change, it developed considerable expertise in the field. The business it conducted was one element of its consulting work, so it developed and emphasized engineering rather than construction. EHC's pricing strategy was to charge according to the total cost of the job, resulting in a lack of interest in smaller and less profitable projects.

In performing its technical services, EHC had no incentive to reduce project costs, since its services were supplied to captive clients. Furthermore, the real incentive was not in the fees themselves, but in the multiplied earnings of the entire system. Consequently, the technical service arm of EHC did not need a marketing/sales organization and was not required to make a profit. This further encouraged the development and application of extra-high-quality, cost-unconscious technology by an elite group of engineers.

Maturity

EHC became a dominant force in the electrical-utility industry. Its impact became so great that it drew government scrutiny, an event that was to be of momentous significance to its future. Essentially, EHC achieved maturity as an organization within twenty years of its birth. Throughout this period, it demonstrated the ideal characteristics of an organization operating in the right fashion in the right environment, with the necessary degree of flexibility to meet the challenges in its path.

Phase 2: The Holding Action

Although its successful momentum continued until 1935, the first major, unrecognized crisis faced by EHC was a change in the federal attitude toward the industry, first manifested in the 1920s. The government became concerned about the power of holding companies such as EHC. The major equipment manufacturer that had created EHC had the foresight to perceive the storm signals, and divested itself of EHC by distributing the stock among its stockholders. Nevertheless, this did not satisfy the government, which initiated an investigation in 1925 into the control of the electric-utility industry. The investigation disclosed that, even though EHC never owned a majority in the stock of any operating electric company, it nevertheless managed to maintain effective control over the entire organization through devices considered unacceptable by the government. In retrospect, it appears that EHC's first major error was to expand physically and financially to such an extent that it drew attention to itself.

Its second major error was to underrate the seriousness of the government's intention to pursue its objective—namely, destruction of the holding-company system. Consequently, EHC failed to develop alternative plans for survival as a different type of organization. The second chief executive concentrated on evading the inevitable rather than on developing strategic plans for long-term preservation of the organization.

The first crisis to be fully recognized was the proposed Public Utility Holding Act (PUHC) of 1935, which directed holding companies to divest themselves of their domestic operating companies. This led to the formal establishment of the service arm of EHC, as a subsidiary engineering company called ENCON. This was a sound strategic move anticipating that, if and when EHC were forced to divest itself of its operating companies, ENCON could then solicit their business as an outside supplier and for a profit.

Henceforth, EHC spent a lot of energy on delaying tactics against PUHC. The struggle temporarily preserved the profits of its stockholders, but it detracted from the careful planning needed to assure the organization's future existence. This period, which lasted until 1953, was characterized as one of protest and defensiveness, subsequently followed by a recalcitrant, backward-looking, unrealistic attitude that did not facilitate the adjustment process. The company did not refocus its energy and assets on a new, more realistic mission. This failure to remain objective prevented EHC from becoming a much larger and stronger organization, and led to a catastrophic takeover by a conglomerate in 1968—without a doubt, the most severe blow dealt to the organization in its seventy-year history.

Phase 3: The Search for New Beginnings

It is significant to note that, prior to the takeover, contact with the outside environment and its associated struggles were essentially handled by EHC, the parent company. ENCON never had to develop a capacity to market its services, which were mostly furnished to former EHC operating utilities who had elected to do business with ENCON, based on habit and top-level personal relationships. Moreover, the storm over the PUHC and the subsequent struggle to overturn it became EHC's fight, while ENCON seems to have concentrated blissfully on what it knew and liked best—technical work.

ENCON's preferential association with operating utilities and its addiction to high-quality, high-priced work resulted in its failure to fully develop two capabilities crucial for today's competitive environment: (1) to estimate costs of projects within a reasonable degree of accuracy and (2) to extract maximum productivity from its technical staff.

Another legacy was the matter-of-fact treatment of its professional staff. Since ENCON was a prestigious organization, perhaps the best in the industry, it was assumed that professional talent would desire to be associated with such an organization, even if concrete rewards and career opportunities were somewhat limited. Evidence indicates that this elitist concept worked until the late 1950s, when sudden mass retirements and the continued exodus of personnel to its competition resulted in a tremendous shortage of capable managerial talent. Yet little was done formally to develop managers until the 1970s.

Characteristics of past practices also emerged as the leadership of the organization was observed. From the beginnings of EHC to the ENCON of 1978, the leadership for the most part could be characterized as managers and executives who delighted in technical issues, and viewed management as an annoying, if necessary, part of the job. The net effect was excessive reliance on a few technical experts who eventually became managers and department heads, but still performed the most significant technical work themselves. This led to a failure to develop a whole generation of technical personnel capable of performing the work unsupervised. More important, development of managers with a true business perspective was neglected.

This management philosophy, centered on engineering practice, had a negative impact on the organization's ability to focus on the reality of the modern business environment. EHC's failure to invest the considerable cash that had been generated through the sale of its subsidiaries, as directed by the PUHC, led to a disastrous takeover, which saw the predator make off with most of the organization's liquid assets. Moreover, EHC was obliterated as an entity, leaving ENCON as the sole remnant of a once-powerful structure. This turbulence and uncertainty caused by a lack of clear objective also led to a gradual and damaging erosion of the company's market share.

Perhaps the historical deficiency with the most impact on the organization's future was its lack of long-range strategic planning. The company had been somewhat sheltered throughout its existence, while reaping the benefits of a developing technology that demanded the particular expertise that the company possessed; there did not seem to be a need for long-range planning.

When the major historical narrative was completed, we were faced with two problems: (1) to provide a meaningful analysis and (2) to educate management on the theoretical premises upon which the analysis was based. Thus it became necessary to expand the Levinson framework with a matrix developed by Lippitt (see Figure 9.1), which enables an examination of the four phases organizations go through when faced by a major crisis (shock, defensive retreat, acknowledgment, adaptation and change). This particular analytical tool helped distinguish the present state of organizational recovery from a state of crisis.

Recommendations to Management

The recommendations submitted to management were quite specific. They included:

1. Strengthening the company's matrix management system by establishing a clear balance of power between the project organization and the technical disciplines. Specifically, this would be done by developing and implementing a more effective planning and scheduling system, establishing a dual performance-appraisal system for the engineers engaged in project activities, instituting a formal program of development for project managers, developing high-level career opportunities in the technical areas, providing training relevant to the project management system, and examining the necessity for personnel adjustments.
2. Redefining the nature of the leadership role to be more flexible, entrepreneurial, and better in touch with the present environment; and developing appropriate skills in the company's managers.
3. Integrating the regional offices into the corporate decision-making processes.
4. Designing and implementing a human resources planning model integrated with strategic and operational planning.
5. Continuing to address the development of long-range planning capabilities.
6. Radically changing the marketing process.

Review, Action Planning, and Implementation

Management Review

The organizational development council worked through the diagnosis and recommendations for six months. The result was a mandate to prepare action plans for implementing the provisions of the recommendations.

Action Planning

The planning and budgeting for action was done by involving the same managers who had participated in the diagnostic effort. Action plans specified what, when, and where things were to be done and who would be responsible for getting them done.

Implementation

Implementation of the action plans involved interventions in several areas. These interventions included:

1. Redirection of the marketing program, with significant input from an essentially new staff hired away from the company's competitors.
2. Design and implementation of a strategic human resources planning process, whose ultimate features included integration with the strategic and operational plans, and the development of a state-of-the-art human resources information system (HRIS).
3. Implementation of twelve interdepartmental conflict-resolution activities, involving a series of intergroup sessions. These sessions were designed to force independent departments to deal with a changed environment that required better teamwork and coordination to ensure the concerted pursuit of the company's goals. This was a major cultural issue, since the thrust was to break down the traditional independence of departments, which previously had been managed as private fiefdoms. They involved meetings between designated representatives of two departments at a time, facilitated by internal consultants. The result in all cases was a definition of mutual problems and goals, and development of action plans with milestones, responsibilities, and follow-up mechanisms.
4. Implementation of several team-building activities, designed to assist existing work groups in defining goals, roles, and responsibilities, while reinforcing the need for interdependence. These activities were conducted in several configurations: (a) family team building, between a supervisor and his or her immediate subordinates; (b) project team

building, designed to help a project manager and his key managers focus better on problems, roles, relationships, and responsibilities; and (c) functional team building, designed to help managers with the same job but in different divisions deal with common concerns.

5. Implementation of an executive-development program, conducted by a team of outstanding faculty provided by a major business school. The faculty agreed to design a program specifically tailored to the company. The program stressed strategic planning and management, finance, contemporary economics, human resources management, management of technology, and government relations. The curriculum even included a cultural update in the arts, theater, literature, and history. In essence, the program was a crash course on contemporary issues and business practices in today's world. Concurrently, the faculty worked with management to significantly improve the company's strategic-planning process.

The remainder of this appendix describes in detail the most significant actions taken by management, and the design and implementation of significant and sophisticated developmental processes appropriate to the organization at the time.

Strategic Human Resources Forecasting, Planning, and Development Systems

Throughout its history, ENCON's resource considerations in planning had been perceived as mostly financial or marketing matters, with perfunctory attention paid to the people end—the human resources who, in the final analysis, make things happen. If considered at all, the impact of human resources on organizational plans was recognized only when implementation of those plans foundered when the right people to lead such programs were either not available or not ready to assume significantly more demanding responsibilities.

This neglect of the human resources element in planning was due to several factors, among which were (1) the perception that human resources, when needed, could be "bought" on short notice and (2) the reluctance to invest in the internal development of people owing to the expense involved, the time required, and the alleged burden it would impose on supervisors and managers.

In the business environment of the late 1970s, however, such attitudes gave way to a genuine concern for how planning for human resources took place, primarily because of the increasing specialization of skills and consequent competition for people who could be effective contributors in a short time. Moreover, there was growing recognition that the ready availability of proper numbers and quality of people often was the chief determinant of the company's ability to execute its strategic plans. These considerations created an incentive for establishing a formal human resources planning function as a means of controlling and directing this most crucial resource through development, training, and succession planning. Moreover, human resources planning became gradually recognized as an important process that could be most useful when integrated with other established planning systems, in order to match people requirements to goals of the organization.

In practice, this meant using sophisticated techniques that combined qualitative methods of human resources development with quantitative methods of processing and analyzing massive amounts of data and many alternatives—a task that could be accomplished only through the judicious use of computer-based human resources information systems and related forecasting capabilities. Effective systems helped clearly define how the organization fit into its environment, diagnosed its degree of readiness in terms of operational capabilities and weaknesses, and evaluated the quantity and quality of resources available to it at the time. Applying the concept to the whole organization also required using relatively new techniques that integrated strategic planning with operational planning and human resources planning at critical interfaces, in order to provide a more meaningful analysis of an organization's resource needs over time.[8]

Human resources planning systems were designed to accurately forecast current and future manpower needs and to assist management in meeting those needs in the most effective and efficient manner. To accomplish these objectives, data from the various subsystems of this model were integrated to produce two essential elements of information: (1) a human resources demand forecast and (2) a human resources availability forecast.

The demand forecast was based on projections of the number of employees required to meet current and anticipated workloads. This forecast took into account both projects and departmental staffing needs, and was communicated on the basis of type and level of skills required.

The availability forecast was based first upon projections of currently available personnel according to type and level of skill. Subsequently it was modified to account for predictable changes in the employment outlook—i.e, new hires, promotions, transfers, terminations, illness/disability periods, and retirements.

In comparing the demand forecast with the availability forecast, the model produced what is termed a variance forecast—i.e., a determination of projected surpluses or shortages in the number of employees required to meet current and anticipated needs.

This approach to integrated forecasting enabled tentative identification of the gap between resources required to execute strategic and operational plans and resources available to the organization. Once the gap was identified, decisions could be made on interventions to close it.

The final step involved reviewing the plans submitted by department heads to top management. In its review, management considered the operational manpower demand forecasts and directed department heads to take necessary steps to provide adequate staffing for active, scheduled, and potential projects. In addition, the new human resources level required heads to staff their departments to meet the needs of corporate strategic plans. Based upon these staffing instructions, appropriate internal and external searches were made until the hiring or assignment of appropriate individuals took place.

While this type of analysis did not produce a "perfect" match between requirements and resources, it did simulate likely conditions, and therefore helped top management to identify imminent major manpower problems.

With this approach, human resources planning and development became an integral part of the strategic-planning process, ensuring the congruence of plans at all levels and the availability of resources when needed, while maintaining the flexibility necessary to make changes.

Integration of Human Resources Development With Corporate Strategy

For the most part, the intent of the system was to forecast employee demand through the strategic and operational plans, and to compare that demand with forecasted availability, the latter computed by adding the results of career paths adjusted for attrition.

Strategic Planning: Managing Toward the Future

For several years, the organization had engaged in corporate planning. The process started with a definition of financial goals and objectives. It followed with an evaluation of the company in regard to its relative strength in areas such as resources and technology, including its present and anticipated financial status, its basic capabilities of production, its situation in the marketplace, the quantity and quality of present human resources, and its position in research and development. A thorough examination of financial goals and objectives enabled regular evaluation of operating results and prospects.

A considerable amount of environmental scanning focused on economic trends, regulatory requirements, technical developments, competitors' actions, and availability of human resources in the economy. To this, appropriate marketing data were added and analyzed.

The integration of internal and external data that were collected led to development of preliminary strategies, their testing by a variety of means, and the selection of primary and alternative strategies.

Training and Management Development Linked With Strategic Planning

By 1983, the company had achieved a significant level of sophistication in strategic planning. At about this time, however, the effects of the economic downturn for the engineering and construction industry became of particular concern.

Previous work done on strategy development clearly indicated that at that point in time, the company had reached its limit in its ability to prognosticate. Moreover, the diagnostic team was experiencing difficulties in developing truly effective strategies and tactics even for identified scenarios, particularly those that required the organization to pursue nontraditional lines of business. Top management also recognized that the skills of a management group that had grown up in basically a single industry needed to be broadened. After several discussions at the highest levels of the organization, a decision was made to seek outside resources to provide knowledge and insight in areas beyond the mainline service business. It was clearly stated that emphasis would have to be on the development of a broader perspective of the business world and on the reinforcement of strategic skills.

After further deliberation, management decided to seek the help of a major, respected educational institution, rather than a consulting organization; the main reason for doing so was the desire to combine new business skills with additional work designed to broaden technically competent executives into individuals highly aware of the world around them, in both the business and the cultural sense.

Several top business schools were invited to review the company's needs. The requirements were quite specific, demanding that, at the end of the program, executives would:

1. Adopt a strategic perspective in planning and implementation, rather than the medium-range, activity-oriented behavior that might have been appropriate in the past but was no longer adequate in today's environment.
2. Stress marketing of services to a greater degree than before.
3. Develop entrepreneurial skills necessary for the desired push into diversification.
4. Manage existing technology and develop or acquire new technology necessary to the diversification program.
5. Acquire knowledge about the workings of government, politics, and the influence process necessary to promote favorable legislative response to major capital-projects funding.
6. Update their knowledge base with the latest concepts and techniques in fundamental areas such as financial management, economics, forecasting, decision making, and human resources management.
7. Provide a cultural update in literature, the theater, arts, and history.

A major northeastern business school was selected as the one with the resources and reputation necessary to do the job. This school exhibited flexibility in working with ENCON to develop a program tailored to meet the needs of their executives. The program, which was designed in conjunction with ENCON, consisted of thirteen two-day sessions conducted once a month. In addition, the cultural update was accomplished during evening sessions. Each session was attended by groups of twenty-five senior managers, including the CEO and COO. The school did an outstanding job of providing a world-class faculty that, over the course of the program, became a genuine resource to the company's management.

Each session of the program was designed to provide new input for two intensive days, followed by specific assignments to be done back on the job. The new information was applied to further work on the existing strategies, and by the end of the first thirteen-month cycle, radical changes were made to existing strategic plans. The sessions enabled the management group to examine the business environment in depth, assess the strengths and weaknesses of the organization, and establish a process likely to lead the company in a new direction.

As a result of the program, a parallel management structure to manage strategic planning was established. It consisted of:

- A corporate strategy group (CSG), composed of the top executives, responsible for the corporate portfolio and new corporate activities
- Seven business-family planning groups responsible for the development and monitoring of group operating plans and for new business areas
- Seventeen business-program planning teams responsible for the actual development and monitoring of specific strategic programs

About a hundred key technical and staff support managers were selected to serve as members of the various business planning teams. Each of these teams, chaired by a group vice president, was charged with analyzing and developing business plans for each of the selected major segments of the company's business portfolio. The implementation of strategic plans developed by these planning teams and the responsibility for contracts and orders for services became the realm of the various operating groups.

Following the development of the strategic programs, an evaluation was made of the financial and human resources necessary to implement those plans. Budgets were set, revised, and finalized for each of the approved plans. On the human resources side, the task was much more complex.

The analysis of human resources requirements to execute the strategic plans focused on statements in the plans that referred to needs for additional staff, as well as indications that the strategy could be implemented only by people whose skills were either uncommon or not readily available in the organization. The following are examples of statements in the strategic plans, and the corresponding questions asked by the human resources planners and training specialists.

Water-Resources Planning and Engineering Capability

> "A water-resources planning and engineering capability will be developed. A total of five members of the consulting engineering staff will be assigned to support the water-resources business development program. Three of these individuals will need to be

developed or hired, and the other two will be existing staff members. There will be a need for people with experience with the federal water-resource agencies and in the water-supply business at the state and local agencies."

Questions

- Which two existing staff members will be used?
- Should we hire or develop the other three specialists? Will it be cheaper to hire such people from the outside, or to train existing employees? If the latter, who will do the training?

Domestic Operating Nuclear Projects

"Use the approach of marketing completion services via a combination of business development people and four teams of experts from Quality Assurance, Construction, Project Engineering, Project Management, Licensing and Plant Services."

Questions

- Who would be the key people on these teams?
- How large would each team be?
- What special skills would be required?

Mothballing of Power Plants

"Identification of candidate plants for mothballing will require personnel who can assess the completion status of deferred units, regulatory status and technical feasibility of mothballing, and eventual reactivation. It will also require individuals familiar with the financial status of the utilities and the options available under the state's Public Service Commission regulations."

Questions

- Do we have people with the necessary experience and skills to identify and prioritize candidate plants?
- Who are they?
- How many people would be required?

Obviously, hundreds of such statements were analyzed, thousands of questions were asked. The end result, however, was a definition of the number and kinds of people required to implement each strategic plan. This strategic demand was added to the operational (immediate and proximate) demand in order to compute the total number of people the organization would need in order to pursue its plans.

Furthermore, the gaps in numbers and skills were identified, and the necessary action to close those gaps was initiated. Action occurred in basically two areas: (1) development of training programs consistent with the needs of people assigned to implement the strategic programs, and (2) recruiting of people with skills not previously found in the company. In order to minimize the cost of training, the organization extensively used the concept of "leveraging technology." This involves utilizing a few recognized experts as key resources or trainers, around whom teams of less experienced but competent employees are assigned. Under the guidance of experts, the employees learn by doing on the job, aided by formal training when necessary.

Strategic Linkage of Human Resources Development

The linkage, or cause-and-effect relationship, between corporate strategies and training and development programs obviously is quite strong at ENCON, as would be expected in any organization in which different strategies require involvement in various technologies, with correspondingly discrete professional disciplines, technical specialties, and experience requirements. Put simply, the engineers needed in nuclear power plant design are not the same as needed in wastewater management or bridge and highway construction. The technologies involved in different "lines of business" can be vastly different, and strategies to shift resources into new markets invariably must consider the varying technical skills and discipline-specific knowledge needed to succeed in each market.

The specialized training and development that may be required in a high-tech industry such as ENCON's were identified by a computerized skills inventory, which listed the types of work in market areas, such as alternative-energy facilities, that were of interest to ENCON. In each type of work, human resources requirements were further defined as involving engineering disciplines, construction experience, or quality-control skills. Other potential markets singled out by strategic planning, such as energy transmission or the military market, required an even greater array of discretely identifiable skills and experience.

Of course, not all the identified market and discipline categories required formal training or separate developmental experience; but vastly different qualifications were needed across the range of technologies involved in the different markets targeted by the strategic plans.

Information in the human resources data base on the skills, talents, qualifications, and career paths of individuals made possible the analysis of both "where we stand" with respect to specific technical skills and "where we would stand" at various times in the future, as a result of existing training and development, career paths, attrition, and other factors. Network-flow availability forecasting, based on career paths, provided a view of the future qualifications of managers and professionals, and indicated gaps or variances between the demand requirements of a given strategy—such as x number of municipal solid-waste plants of a certain type—and the availability of personnel to staff such operations.

In some cases, the variances were too great to be economically "managed." Market conditions, cost considerations, and other corporate-planning factors indicated that human and other resources would be more profitably used by selecting and pursuing another strategy.

Most critically, the analysis of the impact of change—in strategic objectives, operational demand, or human resources—was conducted with an understanding of the interrelatedness of change. For example, different cost estimates of having available a certain number of qualified engineers at a certain time in the future could be presented for management decision. Such a capability, possible only with a fully integrated system that encompasses both demand and availability factors of human resources planning, permitted management interventions that were least costly or otherwise optimal in pursuit of organizational goals and objectives.

Appraisal Systems Tied to Strategic Goals

Performance appraisal is a subsystem of the integrated human resources planning and development process that estimated the availability of human resources to accomplish ENCON's strategic objectives. Guided by needs depicted as short- and long-term demand, performance appraisal permitted the organization to assess the capabilities of the existing managerial and technical work force, based on past performance. A separate system, potential appraisal, used similar organization-specific criteria to assess how well these same individuals might do in the future. Performance appraisals that look at the past and potential evaluations that assess future capabilities, worked together to identify the managers and professionals—their numbers, qualifications, skills, and talents—that would be needed in the years ahead.

For example, performance-appraisal criteria were developed on the basis of organizational needs, rather than on abstract concepts of what is "right" according to general business principles, professional standards, or subjective measurements. If the company were to need a growing number of a certain type of manager, with a specific background in a given technical area and capable of managing with a certain style (say, through extensive delegation of authority on complex projects requiring many disciplines), then criteria reinforcing these qualifications would be built in to the evaluation instruments used in performance appraisal.

As a practical matter, in the case of a highly complex organization such as ENCON, this meant that many different evaluation instruments were required. The rationale was that the same criteria cannot adequately measure the performance of research scientists working on a new technology and project managers handling a relatively standardized construction project; even greater differences existed among managerial, professional, and support personnel.

This approach to performance appraisal can be criticized for allowing too much flexibility. Indeed, allowing many departments to modify the instruments results in a significant administrative burden. It has been correctly pointed out that the assessment and processing of evaluations is surely an easier and less complicated process when only a few forms are used, instead of dozens of different instruments with different criteria for different positions.

However, when the primary objective of performance appraisal (as well as potential appraisal, career planning, and succession planning) is to achieve the availability of human resources dictated by strategic plans, these considerations become secondary. If the future needs of the organization are specifically diverse and dissimilar, so should be the instruments that assess the capabilities of employees to fill those needs.

Computers to assimilate, organize, and access performance- and potential-appraisal information permitted the cost-effective use of a multiplicity of forms and evaluation instruments; they also allowed systems administrators to assess the effectiveness of the systems themselves. For example, ratings of individual supervisors were readily compared with overall company ratings, ratings within a department, or past ratings by the supervisor. Trouble spots were quickly identified for further investigation. Most important, the mechanization of data assured that supervisors who used performance appraisals to help employees improve performance had available to them reliable, comprehensive data, and were guided by the same understanding of organizational objectives.

Career Planning: Basis for Availability Forecasts

The purpose of any career-management system is to merge the vocational goals of individuals with the business goals of the organization. Another, more pragmatic view suggests that career management is a way of harnessing the hopes and personal objectives of individuals to corporate ends. To reinforce the process, developmental activities are provided for individuals with the qualifications, skills, and experience necessary to become significant contributors to the organization.

In a strategically integrated system, however, a career-management system can do even more than this. Career paths can be the basis for availability forecasts that project the availability of internally developed employees, and provide planners with a means of closing the gap between demand and supply.

Such an approach also strengthens the generic purpose of career planning: When employees recognize that their career paths are linked to strategic objectives, that the positions they are working toward in the years ahead will genuinely be needed by the organization, career planning gains credibility and the commitment of its participants. Thus, career paths are no longer an assortment of unrelated wish lists lacking a basis in reality, but become part of a strategic plan that will have the right people in the appropriate positions at the right time.

Conclusions

This case illustrated how organizational "pain" owing to changing market conditions encouraged the management of a company to commission an organizational diagnosis. The report, which took over a year to complete, provided significant insight into the reasons for the organization's inability to deal effectively with a new environment, and it demonstrated that the company's history and culture were in part responsible for that. Subsequent interventions at many levels initiated a program of recovery that helped mitigate the effects of a particularly troublesome decade for the industry.

The effectiveness of linking the major planning systems (strategic, operational, and human resources) was demonstrated. This is a clear case of how a corporate strategy, which was found wanting, justified advanced training for the company's top managers (the executive program), and this training led to acquisition of new skills, which in turn enabled a reexamination of corporate goals and strategies and resulted in new or enhanced strategies. Implementation of those strategies was in the hands of the same people who were trained, who in turn sent their subordinates through a similar process of education and problem solving. Implementation of the enhanced strategic plans was supported, in both the short and long term, by the various human resources programs that not only helped project the number of people required to execute strategic and operational plans, but also enabled the development and retention of the best people in the organization, based on what the strategic plans indicated would be required.

The organizational diagnosis at ENCON was on the cutting edge of such methodology. The venture was helpful in promoting a corporate culture that is client and market oriented, aggressive and forward looking, tolerant of uncertainty, and realistic in its goal setting. The enhanced processes of strategic planning and human resources management were reinforced by a consciousness that the organization and its people were dealing with immediate threats (the severely depressed state of the industry) by improving productivity and enhancing technical know-how, while building for the future through continued emphasis on flexible strategic planning and effective management of human resources.

An empirical evaluation of the strategic orientation of ENCON can be made by comparing its performance to that of its competitors. Whereas, in the last decade, many organizations within the industry experienced severe cutbacks and loss of earnings, ENCON maintained essentially the same staffing level and has remained profitable.

ENCON's diagnosis isolated a number of important facts about the organization. The company saw the need to develop a strong marketing department. It learned where to strengthen its matrix organization. It improved its team-building programs. Top management learned that secrecy about the company's financial affairs created needless anxiety and general pessimism throughout the company. It learned that its pride in the company's past was a strong impetus to change some present practices and work for a more positive future.

But in many ways the strongest and most positive effects of the study concerned not the findings, but the process. People gained tremendous insight into the organization and themselves, as they researched, interviewed, and organized the data. The study was a cathartic experience, and many said it would have been personally significant and satisfying even if it had not generated change. And the study was an energizer. People gained new pride in the organization, confidence in themselves, and zest for their work.

The aftermath of the diagnostic study was not just the planning and implementation of action plans, but the development of a new culture, reinforced by learning new ways of thinking through problems and finding solutions. In fact, the people in the organization internalized such changes in a way that they now routinely employ diagnostic approaches whenever they are faced with problems and challenges.

Notes

Chapter 1

1. Elliott Jaques, *A General Theory of Bureaucracy* (London: Heinemann, 1978). See also Elliott Jaques, with R. O. Gibson and D. J. Issac, *Levels of Abstraction in Logic and Human Action* (London: Heinemann, 1978).
2. Richard Beckhard, *Organization Development: Strategies and Models* (Reading, Mass.: Addison-Wesley, 1969), p. 9.

Chapter 5

1. Paul R. Lawrence and Jay W. Lorsch, *Developing Organizations: Diagnosis and Action* (Reading, Mass.: Addison-Wesley, 1969), p. 2.
2. Harry Levinson, *Organizational Diagnosis* (Cambridge, Mass.: Harvard University Press, 1972), pp. 3–4.
3. Levinson, *Organizational Diagnosis*, p. 3.
4. Levinson, *Organizational Diagnosis*, p. 5.
5. Levinson, *Organizational Diagnosis*, pp. 74–86.
6. Levinson, *Organizational Diagnosis*, p. 74.
7. Gordon Lippitt and Warren H. Schmidt, "Crises in a Developing Organization," *Harvard Business Review* (November-December 1987), p. 103. See also Gordon L. Lippitt, *Organizational Renewal* (New York: Appleton-Century-Crofts, 1969), p. 28.
8. Lippitt, *Organizational Renewal*, pp. 26–41.

Chapter 6

1. Richard Beckhard and Reubin T. Harris, *Organizational Transitions: Managing Complex Change* (Reading, Mass.: Addison-Wesley, 1977), pp. 8–15.
2. Richard F. Beckhard, "Applied Theories Guiding Interventions in Large Systems Change." Presentation delivered at Columbia University Graduate School of Business, Advanced Program in Organization Development and Human Resource Management. Tarrytown, New York, 1986.
3. Boston Consulting Group, "Growth and Financial Strategies: Special Commentary," 1971. See also Bruce Henderson, "Experience Curve—Reviewed," Boston Consulting Group Perspectives, 1974.
4. Daniel H. Gray, "Uses and Misuses of Strategic Planning," *Harvard Business Review* (January-February 1986), p. 90.
5. Gray, "Uses and Misuses," pp. 91–94.

Chapter 7

1. Gordon Donaldson, "Financial Goals and Strategic Consequences," *Harvard Business Review* (May-June 1985), p. 58.
2. Donaldson, "Financial Goals," pp. 59–62.

Chapter 8

1. Abraham Zaleznik and Manfred F. R. Kets de Vries, *Power and the Corporate Mind* (Boston: Houghton Mifflin, 1975), pp. 31–33, 35, 37.
2. William F. Glueck, *Management* (Hinsdale, Ill.: The Dryden Press, 1980), pp. 485–488.
3. Ian C. MacMillan, *Strategy Formulation: Political Concepts* (St. Paul, Minn.: West Publishing Company, 1978).
4. MacMillan, *Strategy Formulation*.

Chapter 9

1. Stephen L. Fink, Joel Beak, and Kenneth Taddeo, "Organizational Crisis and Change," *Journal of Applied Behavioral Science*, Vol. 7, No. 1 (1971).
2. "Behind the Monolith: A Look at IBM," *The Wall Street Journal* (April 7, 1986), p. 25.

Chapter 10

1. Richard F. Beckhard and Reubin T. Harris, *Organizational Transitions: Managing Complex Change* (Reading, Mass.: Addison-Wesley, 1977), p. 9.
2. Beckhard and Harris, *Organizational Transitions*, p. 62.

Chapter 11

1. Arthur Louis, "The Bottom Line on Ten Big Mergers," *Fortune* (May 3, 1982).

Appendix 1

1. Harry Levinson, *Organizational Diagnosis* (Cambridge, Mass.: Harvard University Press, 1972), p. 133.

Appendix 2

1. Cortlandt Cammann, Mark Fichman, et al., "Assessing the Attitudes and Perceptions of Organizational Members," Chapter 4 in Stanley E. Seashore, Edward Lawler III, Philip H. Mirvis, and Cammann, eds., *Assessing Organizational Change: A Guide to Methods, Measures, and Practices* (New York: John Wiley & Sons, 1983).
2. Walter R. Mahler, *Diagnostic Studies* (Reading, Mass.: Addison-Wesley, 1974), pp. 17–19.
3. Jack R. Fordyce and Raymond Weil, "Methods for Finding Out What's Going On," Chapter 11 in Wendell L. French, Cecil H. Bell, and Robert A. Zawacky, eds. *Organization Development: Theory, Practice and Research* (Dallas: Business Publications, Inc., Irwin-Dorsey, Ltd., 1978).

4. Paul K. Lawrence and Jay W. Lorsch, *Developing Organizations: Diagnosis and Action* (Reading, Mass.: Addison-Wesley, 1969), p. 30. See also Philip H. Mirvis, "Assessing the Process and Progress of Change in Organizational Change Programs," Chapter 14 in Seashore, *Assessing Organizational Change*.
5. Mahler, *Diagnostic Studies*, p. 19.
6. Cammann, et al., "Assessing the Attitudes."
7. Cammann, et al., "Assessing the Attitudes."
8. Robert R. Blake and Jane S. Mouton, *Building a Dynamic Corporation Through GRID Organization Development* (Reading, Mass.: Addison-Wesley, 1969).
9. Mark Frohman, Marshall Sashkin, and Michael J. Kavanagh, "Action Research as Applied to Organization Development," *Organization and Administrative Sciences*, Vol. 7, Nos. 1 and 2 (Spring/Summer 1976).
10. Marvin R. Weisbord, *Organizational Diagnosis: A Workbook of Theory and Practice* (Reading, Mass.: Addison-Wesley, 1978).
11. Kurt Lewin, "Action Research and Minority Problems," *Journal of Social Psychology*, Vol. 2 (1946), pp. 34–46; and Kurt Lewin, "Research on Minority Problems," *The Technology Review*, Vol. 48, No. 3 (January 1946), pp. 163, 164, 182.
12. Ronald Lippitt, "Value Judgment Problems in the Social Scientist Participation in Action-Research," Paper at annual meeting of American Psychological Association, September 1950.
13. Wendell L. French and Cecil H. Bell, Jr., *Organization Development: Behavioral Science Interventions for Organization Improvement* (Englewood Cliffs, N.J.: Prentice-Hall, 1984).
14. Peter B. Vaill, "An Informal Glossary of Terms and Phrases in Organization Development," in *The 1973 Annual Handbook for Group Facilitators* (La Jolla, Calif.: University Associates, 1973).
15. Marshall Sashkin, "Models and Roles of Change Agents," in *The 1974 Annual Handbook for Group Facilitators* (La Jolla, Calif.: University Associates, 1974).
16. Weisbord, *Organizational Diagnosis*.
17. Frohman et al., "Action Research."
18. Ronald Lippitt, J. Watson, and B. Westley, *The Dynamics of Planned Change* (New York: Harcourt Brace & World, 1958).
19. D. A. Kolb and A. L. Frohman, "An Organization Development Approach to Consulting," *Sloan Management Review*, No. 12 (1970).
20. Frederick Hertzberg, *Work and the Nature of Man* (New York: World Publishing Company, 1966).
21. Abraham H. Maslow, *Motivation and Personality*, 2nd ed. (New York: Harper & Row, 1970).
22. Robert R. Blake and Jane S. Mouton, *Consultation* (Reading, Mass.: Addison-Wesley, 1976), p. 101.
23. Wendell L. French, Cecil H. Bell, and Robert A. Zawacky, eds., *Organization Development: Theory, Practice and Research* (Dallas: Business Publications Inc., Irwin Dorsey, 1978), p. 18.
24. Alfred J. Marrow, D. G. Bowers, and S. E. Seashore, eds., *Strategies of Organizational Change* (New York: Harper & Row, 1967), p. 26.
25. French et al., *Organization Development*, pp. 17–18.
26. Paul R. Lawrence and Jay W. Lorsch, *Organization and Environment: Managing Differentiation and Integration* (Boston: Harvard Business School Press, 1986), p. 162.
27. Rensis Likert, *New Patterns of Management* (New York: McGraw-Hill, 1961).
28. Rensis Likert, *The Human Organization: Its Management and Value* (New York:

McGraw-Hill, 1967). See also Likert with Jane Gibson Likert, *New Ways of Managing Conflict* (New York: McGraw-Hill, 1976).
29. Chris Argyris, *Intervention Theory and Method: A Behavioral Science View* (Reading, Mass.: Addison-Wesley, 1973).
30. Warren Bennis, *Organization Development: Its Nature, Origins and Prospects* (Reading, Mass.: Addison-Wesley, 1969).
31. Bennis, *Organization Development,* p. 21.
32. Bennis, *Organization Development,* p. 54.
33. "Creating the Adaptive Organization: Organizing for a New Era." Conference sponsored by The Conference Board, New York, July 9–10, 1986.
34. Bennis, *Organization Development,* pp. 77–79. See also Bennis, "The Politics of Change," Chapter 50 in French et al., *Organizational Development.*
35. Warren Bennis, "Theory and Method in Applying Behavioral Science to Planned Organizational Change," *Journal of Applied Behavioral Science,* Vol. 1, No. 4 (1965).
36. Gordon Lippitt, *Organizational Renewal* (New York: Appleton-Century-Crofts, 1969), p. 1.
37. A. K. Rice, *The Enterprise and Its Environment* (London: Tavistock Publications, 1963), pp. 186–198.
38. John A. Seiler, *Systems Analysis in Organizational Behavior* (Homewood, Ill.: Richard D. Irwin, Inc., 1967), pp. 23ff.
39. Robert F. Mager and Peter Pipe, *Analyzing Performance Problems or "You Really Oughta Wanna"* (Belmont, Calif.: Fearon Publishers, 1972).
40. Thomas H. Gilbert, *Human Competence: Engineering Worthy Performance* (New York: McGraw-Hill, 1978).
41. Charles H. Kepner and Benjamin M. Tregoe, *The Rational Manager: A Systematic Approach to Problem Solving and Decision Making* (New York: McGraw-Hill, 1965).
42. Weisbord, *Organizational Diagnosis.*
43. Paul R. Lawrence and Jay W. Lorsch, *Developing Organization: Diagnosis and Action* (Reading, Mass.: Addison-Wesley, 1969), p. 6.
44. Lawrence and Lorsch, *Organization and Environment.*
45. Harry Levinson, *Organizational Diagnosis* (Cambridge, Mass.: Harvard University Press, 1972).
46. Levinson, *Organizational Diagnosis,* p. 4.

Appendix 3

1. Harry Levinson, *Organizational Diagnosis* (Cambridge, Mass.: Harvard University Press, 1972).
2. Richard Beckhard, from "Organization Development," a lecture conducted at the Columbia University Advanced Program in Organization Development and Human Resource Management, New York, 1966.
3. Levinson, *Organizational Diagnosis,* pp. 74–78.
4. Gordon Lippitt and Warren H. Schmidt, "Crises in a Developing Organization," *Harvard Business Review,* Vol. 45, No. 6 (November-December 1987).
5. Levinson, *Organizational Diagnosis,* p. 78.
6. Levinson, *Organizational Diagnosis,* p. 78.
7. Lippitt and Schmidt, "Crises in a Developing Organization."
8. Andrew O. Manzini and John D. Gridley, *Integrating Human Resources and Strategic Business Planning* (New York: AMACOM, 1986).

Bibliography

Argyris, Chris. *Intervention Theory and Method: A Behavioral Science View.* Reading, Mass.: Addison-Wesley, 1973.
Beckhard, Richard F. *Organization Development: Strategies and Models.* Reading, Mass.: Addison-Wesley, 1969.
———. *Organization Development: Its Nature, Origins and Prospects.* Reading, Mass.: Addison-Wesley, 1969.
———. "Applied Theories Guiding Interventions in Large Systems Change." Presentation delivered at Columbia University Graduate School of Business, Advanced Program in Organization Development and Human Resource Management. Tarrytown, New York, 1976.
———, and Reubin T. Harris. *Organizational Transitions: Managing Complex Change.* Reading, Mass.: Addison-Wesley, 1977.
"Behind the Monoloth: A Look at IBM." *The Wall Street Journal* (April 7, 1986).
Bennis, Warren G. "The Politics of Change." Chapter 50 in *Organization Development: Theory, Practice and Research,* Wendell L. French, Cecil H. Bell, and Robert A. Zawacky, eds. Dallas: Business Publications, Inc., Irwin-Dorsey, Ltd., 1978.
———. "Theory and Method in Applying Behavioral Science to Planned Organizational Change." *Journal of Applied Behavioral Science,* Vol. 1, No. 4 (1965).
———. *Changing Organizations.* New York: McGraw-Hill, 1966.
Blake, Robert R., and Jane S. Mouton. *Building a Dynamic Corporation Through GRID Organization Development.* Reading, Mass.: Addison-Wesley, 1969.
———. *Consultation.* Reading, Mass.: Addison-Wesley, 1976.
———. *The Managerial Grid III.* Houston: Gulf Publishing Co., 1985.
Boston Consulting Group. "Growth and Financial Strategies: Special Commentary," 1971.
Cammann, Cortlandt, Mark Fichman, Douglas G. Jenkins, and John R. Klesh. "Assessing the Attitudes and Perceptions of Organizational Members." Chapter 4 in *Assessing Organizational Change: A Guide to Methods, Measures, and Practices,* Stanley E. Seashore, Edward Lawler III, Philip H. Mirvis, and Cortlandt Cammann, eds. New York: Wiley, 1983.
Collier, J. "United States Indian Administration as a Laboratory of Ethnic Relations." *Social Research,* No. 12 (1945).
"Creating the Adaptive Organization: Organizing for a New Era." Conference sponsored by The Conference Board, New York, July 9–10, 1986.
Donaldson, Gordon. "Financial Goals and Strategic Consequences." *Harvard Business Review* (May-June 1985).
Fink, Stephen L., Joel Beak, and Kenneth Taddeo. "Organizational Crisis and Change." *Journal of Applied Behavioral Science,* Vol. 7, No. 1 (1971).
Fordyce, Jack R., and Raymond Weil. "Methods for Finding Out What's Going On." Chapter 11 in *Organization Development: Theory, Practice and Research,* Wendell

L. French, Cecil H. Bell, and Robert A. Zawacky, eds. Dallas: Business Publications, Inc., Irwin-Dorsey, Ltd., 1978.

French, Wendell L., and Cecil H. Bell, Jr. *Organization Development: Behavioral Science Interventions for Organization Improvement.* Englewood Cliffs, N.J.: Prentice-Hall, 1984.

French, Wendell L., Cecil H. Bell, and Robert A. Zawacky, eds. *Organization Development: Theory, Practice and Research.* Dallas: Business Publications, Inc., Irwin-Dorsey, Ltd. 1978.

Frohman, Mark, Marshall Sashkin, and Michael J. Kavanagh. "Action Research as Applied to Organization Development." *Organization and Administrative Sciences,* Vol. 7, Nos. 1 and 2 (Spring/Summer 1976).

Gilbert, Thomas H. *Human Competence: Engineering Worthy Performance.* New York: McGraw-Hill, 1978.

Glueck, William F. *Business Policy: Strategy Formation and Management Action.* New York: McGraw-Hill, 1972.

———. *Management.* Hinsdale, Ill.: The Dryden Press, 1980.

Gray, Daniel H. "Uses and Misuses of Strategic Planning." *Harvard Business Review* (January-February 1986).

Helfert, Eric A. *Techniques of Financial Analysis.* Homewood, Ill.: Richard D. Irwin, 1982.

Henderson, Bruce. "Experience Curve—Reviewed," Boston Consulting Group Perspectives, 1974.

Hertzberg, Frederick. *Work and the Nature of Man.* New York: World Publishing Company, 1966.

Jaques, Elliott. *A General Theory of Bureaucracy.* London: Heinemann, 1978.

———, with R. O. Gibson and D. J. Issac. *Levels of Abstraction in Logic and Human Action.* London: Heinemann, 1978.

Kepner, Charles H., and Benjamin M. Tregoe. *The Rational Manager: A Systematic Approach to Problem Solving and Decision Making.* New York: McGraw-Hill, 1965.

Kolb, D. A., and A. L. Frohman. "An Organization Development Approach to Consulting." *Sloan Management Review,* No. 12 (1970).

Lawrence, Paul R., and Jay W. Lorsch. *Developing Organizations: Diagnosis and Action.* Reading, Mass.: Addison-Wesley, 1969.

———. *Organization and Environment: Managing Differentiation and Integration.* Boston: Harvard Business School Press, 1986.

Levinson, Harry. *Organizational Diagnosis.* Cambridge, Mass.: Harvard University Press, 1972.

Lewin, Kurt. "Action Research and Minority Problems." *Journal of Social Psychology,* Vol. 2 (1946).

———. "Research on Minority Problems." *The Technology Review,* Vol. 48, No. 3 (January 1946).

Likert, Rensis. *New Patterns of Management.* New York: McGraw-Hill, 1961.

———. *The Human Organization: Its Management and Value.* New York: McGraw-Hill, 1967.

———, with Jane Gibson Likert. *New Ways of Managing Conflict.* New York: McGraw-Hill, 1976.

Lippitt, Gordon L. *Organizational Renewal.* New York: Appleton-Century-Crofts, 1969.

———, Peter Langseth, and Jack Mossop. *Implementing Organizational Change: A Practical Guide to Managing Change Efforts.* San Francisco: Jossey-Bass Publishers, 1985.

———, and Warren H. Schmidt. "Crises in a Developing Organization." *Harvard Business Review* (November-December 1987).
Lippitt, Ronald. "Value Judgment Problems in the Social Scientist Participation in Action-Research." Paper presented at the annual meeting of the American Psychological Association, September 1950.
———, J. Watson, and B. Westley. *The Dynamics of Planned Change.* New York: Harcourt Brace & World, 1958.
Lorange, Peter, and Richard F. Vancil. *Strategic Planning Systems.* Englewood Cliffs, N.J.: Prentice-Hall, 1977.
Louis, Arthur. "The Bottom Line on Ten Big Mergers." *Fortune* (May 3, 1982).
MacMillan, Ian C. *Strategy Formulation: Political Concepts.* St. Paul, Minn.: West Publishing Company, 1978.
Mager, Robert F., and Peter Pipe. *Analyzing Performance Problems or "You Really Oughta Wanna."* Belmont, Calif.: Fearon Publishers, 1972.
Mahler, Walter R. *Diagnostic Studies.* Reading, Mass.: Addison-Wesley, 1974.
Manzini, Andrew O., and John D. Gridley. *Integrating Human Resources and Strategic Business Planning.* New York: AMACOM, 1986.
Marrow, Alfred J., D. G. Bowers, and S. E. Seashore, eds. *Strategies of Organizational Change.* New York: Harper & Row, 1967.
Maslow, Abraham H. *Eupsychian Management.* Homewood, Ill.: Richard D. Irwin, Inc., Dorsey Press, 1965.
———. *Motivation and Personality.* New York: Harper & Row, 1954.
Mirvis, Philip H. "Assessing the Process and Progress of Change in Organizational Change Programs." Chapter 14 in *Assessing Organizational Change: A Guide to Methods, Measures, and Practices,* Stanley Seashore et al., eds. New York: Wiley—Interscience, 1983.
Rice, A. K. *The Enterprise and Its Environment.* London: Tavistock Publications, 1963.
Sashkin, Marshall. "Models and Roles of Change Agents." In *The 1974 Annual Handbook for Group Facilitators.* La Jolla, Calif.: University Associates, 1974.
———. "Organization Development Practices." *Professional Psychology,* No. 4 (1973).
Seashore, Stanley E., Edward E. Lawler III, Philip H. Mirvis, and Cortlandt Cammann, eds. *Assessing Organizational Change: A Guide to Methods, Measures, and Practices.* New York: Wiley—Interscience, 1983.
Seiler, John A. *Systems Analysis in Organizational Behavior.* Homewood, Ill.: Richard D. Irwin, Inc., 1967.
Selfridge, Richard J., and Stanley L. Sokolik. "A Comprehensive View of Organization Development." *MSU Business Topics,* Winter 1969.
Vaill, Peter B. "An Informal Glossary of Terms and Phrases in Organization Development." In *The 1973 Annual Handbook for Group Facilitators.* La Jolla, Calif.: University Associates, 1973.
Weisbord, Marvin R. *Organizational Diagnosis: A Workbook of Theory and Practice.* Reading, Mass.: Addison-Wesley, 1978.
Zaleznik, Abraham, and Manfred F. R. Kets de Vries. *Power and the Corporate Mind.* Boston: Houghton Mifflin, 1975.

Index

A

acquisitions (case study), 175–180
action implementation, 242–243, 267–268
action planning, 11, 155–160, 241, 242, 267
action research, 239–243, 245
administrative forms, *see* forms, administrative
administrative task clusters, 40–41
Allegis Corp., 117
analyst's role, 12, 24
Argyris, Chris, on sensitivity training, 246–247
AST Research, 120
attitude surveys, 235–239
authority of leaders, 130–135

B

background research, 105
Beak, Joel, on organizational crisis, 144–145
Beckhard, Richard, 211n, 260
   on core mission, 91, 158–159
   on organizational development, 7
   on power, 134
behavioral science models, 234–249
behavioral scientists, 24–25
behavior modification, 244–245
Bell, Jr., Cecil H., 236n
Bennis, Warren, on organizational development, 247–248
Blake, Robert R., 239
Boston Consulting Group, 97
business environment, *see* environment, business
business planning, *see* strategic planning

C

Cammann, Cortlandt, on attitude surveys, 236

career management, 6, 276
case studies
   mergers and acquisitions, 165–180
   organizational diagnosis, 258–278
   strategy development, 175–180
   team building, 180–190
change
   action research models, 240, 243
   behavior modification, 244–245
   case studies, 165–190
   commitment to, 11, 38, 193
   as a crisis phase, 146
   organizational, 158
   perceptions of, 47
   resistance to, 10, 257
Chrysler Corp., 4
classification of data, *see* data classification
clients, *see* sponsors
common-size analysis, 114
Compaq Computer Corp., 120
comprehensive diagnosis, 16–20, 234, 251–257
confidentiality, 57, 71–72
conflict, 144
conflict management, 135–136
consultants
   client-analyst relationship, 242
   orientation as experts, 10
   role of, 12, 24
   use of, 183–184, 254–257
consultants vs. internal managers, 9, 13, 24
contributors, list in final diagnostic report, 149–150
core mission, consensus on, 158–159
Core Mission and Strategic Planning Issues Analysis, 59, 211–216
core-mission statements, 59–60, 91–92
corporate culture, 83–89, 132, 135, 166–175
corporate history, *see* history, corporate
corporate planning, *see* strategic planning
credibility of final diagnostic report, 151, 152
crises, organizational, 144–146
crisis intervention, 10, 174–175

D

data analysis, 11
  corporate history and culture, 83–89
  planning, strategy, and structure, 90–110
  preparation for, 77–79
  processes, 130–140
  resources, 111–129
data bases, 58–59, 61
data classification, 74–79
data collection
  in action research, 240, 242–243
  methods, 39–40, 199
  scope, 39–40
data gathering, 9, 11, 12, 51–69
data managers, 44
data processing, 70–79
data recording guide, 70
data reevaluation after intervention, 11
decision making, 7, 137, 250–251
defensive retreat during crises, 146
Dell Computer Corp., 120
developmental diagnosis, 8, 192
diagnosis, *see* organic diagnosis; organizational diagnosis
diagnosis, special applications
  case studies, 165–190
diagnostician's role, 23–25
diagnostic models, 12–15, 234–257
diagnostic reports, 148–152, 220–227
diagnostic teams
  appraisal of, 161
  composition of, 42, 200
  following data transcription, 76–77
  interviews with, 45
  and management involvement, 47–48, 193, 200
  member selection of, 31–32, 35–38, 43–44
  responsibilities of, 44–45
  training, 45–48
differentiation, organizational, 251–252
diversification, 175–180

E

Ebasco Services, 211n
environment, business
  data analysis, 90–110
  demands, responding to, 159–160
  strategic planning in the, 3–4
equipment control log, 70, 217
ethical guidelines, 46
evaluation of action research, 241, 243
evaluation of organizational diagnosis, 160–162
experts, defined, 24

F

facilitators, 7–8, 25
fact finding, 14, 39
family-group teams, 180–181
feedback, action research, 241, 242
feedback, diagnostic, 11, 12, 105, 140–154, 192
financial resources
  commitment of, to organizational diagnosis, 34, 193
  data analysis, 111–118
  and organizational diagnosis budget, 43
  in sample proposal structure, 199–200
Fink, Stephen, on organizational crisis, 144–145
Fordyce, Jack, on questionnaires, 237
forms, administrative, 70
forms:
  document-review control cover, 219
  equipment control log, 70, 217
  interview control log, 70
  master interviewing schedule, 209
  master project checklist, 202–208
  transcription control log, 217
French, Wendell L., 236n
Frohman, A. L., on descriptive analytic theory, 242
functional teams, 180

G

General Electric, 92, 118, 119
Gilbert, Thomas H., on performance analysis, 250
goals
  as an interview topic, 60–61
  failure to meet, 143–144
  of financial management, 113–118
  project teams, 186
  setting, 7
  specificity of, 91–92
  and strategy implementation, 99
Gray, Daniel, on strategic planning, 101
GRID training model, 239

H

Harris, Reubin, on core mission, 158–159, 239
Hertzberg, Frederick
  on job enrichment, 243–244
  on participative management, 7
historical methodology applied to organizational diagnosis, 261–266

Index 289

history, corporate, 83–89, 247–248
human resources
　case study, 183
　data analysis in, 111, 121–129
　organizational diagnosis administration, 41–43
　proposal structure, 199–200
　strategic planning in, 268–278

I

Iacocca, Lee, 4
IBM, 96, 118, 119, 120, 147
intergroups, 7, 180
interpersonal relations during crises, 146
intervention, crisis, *see* crisis intervention
interventions, 7–8, 160
　behavioral science models of, 234–249
　comprehensive models of, 234, 251–257
　special-purpose models of, 234, 249–251
　team building (case studies), 180–190
interview control log, 70
interview data-recording guide, 210
interviewees, selection of, 40–41
interviewing process, 61–69
interviews
　content, 59–61
　as a data-collection method, 39–40, 199
　of diagnostic team, 45
　scheduling, 43, 51–58, 199, 209
　transcripts of, 70–74
interviews vs. questionnaires, 62

J

Jaques, Elliott
　on abstraction levels, 4
　on management capabilities, 140
job enrichment, 243–244

K

Kepner, Charles H., on problem solving and decision making, 250–251
Kets de Vries, Manfred F. R., on leaders, 131
Kolb, D. A., on descriptive analytic theory, 242

L

Lawrence, Paul R., on organizational differentiation, 251–253
leaders
　authority and power of, 130–135
　needs and wants of, 256–257
leaders, project, *see* project leaders
Levinson, Harry
　on comprehensive analysis, 253–257
　on consultants, 254–257
　on corporate culture, 84
　on corporate growth cycles, 87
　on data "immersion" process, 78
　on developmental phases, 262
　on language use, 58
　on presentation techniques, 153
　on problem assessment, 9, 28–29
　on transference, 192, 255
　Organizational Diagnosis, 253, 259
Lewin, Kurt, on action research, 245
Likert, Rensis, on participative management, 246
Lippitt, Gordon, on corporate growth cycles, 87–88, 262
Lippitt, Ronald, 242
Lorsch, Jay W., on differentiation, 251–253

M

MacMillan, Ian C., 134, 211n
Mager, Robert F., on performance analysis, 249–250
Mahler, Walter, on attitude surveys, 237, 238
management development, 6, 128–129
management review of organizational diagnosis, 155–157, 267
management succession, 6
managers
　decision-making, 4–5
　participation of, on diagnostic team, 47–48, 193
marketing strategy, 96–97
Maslow, Abraham, on self-actualization, 243–244
Menninger, Karl, 256
mergers (case study), 165–175
Michigan Organizational Assessment Questionnaire, 238
middle management, presence of, at final presentation, 152
middle management, schism with top management, 134–135
morale, 245
motivation of employees, 243–244, 245
motivation to change, 9, 27, 29–30
Mouton, Jane S., 239

N

National Cash Register, 118

O

objectives, organizational, 60–61, 92, 99
objectives of organizational diagnosis, 149, 160, 192, 198
objectives of project teams, 186
objectives of team building, 7
O. M. Scott Co., 91
operational planning, 102–103
organic diagnosis, 13–20, 193
organizational charts, 40, 59, 104, 132, 239, 249
organizational development, *see* organizational diagnosis, focus of developmental
organizational development councils
  budgeting time for, 200
  establishment of, 32–33, 259–260
organizational diagnosis
  action planning in, 155–160
  administrative systems in, 38–43
  commitment to, 34, 193
  diagnostic techniques, value of, 8–10
  distinguished from consulting, 10–11
  evaluation of effectiveness, 160–162
  example of, 258–278
  final approval of, 34–35
  issues and problems in, 191–194
  management review of, 155–157
  as a management tool, 3–20
  master project checklist for, 202–208
  models of and approaches to, 12–15
  organic approach to, 13–20, 193
  origins and concepts of, 1–20
  preliminary assessment and startup of, 23–28
  process distinguished from content, 10–11
  process overview, 16–20
  project organization, 35–38
  proposal presentation, 33–34
  report preparation, 143–148
  report presentation, 152–154, 201
  report recommendations, 148, 230–233, 266
  report structure, 148–149
  report writing, 150–151
  resistance to, 191–192
  resource requirements, 41–43
  success, conditions for, 193–194
organizational diagnosis, focus of
  developmental, 6–8, 15–16, 29–30, 192
  and effect on interviewee selection, 41
  remedial, 8, 15, 25, 192
organizational diagnosis, scope of, 8, 15–16, 29–31, 38–40

organizational planning, *see* strategic planning
organizational structure, *see* structure, organizational

P

participants, list in final diagnostic report, 150
participative management, 7, 131, 246
percentage-change analysis, 115
perceptions
  effect on behavior of, 14–15
  attitude surveys to determine, 235–239
  of core-mission statement, 59–60
  data gathering on, 39
  interviewing techniques to determine, 65
  of middle management, 135
  of diagnostic team, 45
  value of, 58
performance, drop in, 144
performance analysis, 140, 249–250
performance appraisals, 6, 125–128
  of diagnostic team, 161
performance planning, 7
physical resources, 111, 120–121
  case study, 182–183
  and equipment control log, 70, 217
  proposal structure, 200
planning, strategic, *see* strategic planning
political capability, 134
political environment, 29–33
political support system, 35–38
power, 130–135, 260
Praxis Consulting Organization, 250
presentation techniques, 152–154
problem diagnosis, 8–11, 15–16
problem solvers, defined, 24
problem solving
  as an objective of team building, 7
  barriers to success in, 3–5
  Kepner-Tregoe Analysis (KTA) method of, 250–251
  participative, 7
  practices, 136–137
process consultation, 8
productivity, 138–140, 245
project administrators, 44
project leaders, hostility towards, 192
project managers, 42, 186–187, 200
project teams, 180, 185–190
proposals, presentation of, 33–34
proposal structure, 198–201

Q

questionnaires
  as data collection methods, 39, 199
  to evaluate organizational diagnosis, 161–162
  vs. interviews, 62
questionnaires:
  attitude surveys, 235–239
  Core Mission and Strategic Planning Issues Analysis, 59

R

Radio Corp. of America, 118
ratio analysis, 114–115
recommendations, diagnostic, 148, 230–233, 266
remedial diagnosis, 8, 25–30, 192
resistance to change, 10, 257
resistance to organizational diagnosis, 191–192, 260
respondent population, 40–41, 199
reward systems, 138
Rice, A. K., on organizational differentiation, 249

S

Schmidt, Warren, on corporate growth cycles, 87–88, 262
scouting, client-consultant disclosure, 242
self-actualization, 244
sensitivity training, 246–247
shock during crises, 146
Singer Co., 89
Skinner, B. F., 138, 244–245
social consciousness, 247–248
sociotechnical systems theory, 249
special purpose models, 234, 249–251
sponsors
  authority of, 26, 30–31
  budgeting time, 42, 200
  client-analyst relationship, 242
  preliminary assessment of, 26–27, 30–31
  report presentation to, 201
strategic advantage profiles, 107–110
strategic business units, 97–99
strategic-issues analysis, 39, 90–110
strategic-issues interviews, 59–61
strategic planning
  activities, 5–6
  business environment, 3–4, 90–110
  case study, 175–180
  and Core Mission and Strategic Planning Analysis, 59, 211–216
  data analysis, 90–110
  in human resources, 268–278
  and training, 270–272
  value of organizational diagnosis in, 193–194
strategy implementation, 11, 99–101, 111
strengths, organizational, 147
structure, organizational, 6, 103–105, 148–149
survey-research methods, 39, 199
Sylvania, 118

T

Taddeo, Kenneth, on organizational crisis, 144–145
target population, 40–41, 199
task forces, 157–158, 176
technological resources, 111, 118–120
Tichy, Noel, 211n
topical analysis summary, sample, 228–229
training, relationship to performance, 250
training, strategic planning and, 270–272
training programs
  for diagnostic teams, 45–48
  for new employees, 86
training programs:
  GRID, 239
  sensitivity training, 246–247
transcription control log, 70, 217
transcripts of interviews, 70–74
Tregoe, Benjamin B., on problem solving and decision making, 250–251
Trist, Eric, on sociotechnical systems theory, 249
turnover, 122–127

W

Watson, J., 242
Watson, Thomas J., 147
Weil, Raymond, on questionnaires, 237
Weisbord, Marvin
  action research model of, 240, 242
  six-box model for organizational diagnosis of, 251
Westley, B., 242

Z

Zaleznik, Abraham, on leaders, 131

	DATE DUE
NOV 13 1995	
	MAR 15 1996

```
         5977
HD
58.8        Manzini, Andrew O.
.M29            Organizational
            diagnosis
```

CHAMPLAIN COLLEGE LIBRARY

T 5977